Farmers National Bank
&

Snappy Tomato Pizza Company

*Both proudly serving the Simon Kenton
Pioneer community*

We congratulate all the **Heroes** from
Pioneer Spirit!

PIONEER SPIRIT

PIONEER SPIRIT

One High School's Rise
FROM TRAGEDY TO GLORY

Brian —
Live The Pioneer
Spirit!
Eric Deters
10-19-06

ERIC C. DETERS

A̶P™

ACCLAIM PRESS

MORLEY, MISSOURI

Acclaim Press

ACCLAIM PRESS, INC.
Your Next Great Book
P.O. Box 238
Morley, MO 63767
(573) 262-2121
www.acclaimpress.com

Book Design by:

GRAPHIC DESIGN

Publishing Rights: Acclaim Press

Library of Congress Catalog No.: 2006934911
ISBN: 0-9790025-0-8
Printed in the United States of America
First Printing October 2006
10 9 8 7 6 5 4 3 2 1

Additional copies may be purchased from Acclaim Press.

This publication was produced using available information. The Publisher regrets it cannot assume responsibility for errors or omissions.

CONTENTS

DEDICATION

*I dedicate this book to Mary Ann Zimmerer, my
wife and cheerleader from the
Simon Kenton Class of 1981,
and Erica, Charlie Ann and Parker, my three
future Simon Kenton graduates, and my parents,
Charles and Mary Sue Deters*

Introduction

E ric Deters has identified a disease, "Kentucky School Basketball Mania," and no one has yet found a cure.

This book traces two events that are very familiar to me. One deals with a prime example of the disease that I just described. The other is a tragic news story I covered when I was with Channel 12 News in Cincinnati.

First, let's deal with the mania. A surprising number of Kentuckians can tell you the long-ago story of tiny Carr Creek slaying the dragons in the state tournament. Less known, but just as dramatic, was the victory of even tinier Cuba in the 1950's, which took the trophy home, some said, by copying the moves of the Harlem Globetrotters, including Goose Tatum and Marcus Haines. And, of course, there is the enduring legend of King Kelly Coleman.

Mr. Deters traces an equally unlikely championship team. There had been no champion at the state level from the Ninth Region – the area in Northern Kentucky across the Ohio River from Cincinnati – in the history of the state tournament.

In the interest of full disclosure, let me point out that I am a native of what came to be called the Tenth Region, also north and also in Kentucky, but just as competitive with the Ninth as with any other region in the Commonwealth.

As you will see in this comprehensive account, Simon Kenton High School reached its defining moment in athletics against the Mason County Royals. As it happens, I was born in Maysville, Mason County's major city.

In fact, it should be pointed out that the Tenth Region had a distinguished record in the state tournament. The Maysville Bulldogs – predecessor to the Mason County Royals – had been state champs in the 1940's. For that matter, Brooksville High School, now replaced by Bracken County, the county in which Nina and I live and also in the Tenth Region, had been the improbable state champs seven decades ago. In fact, the Mason County Royals would themselves claim the state trophy in more recent years.

Now to the backstory. In the fall of 1980, I was the managing editor and anchor of Channel 12 News in Cincinnati. As a native Kentuckian, I tried to make sure that Northern Kentucky, which accounted for about one quarter of the Greater Cincinnati community, received the attention it deserved but had been denied for years.

One October day, we heard the melancholy flash that there had been an explosion at Simon Kenton High School. There were many injuries and there might be fatalities, we were told.

By then, we at Channel 12 had many good sources in Northern Kentucky, so in a very few minutes I knew that the cause of the tragedy was an error in testing gas lines by the Union Light, Heat and Power Company. We went to the late afternoon news conference loaded for bear. A student had died. We were suspicious that there might be a cover-up. I sent a reporter armed with tough questions.

Here's what happened. The ULH&P spokesman opened with a statement. He admitted it was all his company's fault. He said it was an inexcusable error and he wished he could turn back the clock. He took responsibility on behalf of his employers. He said he believed the incident would lead to major changes in the way power companies everywhere did business. The young student's death would not be in vain.

In other words, the company told as much of the truth as it knew at that moment. It took the sting out of our aggressive questioning. It was so unusual that I now use it in seminars as an example of what companies should do as a first response when confronted with terrible events. Surprise reporters with the truth.

The distance from that tragedy to Simon Kenton's triumph just a few months later are the narrative that Mr. Deters will now describe.

It is a unique story. It will resonate with every person who remembers his or her high school journey, and how it shapes them, even now.

Nick Clooney
Augusta, Kentucky

Foreword

At the 1981 Kentucky State High School Basketball Tournament I sat close to the floor, always a passionate High School basketball fan even before I became the University of Kentucky basketball coach. But at this final game of the tournament, I had a special interest; Simon Kenton High School and its phenomenal rise to the championship game and its All-State athlete, Troy McKinley. What I wasn't aware of at the time was the inspirational drama that was exploding before my eyes as Simon Kenton won the High School Basketball State Championship in Rupp Arena.

Now as I read Eric C. Deters' saga, *Pioneer Spirit*, I can only wish that as I watched, I had known the magnitude of the epic that was unfolding that night in Lexington's Rupp Arena.

Simon Kenton, fans, parents of the players and cheerleaders, teachers, administrators and all from the Ninth Region knew the story and were seeing much more in the event and the near miracle that was coming to fruition as the last seconds ticked off the clock on the scoreboard above all of us. Few of the 21,000 plus fans in Rupp fully appreciated the enormity of the story behind this team, this school and the proud residents of this northern Kentucky community.

Thanks to Eric C. Deters, all can relive one of the most inspiring stories of a team and most of all an entire community that overcame dramatic and even tragic events, to develop the united spirit that is necessary to achieve greatness. This is a "warm" "feel good" kind of story that has a personal touch and in depth contact with all that are involved.

I now relive that moment in Rupp Arena and now marvel at what I was missing that Saturday night. Coach Larry Miller, his courageous players, the loyal cheerleaders, supportive administrators, proud faculty, relatives and fans were understandably in a state of disbelief that what was considered impossible had been achieved. The joy was much more than winning a championship, it was a life experience in what can be accomplished when a team, a school and a community can unite, believe and persevere to overcome the worst of adversity.

I wish that I had known at the time what that march to victory entailed.

I will enjoy the movie. (It has to be made.)

Joe B. Hall
Former University of Kentucky Basketball Coach

PREFACE

"The beginning is the most important part of the work."
  ~ Plato

Igrew up on a nearly one-thousand acre horse and cattle farm a few miles outside the small tranquil town of Independence, Kentucky in the northern section of the state. I was the middle child of eleven children of Charles and Mary Sue Deters. Our father practiced law and our mother stayed at home to care for us. According to our mother, our father chose to raise us in the country so he and our mother would be the greatest influence in our lives. It worked. Besides the number of children, further proof of my Catholic roots is evident by my father representing the local Catholic bishop and several religious orders. My parents frequently hosted clergy for dinner and holidays. Also, Mom and Dad prayed the rosary with all of us after dinner during the months of May and October, the Blessed Mary's months of honor in the Catholic faith. For Lent, my mother diligently tied a purple bow with a ribbon around our one television. For a long forty days, we reluctantly abstained from television. In addition to these seasonal rituals, our parents stressed Catholic education.

With the exception of my first year of formal schooling at Kenton Elementary, the closest public grade school to our home, I attended Catholic grade school, high school, and college without ever leaving Northern Kentucky. I attended Kenton Elementary for only one year because for a reason unknown to me, the local Catholic grade school in 1969 failed to offer first grade. Ms. Wagner taught me first grade at Kenton Elementary. One room down, Ms. Bates taught first grade to a girl named Mary Zimmerer. The Catholic grade school, St. Cecilia, is located in "downtown" Independence. St. Cecilia is the church my family attended every Saturday night or Sunday morning. Despite the parental intention of Catholic education, my 'farm-boy' older brothers, Thad and Jed, chose not to attend a suburban Catholic parochial high school. My parents allowed my older brothers to attend and graduate from Simon Kenton High School in Independence, Kentucky. Thad graduated in 1977 followed by Jed in 1978. However, both of my older brothers attended grade school at St. Cecilia. I would fail to follow my brothers' path to Simon Kenton High School. Instead, I chose to skip the seventh and eighth grades to attend my father's alma mater, Covington Latin School, the only accelerated college prepatory school in the country. I began high school at age twelve and graduated at the age of fifteen.

My reluctant choice of Covington Latin School over Simon Kenton High School resulted in my missing out on being a member of one of the most memorable senior years any high school class ever experienced. Born August 6, 1963, if I had attended Simon Kenton, my graduation year would have fallen on 1981. As trivial as it sounds to me today, the only reason I chose Covington Latin School over Simon Kenton High School is from the fear my St. Cecilia classmates would discover I wet the bed.

As I struggled through Covington Latin School and later breezed through Thomas More College, I still hung out with friends who attended Simon Kenton High School. This began with following my older brothers and their friends around. In 1980-1981, rather than being a senior at Simon Kenton High School, I found myself a sophomore at Thomas More College, a private Catholic college in Northern Kentucky's suburbs. However, I still attended home Simon Kenton football and basketball games. Without fail, every time I attended a game and watched the action from the sidelines or stands, I regretted my Covington Latin School decision. I passed up a high school five miles from my home to ride a mass transit bus over an hour to and from school every day for four years. In addition, the Covington Latin Trojans never fielded a football team. The varsity basketball team, which I played on, won only two games my senior year in large part because we played teams consisting of players two years older. My only basketball claim to fame is guarding the now-famous actor George Clooney of Augusta High School in a box and one defense. We lost the game. The crowd in the Augusta gym loved George Clooney just as much then as I'm sure they do now.

Covington Latin also refused enrollment to girls. Compare this unpleasant reality to my seeing pretty girls everywhere at the Simon Kenton High School games I attended. One girl always stood out, a cheerleader named Mary Zimmerer, the same girl Ms. Bates had taught at Kenton Elementary.

Despite her being out of my "league," I always dreamed of Mary Zimmerer. Most men have been asked the Ginger or Mary Ann question. I always answered Mary Ann. Mary Ann Zimmerer was truly a Mary Ann. I enjoyed a few memorable chance encounters with Mary. Of course, she fails to recall any of them. I accepted that I would never date anyone as special as Mary Zimmerer.

From a distance all my teenage years, I watched the Simon Kenton Pioneers play football and basketball. Oh, how I was jealous! Billy Meier, Greg Ponzer, Sean Dougherty, Troy McKinley, Dave Dixon, Dave Medley and Alan Mullins lived the life from my perspective. They played football and basketball in front of all their beautiful female classmates, including Mary Zimmerer. Meanwhile, I diligently studied three to four hours a night simply to pass my courses at Covington Latin School.

As I reached the age of forty-two, I couldn't believe no one had written the remarkable story I witnessed from the sidelines and stands. In November, 2005, beginning with the Simon Kenton High School head boys' varsity basketball coach Larry Miller, I conducted extensive interviews of coaches, players, cheerleaders, teachers, fans, and administrators. Considering my educational path to Covington Latin School rather than Simon Kenton High School, I believe it is ironic that I'm now not only married to Mary Zimmerer, but the one writing this book. I barely knew a single member of the storied basketball team, the cheerleaders or coaching staff until later in my life. Mary claims she only remembers there were "a lot of Deters" and we each looked alike. Later, as an attorney, I performed legal work for several members of the team. I believe I never held a conversation with Dave Dixon or Dave Medley until writing this book.

This story, an enjoyable journey through time over twenty-five years ago, is filled with more twists than my authorship. In 1981 and today, everyone passionately cared about basketball in Kentucky. At Simon Kenton High School, seven tough young men would be led by three brash young coaches to the highest peak of success on the basketball court. Eight talented and attractive young women led by a free-spirited young art teacher cheered on the players and coaches. Life lessons would be learned. Friendships would be forged to last a lifetime. However, there would be no top of the mountain without the proverbial valley below. The valley would be an unexpected and tragic natural gas explosion which unmercifully tore through Simon Kenton High School, killing a classmate, injuring over thirty students, staff and firefighters, and destroying half the school building. The determined march out of the valley began with an unprecedented move, night school for the Simon Kenton High School students at a neighboring high school which also happened to be the Pioneers' arch rival.

The story takes place primarily from 1980-1981. Oddly and prophetically, the 1980 yearbook staff of Simon Kenton High School, the year before the school explosion, titled the yearbook "Exploding." Following this undesired "prophecy," the Class of 1981, a class of young heroes, chose as their class song "The Best of Times" by Styx. The Class of 1981 chose as their class motto an equally prophetic inspirational phrase:

"If you can dream it,
You can do it.
If you can imagine it,
You can achieve it."

And they would. The 1981 yearbook staff chose the more upbeat and optimistic theme of "No Stopping Us Now". No one would. As you read this story, you will find similar and recognizable parallels to your own childhood and high school years. The difference is found in the dramatic unexpected events which the Simon Kenton Pioneers overcame by force of will. The title of this book is meant to focus on the indomitable spirit displayed by everyone who played a role in this story: the players, coaches, teachers, firemen and students. I only regret I could not possibly place everyone's story from the events in the book. However, I'm honored to receive the opportunity to write this inspirational story. It's a story of a group of young basketball players, cheerleaders, coaches, firemen, teachers, staff, parents and students. Student-heroes who captured the pioneer spirit of their own school's namesake.

PIONEER
SPIRIT

One High School's Rise
FROM TRAGEDY TO GLORY

The Art Room

"What is past is prologue."
~ Shakespeare

Thursday, October 9, 1980
Simon Kenton High School
Independence, Kentucky
11:53 a.m.

An ominous hissing sound seeped from behind the concrete block wall separating Linda Whittenburg's art room from the boiler room. As art students cheerfully painted the classroom's windows with seasonal Halloween themes, Ms. Whittenburg teased her student aide, Glen Bridges, as he struggled to clean the sink. The students stood on chairs to reach the ground level windows. Robert Williams, the only young artist not standing along the windows, helped those painting by mixing their paint and handing them brushes.

Everyone in the room turned their heads toward the hissing sound. Before anyone could speak, think, or react, the concrete block wall exploded.

The explosion left no one in the art room standing. Broken concrete, smoke, dust and flames consumed the room. Debris covered the students and their young teacher. Disoriented, Ms. Whittenburg and her students struggled to their feet and searched for an exit. Concrete blocked the exit from the room to the hall. They stumbled to a closet which led to another art room. As they worked their way out, covered in paint, soot and dust, no one realized it, but Robert Williams was not with them.

CHAPTER 1
A Pioneer Named Simon Kenton

"What we do in life echoes in eternity."
~ Maximus from the movie *Gladiator*

Simon Kenton High School is named for a consequential early pioneer in our country's history. Kenton County, the location of Simon Kenton High School in Kentucky, is also named in honor of this early historical figure. The northern border of Kenton County strategically lies directly across the Ohio River from Cincinnati, Ohio.

In 1755, Mark Kenton, Sr., an Irish immigrant to America, and his wife, Mary Miller Kenton, a Virginia native of Scott-Welch descent, brought a son named Simon into the world. The Kentons raised Simon in the Bull Run Mountains of Prince William County, Virginia.

Simon Kenton rapidly grew into a brawny young man with little apparent ambition. He despised school and disclaimed the farming life his father struggled in to sustain his family. However, Simon appreciated the outdoors. By the age of fifteen, he became an accomplished hunter. Meanwhile, Simon's uncle enthralled his nephew with lustrous stories and splendid tales of the western frontier bordering the Ohio River.

The "middle ground," as Simon's uncle referred to the distant frontier, contained unlimited quantities of wild game for the steady aim of a hunter. Simon's uncle further claimed schools of fish clogged the creeks and flocks of birds blackened the blue sky when flying overhead. Blazing trails, fighting savage Indians, establishing settlements and hunting the abundant prey consumed Simon Kenton's dreams.

When he was still a teenager, Simon fell in love with a resplendent young woman named Ellen Cummins. However, Ellen loved and planned to marry another man, Willie Leachman. In foolish youthful bravado, while bearing the heavy pain of losing Ellen's heart and hand, Simon Kenton imprudently appeared at the church on the day of Ellen's and Willie's wedding.

Before the solemn ceremony, Kenton demanded Willie Leachman step outside the church for a physical confrontation. Kenton unwisely chose a poor venue to challenge Leachman. Leachman's loyal guests joined in the provoked fight, and, rather than deliver a beating, Simon Kenton received a pummeling. Time sometimes tempers vengeance. Other times, as in Simon Kenton's case, time fueled the vengeful fire which burned in his breast. Kenton soon sought vindication for the humiliation he had suffered. For an entire year, his anger smoldered. When he finally caught Leachman alone, Kenton beat Leachman so severely that he believed he had killed the target of his vengeance. Murder was not the intention of Simon Kenton, only retribution.

Desperately fearing his own hanging or lengthy imprisonment for murder, Simon Kenton fled Virginia without furnishing his family notice of his hastened departure or his intended destination. He speedily traveled west by

Simon Kenton

horse toward the bountiful territory his uncle had described. Unknown to the frightened Simon Kenton, Willie Leachman had fortunately survived. The mistaken notion that he had committed murder led Kenton into the untamed and uncharted American wilderness where he developed legendary status as the frontiersman he earlier dreamed to be. Altering his name to Simon Butler to cleverly mask his true identity, Simon Kenton reached the hallowed territory known as "Kaintuckee." The native American indians coveted the territory as their hunting preserve. Kenton would fail to garner the popular notoriety of Daniel Boone and George Rogers Clark. Yet, he once saved Daniel Boone's life by hoisting the seriously wounded man over his shoulder and carrying Boone to the guarded safety of a fort as a heated Indian battle waged around them.

Simon Kenton eventually reclaimed his rightful name upon learning of Willie Leachman's survival. During his long and adventurous life, Kenton fulfilled the promise of blazing trails, founding settlements and establishing critical commercial routes leading to the American west. Kenton also proudly and dutifully fought with the colonists during the American Revolution. In addition, he fathered nine children. An unfair and unjust stain on his record included serving time in a debtor's prison for having been unable to pay his debts.

In 1778, an Ohio Indian tribe boasted the capture of Simon Kenton. Members of the tribe unmercifully beat him before tying him "spread eagle" on the cold ground and leaving him for a night of suffering. In the early morning, the Indians cut Kenton free, tied him to the back of an unbroken wild horse, and sent him on a brutal ride through a heavily wooded area where wicked tree branches repeatedly struck his torn and battered body. Following the horse torture, the Indians forced Kenton to run the dreadful gauntlet. Every present member of the tribe, including women and children, formed two long lines facing one another a quarter mile long. As he was forced to run through the middle of the lines, the Indians struck Kenton with clubs, tomahawks, sticks, switches and knives as he staggered through his punishment. He ran the gauntlet nine times. Few rugged and sturdy men ever survived the fierce gauntlet. However, Kenton not only lived; he eventually escaped from his captors.

Simon Kenton lived the majority of his active frontier life in settlements and outposts scattered along the Ohio and Kentucky wilderness. Those settlements usually formed near rivers, the interstate highways of the time. One of Simon Kenton's favorite settlements along the Ohio River, fifty miles upriver from present day Cincinnati, was Maysville, the largest town in Mason County. Kenton assisted in the settlement of the community, lived much of his eventful life there, and the bridge over the Ohio River in Maysville was named in his honor.

Simon Kenton would echo in eternity. Two long centuries after he explored the Kentucky wilderness, a school and county which bore his name would ironically collide with another school from the county he settled. The classic epic battle would not involve Indians, but basketball, a game Simon Kenton never played.

CHAPTER 2
Independence, Kentucky

"Bloom where you are planted."
~ Anonymous

In 1840, when community leaders led the creation of Kenton County out of Campbell County, state law required county seats to lie in the geographical center of the county. An early pioneer to the Independence area by the name of John McCullum generously donated land at the center of town for the county seat. A short road in the heart of Independence still bears McCullum's name. In 1842, the town formally incorporated the city. The founding fathers of the town bestowed the name Independence to celebrate Kenton County's separation from Campbell County. To this date, out of 120 counties in Kentucky, Kenton County and Campbell County remain the only two counties with two courthouses. Each has one in their most populated cities along the Ohio River on their northern boundaries and the one at the "center". In Kenton County, that "center" is Independence.

Kenton County, Kentucky is the state's third most populated county and northernmost geographically. Long and narrow, Kenton County begins at the Ohio River on its northern border and cuts through urban neighborhoods, then affluent suburbs and finally farming communities at the county's southern border.

Independence is a small country town, as well as one of the fastest growing cities in the state. Geographically, Independence contains more square miles than any of the over twenty incorporated towns in Kenton County, Kentucky. While subdivisions bulging with young families have taken the place of livestock and crops, Independence retains a small town feel comparable to the rural country town it was in the 1970'a and 1980's. The historic courthouse, light business district and sprawling cemetery in its downtown yield to the new shopping center, grocery store, schools, restaurants, police station, parks, senior citizen center and sidewalks which followed the new residents to town. The main arterial road, Madison Pike, gently curves along the high geographical ridge which transverses through Independence.

The citizens of Independence enthusiastically celebrate the patriotic holidays as appropriate for a town named Independence. Memorial Day and the Fourth of July involve lengthy parades, community festivals and extensive fireworks to conclude the celebration.

In 1970, Independence claimed a population of only 1,784. By 1980, the population swelled to 9,310. In 1980, Mason County's population was double the size of Independence. However, in 1980, prior to the present sewer system, extensive waterlines and road improvements, Independence contained a spattering of small family grocery stores named Butler's, Riley's, Roxie's, Johnny's and the Cherokee IGA, not the national Kroger chain. The locals in Independence in 1980 drank or dined in the only sit-down restaurant in Independence, a tavern across from the Courthouse called Ponzers. The owners of Ponzers, Sue and Vic Ponzer, raised four boys and a daughter in Independence. The youngest, Greg, would star in football, baseball and basketball at Simon Kenton High School.

CHAPTER 3
Simon Kenton High School

"To sow schools is to reap men."
~ Anonymous

In February 1894, Reverend and Mrs. G.W. Dunlap organized a private high school in Independence, Kentucky. In 1898, the Dunlaps sold their school to C.V. Lucy and his mother who operated the school until the Kenton County School Board took over management. In 1912, the Kenton County School Board built a new building. The newly constructed school contained eight rooms. In 1924, the School Board added a brick auditorium as a separate structure. In September 1937, the Independence High School, as it was then called, closed and the area students attended the modern Simon Kenton High School.

Born January 16, 1928, Randall Wagner remembers the old gym at the old Dunlap School being too confined for proper basketball play. "The baskets were against the wall so you couldn't drive in," Randall recalls of the limitations. Randall actually played grade school basketball in the cramped gym.

After high school, Randall Wagner served in World War II in the Merchant Marine as a member of the United States ambitious plan to daringly invade Japan. Thanks to the atomic bomb, Randall never experienced live action. He credits President Harry Truman with saving his life. In the late 1940's, after Randall's honorable discharge from military service, he began attending each home Simon Kenton basketball and football game.

Randall Wagner also helped create the football program at Simon Kenton High School. A hundred dedicated volunteers signed a bank note at the Independence Bank. The group of benefactors borrowed $30,000 to construct a football complex at the high school. Once indebted, the group worked feverishly to pay off the note from concession stand sales.

"That's the way we started football. Agnes Caldwell made five gallons of hot chocolate at Piner and my mother did the same at Kenton Elementary. On Friday afternoon, we'd run over to the ice house at Erlanger and pick up all the ice. We sold fountain drinks. We made a lot on fountain drinks," brags Patsy Wagner, Randall's wife. "Betty Sue Cook and I served hot dogs and hot chocolate. We worked every game."

Patsy's concession stand friend, Betty Sue Cook, is the matriarch of the Rich family. When only three weeks old, Betty Sue's father left home, never to return. Betty Sue's mother, grandmother and Aunt Mary operated their dairy farm and raised their tobacco crop on their own. Aunt Mary cooked and managed the household chores while the three generations of Rich women worked in the fields and barns. Now seventy-seven years old, Betty Sue's blue eyes still twinkle and she remains as active as ever. In 1951, at age twenty-three, Betty Sue began work at the Kenton County School Board's central office immediately adjacent to Simon Kenton High School. Today, Betty Sue remains employed at the School Board in a part-time position. She and her husband James live on the 165 acre farm Betty Sue worked with her family. Betty Sue Cook was graduated from Simon Kenton in 1946. Betty Sue attended her first basketball game on any level at Piner Elementary when at only three weeks old, her mother placed the infant Betty Sue under a chair at the game. Her mother cooked at Piner Elementary for forty-two years. And her boys each played baseball and basketball. Betty Sue attended their games and drove them everywhere they needed to go for practice and games. When she failed to appreciate a call by an umpire or referee, she never hesitated to express her opinion directly to the umpire or referee. All three of the Cook's sons were graduated from Simon Kenton High School. Like Randall and Patsy Wagner, Betty Sue and James Cook began attending all the home Simon Kenton football and basketball games.

The current football field at Simon Kenton is named for Chlorine "Jake" Menifee. "Jake" became a Board of Education member and later meddled in the basketball program. Randall Wagner admits Jake could cause problems. "But you knew Chlorine was coming from his heart. He was going to do all he could for Simon Kenton," Randall Wagner observed.

Patsy and Randall Wagner met at Union College in Kentucky and married in 1948. Similar to the Cooks, the Wagners were blessed with three sons. Patsy Wagner taught school at the old Independence School from 1948-1950. Patsy then took a sabbatical from teaching until her youngest son began school. Patsy later taught at Kenton Elementary for twenty-five years and subbed for sixteen more years. She taught at Kenton Elementary when Dave Medley, Billy Meier, Greg Ponzer, Alan Mullins, Mary Zimmerer and Jill Brueckner attended the school. These boys and girls became members of the Simon Kenton High School 1980-1981 varsity basketball team and cheerleading squad respectively.

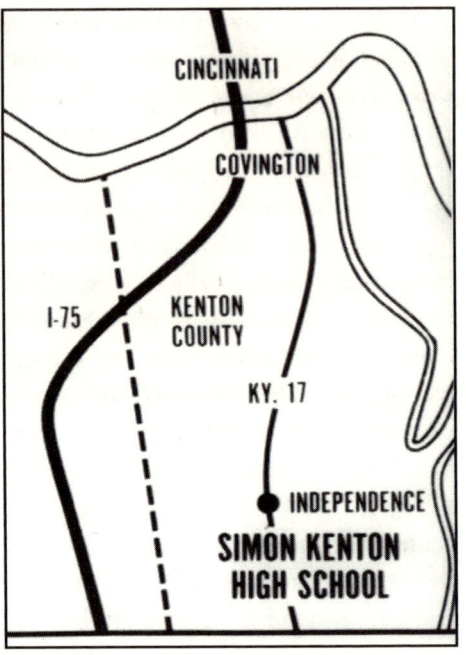

In 1970, leukemia struck Randall, and the doctors coldly suggested Patsy take a vacation and enjoy life as she waited for Randall's inevitable death. "They told us Randall had three weeks to three months, certainly not six months to a year, to live. I said to the doctor, 'If you think that I'm going to Florida and sit in the sun and watch somebody I love die, you have another thought coming. There is help somewhere and I intend to find it.' We found it at M.D. Anderson in Texas," Patsy recalls.

Randall Wagner survived leukemia. Thirty-five years later, he's still attending all the Simon Kenton basketball games. He sits in the top row of the gymnasium with his wife Patsy and their dear friends, Betty Sue and Jim Cook, and yells like hell at the referees, the players and anyone else relevant to the game. It's a sight to behold and hear.

The School Board constructed Simon Kenton High School on twenty-three acres one-half mile south of downtown Independence. Later, the School Board purchased 5.5 additional acres to add a fresh water lake for the water supply for the school. On October 22, 1936, the Kenton County School Board named the school Simon Kenton High School and dedicated it on Sunday, September 5, 1937. Simon Kenton opened for business on September 13, 1937 with an enrollment of 496 students.

The school's physical structure remained the same until 1956 when the School Board added a bi-level with seven modern classrooms. In 1962, the School Board erected a new cafeteria to the south side of the school and several classrooms in the basement of the addition. The next major modification to the school grounds involved the draining of the lake after Robert Blanton, a 1970 Simon Kenton Senior, drowned while swimming in the lake.

In 1969, the School Board built a north wing for a new library and science and mathematics classrooms. The School Board also added a new parking lot in the front of the school.

Construction in 1980 at Simon Kenton involved a baseball field and a rubber-based track encircling the football field. Also, for the first time in its history, the school enjoyed their own tennis courts. A new large addition provided rooms for health, graphic arts, welding, industrial arts, band, chorus, a weight room and a new gym which seated 1450.

The contractor, Klensch Construction, completed the gymnasium one day prior to the first home basketball game for the 1980-1981 basketball season. The first Simon Kenton team to ever play in the new gymnasium would never be forgotten.

CHAPTER 4
Basketball in Kentucky

*"If winning doesn't matter, then why is there a score-
board in every gym in America?"*
~ Coach Rupp, University of Kentucky

The first dream of any young boy in Kentucky who first dribbles a basketball is to play on his local high school varsity team. The second dream
is to play for the University of Kentucky Wildcats and wear the blue
and white. Marquette coaching legend, Al McGuire once said, "The kids
in Kentucky start listening to the games on the radio when they are still
being burped on their father's shoulder." Cut a boy, girl, man or woman in
Kentucky and he may bleed blue. Heck, their dog probably bleeds blue. The
sole exception may be some, but not all the basketball players or fans growing
up in Louisville. Many of these Kentuckians bleed Cardinal red rather than
Wildcat blue. Regardless of color, they bleed basketball. Basketball matters
in Kentucky. Kentucky is divided into 120 counties. With the exception
of the few counties with larger cities, in each of the 120 counties the entire
social fabric of the community centers around high school basketball or football, politics and church. It's a way of life in Kentucky. Basketball drama
comes alive when five players from each team step to the court, the whistle
blows and a referee tosses the ball up to begin the game. Unlike a play in a
theater, from the time of the ball toss, there is no script.

James A. Naismith invented the game of basketball in 1891 at the Young
Men's Christian Association (YMCA) Training School in Springfield, Mas-
sachusetts. The first reported basketball games in Kentucky were played at
the Louisville YMCA. In 1903, college basketball was played for the first
time in Kentucky at Kentucky University (KU) in Lexington at the Lexington YMCA.

The first Kentucky State High School Basketball Tournament, eight teams by invitation only, was played in 1916 in the City of Danville. This high school tournament event moved to the University of Kentucky two years later after the formation of the Kentucky High School Athletic Association (KHSAA). The University of Kentucky actually oversaw the tournament until 1938. Since 1928, the KHSAA have played the Kentucky boys' state basketball tournament in Lexington or Louisville.

Larger schools won the majority of the early high school championships. However, talented players and teams from little-known towns from all over Kentucky challenged and occasionally won. Each school of each Kentucky county holds their own hoop legends dear and close to their basketball hearts. One of the most famous basketball games in Kentucky history is Ashland's four-overtime victory over little Carr Creek in the 1928 state championship final. Only eighteen boys attended Carr Creek at the time. Called the "barefoot boys", Carr Creek joined numerous other small town state tournament champions over the years.

In 1931, Adolph Rupp, after coaching basketball only at Freeport High School in Illinois, was hired as the University of Kentucky basketball coach. In 1948, Adolph Rupp, with his "Fabulous Five", won the University of Kentucky's first National Collegiate Athletic Association (NCAA) championship. The "Fabulous Five" Cliff Barker, Ralph Beard, Alex Groza, Kenny Rollins, Wallace "Wah Wah" Jones, Dale Barnstable and Joe Holland also played in the Olympic Games in London, England in 1948 and the U.S. team won the gold medal. My mother, Mary Sue Krippenstapel, knew "Wah Wah" Jones when she attended high school with him in Harlan County. The Wildcats repeated as national champions in 1949, 1951 and 1958. The Wildcats lost to Texas Western in the championship game of the 1966 NCAA tournament. *Glory Road* is the recent movie depicting the integration of basketball in the face of Adolph Rupp's alleged resistance. Regardless, Adolph Rupp, at the time of his retirement, retired as the winningest college coach of all time, 879 wins and 190 losses. Numerous players from Kentucky high schools played under Rupp and assisted in his total victory tally.

The Kentucky State High School Tournament broke the color barrier earlier than the national college scene. In 1957, three blacks played on the Hazard high school boys team. Lexington Dunbar and Covington Grant competed with all black teams in the Sweet 16 in 1958. James Ricketts of Louisville Manual in 1959 became the first black player to play in the championship game. Two years later, Louisville Dunbar became the first all-black team to advance to the finals.

Joe B. Hall followed Coach Rupp at the University of Kentucky. The University of Kentucky lost in the championship game of the 1975 NCAA tournament to John Wooden's UCLA. After winning the 1976 NIT in the 1978 NCAA tournament, the University of Kentucky defeated Duke University to win the national championship behind Jack "The Goose" Givens. Rick Pitino, coach of the New York Knicks of the NBA, became the University of Kentucky basketball coach in 1989 and proceeded to resurrect the program after a painful NCAA investigation and sanctions. Pitino led the team to a national championship in 1996 and the finals in 1997. In 1997, after Tubby Smith replaced Pitino, who left to coach NBA's Boston Celtics, the Wildcats won another national championship in 1998. A remarkable feat - three final games in three years.

Since 1933, the University of Kentucky has won 40 Southeast Conference Championships. They won the NIT in 1946 and 1976.

In 1971, Denny Crum accepted the head coaching position of the Louisville Cardinals. Crum had played for John Wooden at UCLA. The Louisville Cardinals won two national championships in 1980 and 1986. Louisville dominated the former Metro conference and now under Rick Pitino will challenge every year for the Big East title.

Kentucky's basketball scene always has focused on high school and college basketball. However, Kentucky briefly sported a professional team. The Kentucky Colonels, based in Louisville, played in the professional basketball Association formed in 1967. However, the ABA folded in 1976. Despite discussions and dreams, no NBA team has ever located in Kentucky. No matter, high school and college basketball is king in Kentucky.

As basketball has been played through time in Kentucky and despite the glory achieved at the college level, basketball's purest form remains at the high school level. However, before high school, there is booster, grade school and middle school basketball to play.

CHAPTER 5
The Beginning

"Do not go where the path may lead; go instead
where there is no path and leave a trail."
~ Emerson

Championship athletic teams, as Rome and the other major great cities of antiquity, are not built in a day. Yet, providence and circumstances sometimes intervene and collide with destiny's fate. Billy Meier, Sean Dougherty, Troy McKinley, Alan Mullins, Dave Dixon, Dave Medley and Greg Ponzer happened to "come along" together at the same time and place in Independence, Kentucky.

Billy Meier's parents were Kathleen and Norman Meier. Billy lived contentedly on the short Apple Drive as a youngster. Apple Drive intersected Madison Pike less than a half mile south from Simon Kenton High School. About thirty small aluminum siding homes dotted both sides of the narrow asphalt street. Later, the Meiers moved a hundred yards south of Apple Drive on Madison Pike to a small house under huge oak trees. This house bordered Independence's only free standing pharmacy, Nie's. Billy grew up with an older sister, Karen, and a younger brother, John, who played junior varsity Billy's senior year at Simon Kenton High School. From childhood, Billy enthusiastically played baseball, football and basketball whenever and wherever the opportunity presented, whether organized games or with his friends.

Bill and Barbara Dougherty had two children, Sean and his younger sister, Kelly. Bill worked for years as a teamster truck driver for a company named Parsac. Later, Bill owned his own paper route for the daily morning newspaper, the *Kentucky Enquirer*. Barbara supplemented the family's income by waitressing at Independence's Ponzer's Tavern. Barbara, a petite and pretty brunette, always exhibited a cheerful countenance. Customers loved Barbara, so they tipped well. The Dougherty family lived on Mayflower Drive off Don Victor Drive about one mile from downtown Independence and three miles from Simon Kenton High School. Mayflower was a short narrow dead end street with about ten homes on both sides. The Doughertys enjoyed a backyard swimming pool. Encouraged by his father and relishing the excitement of the competition, Sean participated in every sport offered by the local Taylor Mill Booster organization.

Troy McKinley is the oldest child of Leroy "Bones" and Mary McKinley, Simon Kenton High School sweethearts, Class of 1958 and 1959 respectively. "Bones" received his nickname from a Simon Kenton Assistant Coach, Lafe Miller who assigned him the name when Leroy's skinny and boney body unexpectedly leaped up in the middle of a group of players during practice to grab a rebound. Mary McKinley's grandparents served as custodians at Simon Kenton in its early years and her grandmother worked in the school's cafeteria. Troy had a younger sister, Joy, and a younger brother, Jeff. In 1981, Joy cheered for the junior varsity squad. Jeff later played varsity basketball for Simon Kenton. Bones sold insurance at a small office in the Independence area. The McKinleys lived two miles south of Simon Kenton High School on Madison Pike in a small but cozy white framed house where Bones McKinley was born. Before the Madison Pike address, the McKinleys lived on Mayflower near the Doughertys. Troy grew up playing basketball, baseball and riding motorcycles, his favorite youthful pastime.

Alan Mullins is the youngest of three sons of Jesse and Ruth Mullins. The Mullins moved, when Alan was only one, to Walnut Hall Drive, a dead end street off Madison Pike, less than a mile from Simon Kenton High School. Alan, as the youngest of three boys, played sports against older and stronger competition. Alan played peewee football at only six years of age. Alan's mother was a homemaker looking after her sons and his father worked for Southern Railroad.

Dave Dixon's parents were Wilford and Dorothy Dixon. Dave's father worked as a set-up man at Lingo Manufacturing in Florence, Kentucky. His mother worked in product design at Stretch Sew manufacturing in Florence, Kentucky. Dave also had three sisters, Dottie, Sara and Kathy. The Dixons lived less than a mile south from Troy McKinley on Madison Pike. Along with Sean Dougherty and the others, Dave Dixon played sports in the Taylor Mill Booster organization which a group of recreation-minded men created in the 1950's. As a youngster, Dave was so skinny, you could have used him for a whip.

Dave Medley's parents were Bob and Pat Medley. Dave's brother, Mike, played basketball at Simon Kenton and graduated in 1980 where he also secured the honor of valedictorian. Dave's sister, Laura, also attended Simon Kenton. Laura currently teaches English at the school. The Medleys lived on Maple Tree Drive, a few miles from Simon Kenton on a street which intersects Madison Pike. Maple Tree is lined with large maple trees along its sidewalks so the street is aptly named. Pat Medley worked for the IRS in Covington while Bob pursued a career as an engineer for the CSX Railroad. Bob Medley worked for CSX for forty-three years. He retired in 2001, and as cruel fate would have it, died a year later of cancer. Bob attended Walton-Verona during his high school years. He played basketball at Walton-Verona before summarily quitting after a falling out with the coach. This Walton-Verona connection is the first reference to what is a rather surreal connection/rivalry between Simon Kenton and Walton-Verona.

Greg Ponzer is the youngest son of Vic and Sue Ponzer. Greg's siblings, in order, were Vic, Jr., Joyce or "Sweety", Mike, Guy and Greg. The Ponzer family contentedly lived on 12th Street in Covington, Kentucky until Greg reached the age of two. The Ponzers then moved to Roselawn Drive in Independence. Roselawn is directly across the street from Simon Kenton and Kenton Elementary as Roselawn intersects with Madison Pike. Greg attended both these schools in close proximity to his home. Vic, Sr. labored at the Bavarian Brewery a short stroll down the street where his family lived in Covington. Like Alan Mullins, Greg also played sports against his older brothers. Greg remembers the competition often led to violent fights. Vic, Sr. soon left the brewery job and opened up Ponzer's Tavern in downtown Independence across from the Kenton County Courthouse. Ponzer's served as the only sit-down restaurant and bar in Independence for decades. During the entire time Vic owned and operated the tavern, Vic jokes he never ate a single meal in the place because he never had time. His wife Sue cooked in the tavern's kitchen. The first Ponzer's Tavern burned to the ground. Vic and Sue reopened the tavern in a larger building. The Tavern served as the social and rumor center of the town.

"He knew everybody's business, but also everybody knew our business. As soon as I or my brothers acted up, which we had a tendency to do, he was the first one to find out. So as kids, we learned very early, you didn't keep anything from Dad because he was going to find out anyway from somebody else," Greg Ponzer explains.

These seven boys never tasted a silver spoon. They each hailed from solid small town working class parents. As everyone knows in America, the land of hopes and dreams, station in life and on the basketball court is earned by merit, not class.

CHAPTER 6
Seven Boys

"Leaders aren't born, they are made. And they are made just like anything else, through hard work."
~ Vince Lombardi

Troy McKinley epitomized the quiet, soft-spoken athlete who preferred to excel on the basketball court with little fanfare. He never sought or felt comfortable with public adulation. Smack talk, a modern day sports given, would be foreign to him. Giving him the benefit of a half inch, by his senior year in high school, Troy stood six foot six in his bare feet. He possessed a very angular body structure. He wore his blonde hair parted in the middle and feathered back on the sides. In the late 1970's and early 1980's, this hairstyle became the most popular among male teenagers. Troy's hands could grip and palm a regulation basketball. He grew early and often as a youngster, towering over his grade school and middle school classmates and teammates. He possessed a large square nose which he inherited from his father. His eyes cast a gentle gaze. His light skin complexion resulted in sunburn if left unprotected or uncovered. If compelled to describe Troy in a word, the word is quiet. Yet, Troy possessed an extremely focused and intense determination which never needed verbal affirmation. An introvert by nature, Troy still mingled socially and made, nurtured and maintained friends with little difficulty. Few can be classified in the category of someone "everyone likes" or "doesn't have any enemies". Troy is one of them. Troy always chose to lead by quiet example.

Dave Dixon's personality at first blush appeared the part of a quiet intro-vert. This first impression unintentionally disguised an extremely tough and determined young man. In old Westerns and even modern films, the hero often partners with a quiet sidekick who at certain critical moments surprises the audience with wit and spunk, catching everyone off guard. Dave possessed this trait. Yet, Dave Dixon proved to be more than just a "sidekick" or Tonto to Troy McKinley's talents and skills. Dave Dixon had absolutely no problem sticking it to an opponent physically or verbally. Unlike Troy, Dave talked smack to his teammates in practice and opponents at game time. His thin and long body stretched out six feet six inches by his senior year.

Dave's quiet nature differed from Troy McKinley's. Unlike Troy, Dave never hesitated to crack a jaw and never backed down. Dave Dixon was tougher than a pine knot. He reveled in the challenges he faced athletically. Slightly socially reserved, Dave still enjoyed being in the "in crowd" by virtue of his athletic talents and relationships. For example, his first cousin, Tami Elliott, a cheerleader, may have been the most popular girl at Simon Kenton when she attended the high school the same time as Dave. More than any of the other players, Dixon possessed a complexity.

William is a popular given name. Bill is the common short derivative. However, you have to be special to be a Billy. Billy Meier was special in more than one way. First, there was the natural and raw physical attributes. Tall at six foot six, he had penetrating blue eyes transfixed on a face with perfect angles. He often wore a mustache in high school. No girl or woman would ever deny Billy's irrefutable good looks. Yet, they weren't Rob Lowe pretty; they were Matthew McConoughey handsome. Billy was a man's man. The most muscular and "built" of the players, he exuded athleticism.

Billy also possessed great humor, a happy-go-lucky disposition and plenty of charm. He was all boy. He laughed and joked and never took life too seriously. He would form a natural alliance with the teammate most like him in disposition and athleticism, Greg Ponzer.

Billy Meier grew fast between middle school and high school. He was tough, strong and never afraid to mix it up. Unlike his other six foot six teammates, Dave Dixon and Troy McKinley, Billy was not quiet or socially reserved. Billy mixed it up with anyone. Girls flocked to him and he partied. Yet, parties never distracted him from sports. He loved competitive sports and he excelled in all the ones he played. Of all the players, Billy Meier was the most complete and consummate jock.

One player claimed the title as the physical and undisputed emotional leader of the team, Greg Ponzer. How probably the least skilled basketball player by his own admission became the emotional leader is a significant credit to Greg. Greg grew up the youngest of a sports family containing three older brothers. The Ponzers played and fought like hell. It helped forge Greg into the fiercest of competitors. At only five foot ten, Greg lacked height. However, God blessed him with the legs of a bullfrog. He would be the antithesis of the cliche "white men can't jump." From years of training and football, Greg developed an athletic body. Genetics also deserve credit. Greg's father, to this day and at over seventy, is still spry enough to whip most men. All the Ponzers played more than one sport. Greg played guard like the safety he played on the football field: fast, tough, hit what moves. He grew thick wiry hair which could grow into what appeared to be an afro. Along with Billy Meier, Greg was a raw athlete. Also, similar to Billy Meier, they could be boisterous and the life of the party. Michael Jordan admits even if he plays you in croquet, he's going for a win. So would Greg Ponzer. Harboring a hot temper, Greg never minded a physical altercation on or off the field. He also used a sarcastic wit on friends and foes alike. Popular from grade school, he never minded the limelight. Since his father owned the local tavern, drinking in high school became a foregone conclusion. His partner in crime would often be his buddy from grade school, Billy Meier.

Greg always stuck it in the eyes of his opponents. He would reach inside their heads and take them out of their game. He became the hockey version of an enforcer on the basketball floor. Every championship team needs a Greg Ponzer.

If you used a car model to describe an athlete, you'd pick a Ferrari to characterize Alan Mullins. While Greg Ponzer and Billy Meier matched up with anyone athletically and competitively, no one ever labeled their style "smooth". Alan Mullins exuded smooth. While Billy and Greg played "hostile", Alan played "agile" and "mobile". To borrow the often used phrase, Alan Mullins was faster and quicker than greased lightning. At five foot ten, Alan never bashed the boards, but in open court he glided across the floor smoother than a Ferrari across the Autobahn.

Similar to the Ponzer family, genes blessed Alan athletically. Everyone played sports in the Mullins family, including Alan's older brother Danny, another Simon Kenton sports star. Physically, Alan carried only a smidgen of fat on his slender frame. Strong and toned arms and legs served him well. Alan could stop on a dime, shift gears and fly to the ball.

Alan wore his blonde hair parted in the middle and feathered back on the sides. His face revealed a strong set jaw line. Alan appeared cast as a Spartan foot soldier. Similar to Dave Dixon, Alan was quiet and unassuming. Also like Dave Dixon, Alan was tough, focused and determined. He developed into the consummate point guard. No team wins a basketball championship on any level without a dependable point guard.

Sean Dougherty looked like the teenage heartthrob from the 1970's, David Cassidy. However, David Cassidy probably never starred in four high school sports. The shortest player on the team at five foot seven, Sean could still probably claim the title as the quickest player. Alan Mullins could burn it. Sean Dougherty could turn it. Growing up through middle school, Sean's best friend was Greg Ponzer. They would compete in everything, from sports to dates. It would begin in grade school where the two played basketball at different schools.

Physically tougher than Sean, Greg was not as quick. Not as boisterous as Greg or Billy, Sean possessed a serious side. Sean also carried a little insecurity which would manifest itself through competition and his need to always to prove himself. Sean became part of the gang who ruled the roost. Popular, he never shunned attention. Circumstances would require Sean place the team first and accept the dreaded role of a competitor with confidence - the role of sixth man.

Dave Medley, like Sean Dougherty, served as an unsung and unheralded hero because like Sean, Dave Medley was not a starter. The only other bench player other than Sean to play significant minutes, Dave Medley backed up the "Big Three" of McKinley, Dixon and Meier. Also from an athletic family where his older brother Mike starred with Alan's older brother Danny on the basketball team in 1979-1980, David Medley loved basketball. But for those he backed up, Dave Medley could start. The most scholastically intelligent player on the team, Dave graduated fourth in his high school class. Dave shared the Dixon and Mullins traits of quiet demeanor covering up focus and determination with mental and physical toughness. He also grew the biggest hair of the players. Similar to Greg Ponzer, his wiry hair grew out like an afro. Chunky, Dave bodied up and pounded with the best of players. He became a refrigerator in the paint. Dave Medley, despite being cerebral, threw elbows. He would be involved in a most unique and unprecedented fight in middle school which many politically correct observers today might consider reprehensible, but must be judged quite hysterical.

CHAPTER 7
The Coaches

"The coach is first of all a teacher."
~ John Wooden

At six foot four, Larry Miller played a solid game of basketball. Only thirty-one when he coached the Simon Kenton Pioneers during the 1980-1981 season, he remained in competitive physical condition. Larry Miller wore his dark hair short and parted it from the side. He could have played a lawyer or businessman in a movie or Broadway production. His angular jaw, Roman nose and blue eyes provided him handsome good looks. Sometimes Larry wore huge lens glasses which gave him the look of a principal or professor. But he wasn't a lawyer, principal or anything other than a driven, focused and passionate basketball coach. He also defied the image of a "jock" coach by teaching high school physics. Marv Levy, the former NFL Buffalo Bills football coach, taught and inspired his football players with lessons from history. Coach Miller used his knowledge of movement to develop his defense and offense.

Coach Miller smiled easily, but also could express his thoughts at times with a stern glance. He loved conversation, a good story and a funny joke. He cared about his wife, his family, his players, his students and his friends. Therefore, whenever they required his time he gave it generously. Beneath this exterior existed a man with a plan to reach his objectives. The energy to achieve revealed itself in his long quick step, his firm countenance and the clear conviction in his voice. Nothing distracted Larry Miller from his objective, not even an explosion which destroyed his gym. He wanted to win. He needed to win. He loved to win. He had to win. He would work, study, plan and organize for his singular objective: Winning.

Assistant Head Coach Dave Schadler literally saw eye to eye with Larry

38

Miller. At six foot four, they equaled each other's height. The similarities ended with height. Unlike the happily married Larry Miller, Dave Schadler played the active bachelor. His personality conformed to his marital status. Fun loving, laid back and rarely serious, Dave Schadler proved complementary to the intense Coach Miller. Many marriages discover strength in opposing personalities. The Miller and Schadler coaching union remarkably worked in the paradox of their differences. As Miller relentlessly drove and pushed, Schadler consistently smoothed and soothed the wounds caused by Coach Miller's punishing practices. Happy-go-lucky, Coach Schadler not only stood tall; he possessed a huge wing span of arms. He wore thick brown hair and a mustache. Sometimes he wore glasses. Coach Schadler had played college basketball for a while, so he used his personal physical skills to teach the game by example. He bonded with the players by being one of them, he casually looked the other way or gave a subtle wink and a nod when he knew Greg Ponzer and Billy Meier had tied one on. He banged on the boards with Meier, Dixon and McKinley to prove he could practice what he preached. The players respected Coach Miller. They became pals with Dave Schadler. This dual relationship proved valuable to Coach Miller. Miller pushed hard. Rather than breakdown, Schadler massaged the players through the stress. He served as the buffer between the players and their head coach.

Bill Pelfrey, Jr. learned to coach from his father. At five foot seven, Bill, Jr. stood in the shadows of Coach Miller and Coach Schadler literally, but not figuratively. His father, Bill Pelfrey, Sr., had coached the 1980-1981 varsity boys at Simon Kenton when the boys attended Twenhofel Junior High as seventh graders. Bill Senior, gray-haired, bespeckled, and short, always dressed professionally in a suit and tie. He focused all his energies on the serious business of fundamentals and basic skills. Bill, Jr. took his basketball coaching as seriously as his father. Handsome, blue eyed and clean cut, Bill, Jr. spoke with a slight southern Kentucky accent which reflected his mountain heritage.

Collectively, these four coaches, Miller, Schadler, Pelfrey Sr. and Pelfrey Jr., as John Wooden eloquently stated, would teach their players the game of basketball beginning with the fundamentals.

CHAPTER 8
Grade School

"I never had any friends later on like the ones I had
when I was twelve. Jesus, does anyone?"
~ Last line to the movie *Stand By Me*

Kenton Elementary is located a hundred yards from its "big brother" Simon Kenton. Kenton Elementary is south of Simon Kenton on the same road, Madison Pike. Today, only a gravel parking lot and the high school baseball field separates the two schools. In the 1970's, a lake lay between them. A young man drowned in the lake which resulted in the lake's subsequent draining. The baseball field and a parking lot replaced the lake. From 1969 to 1975, Charles Miller served as Kenton Elementary's principal. The school consisted of a gym, cafeteria, small administrative office, music room, library and classrooms for students on two floors and a basement. Since the student body for grades one to six totaled several hundred, more than one class existed for each grade level. For example, Ms. Bates, Ms. Cooper and Patsy Wagner, Randall's wife, each taught a first grade class. Warm and inviting, the parent-teachers association cared for and supported the school.

The basketball court had a tile floor. The stands consisted of concrete steps sloped from the floor to the ceiling. Directly across from the stands and along-side the court stood a wooden stage complete with curtains which the school used for plays, assemblies and student music programs. Wooden backboards complete with the iron rims hung from the rafters.

The success of Adolph Rupp's University of Kentucky teams during the era led to the school's logical adoption of the Wildcat mascot. Kenton Elementary also chose Kentucky's blue and white colors as its own.

Two main roads traverse north and south through Kenton County. One, Madison Pike, led to both Simon Kenton and Kenton Elementary. The other,

Taylor Mill Road, ran only a mile or two parallel to the east of Madison Pike and led to Whites Tower and Twenhofel Middle School. Taylor Mill Road is named after an old mill and is the main north-south corridor stretching from Covington through Taylor Mill and then south through Independence.

Whites Tower Elementary rests at the intersection of Harris Pike and Taylor Mill. From Harris Pike, directly east, Whites Tower is only a mile or two from Simon Kenton High School. Directly behind Whites Tower is the Kenton County Fairgrounds which in the 1970's hosted the Kenton County Fair the second week of August. Built in 1964, Whites Tower shared the same amenities as Kenton Elementary. Two miles apart by road, less than that as the crow flies, Whites Tower and Kenton Elementary boasted a competitive basketball rivalry in 1974 and 1975 when two groups of young boys battled for 5th and 6th grade supremacy. It is fitting the Whites Tower school chose the Bearcats as their mascot, the same name as the University of Cincinnati. Whites Tower's colors even included the red from the University of Cincinnati. As basketball fans in Northern Kentucky assert, the University of Kentucky Wildcats can beat the University of Cincinnati Bearcats any day of the week. The Whites Tower Bearcats and Kenton Elementary Wildcats carried on their own arguments regarding superiority.

By virtue of the location of their homes, Troy McKinley, Dave Dixon and Sean Dougherty attended Whites Tower and played on the 5th and 6th grade teams in 1974 and 1975. Billy Meier, Greg Ponzer, Dave Medley and Alan Mullins attended Kenton Elementary where they too played basketball. The players fail to remember too many details regarding their years playing against each other in grade school except the games always ended up being excessively competitive. In the 6th grade, Kenton Elementary won the league, but Whites Tower won the tournament. The two schools both beat the other schools in their league.

"As I remember, we played only ten or eleven games in the season," Troy McKinley recalls. "I believe it was always between us and Kenton Elementary for the title. We had a pretty good team. We lost only one or two a year."

"When I was a fifth grader, Greg, Billy and those guys were sixth graders, and we played in a tournament with the championship game. Whites Tower was unbeatable because of Troy, but we beat them in the championship. Later that spring, because of our victory, we rode in a big float in the Memorial Parade," Alan Mullins remembers.

Bones McKinley remembers, as many parents do, his son's sixth grade better than his son does. "In the sixth grade, Kenton Elementary beat Whites

Tower in the regular season, and Whites Tower beat them in the championship of the tournament. It was the only game either team lost in the sixth grade," recalls Bones of the season. (The rivalry continues as Mullins and McKinley fail to agree on who actually won the tournament.)

Dave Dixon remembers himself, Troy McKinley, and a boy named Terry Saylors towering over their classmates at Whites Tower. The Whites Tower coach still unmercifully cut the five foot six Dave Dixon from the fifth grade team. The Coach, Ivan Cooper, actually bought the house where Dave Dixon's uncle lived the prior year. Dave thought this connection would certainly help him make the team. It didn't.

"So I thought, well, I ought to be able to make the team now. My uncle sold the coach this house. But Coach Cooper cut me from the team my fifth grade year. I told myself I'm going to do what I can to make this team in the sixth grade. In the sixth grade, I made the team. I became the second leading scorer behind Troy McKinley. We won the elementary school championship. We beat Kenton Elementary," Dave Dixon recalls of the rivalry.

While Coach Cooper coached Whites Tower, Coach Spaw coached the Kenton Elementary Wildcats.

Regardless of who won, the players from the two teams both remember they played the elementary championship at Simon Kenton High School. Dave Dixon's uncle, Shirley Elliott, held the athletic director position at Simon Kenton at the time. "When we walked into Simon Kenton's gym for the championship game, I thought I walked into the mecca of basketball," Dave Dixon recalls of playing in the high school gym.

During these years of the Whites Tower and Kenton Elementary competition, both teams also played Walton-Verona Elementary where three competitive youngsters in their own right named Andy Burns, Curtis Carpenter and Johnny Anderson played basketball. The players from these three grade schools would have a fateful meeting a half dozen years later in high school. In the game which awaited them in high school, the boys from Whites Tower and Kenton Elementary teamed up against the Walton-Verona players. It would be one of the greatest high school basketball games anyone ever witnessed.

CHAPTER 9
Going to State

"A life is not important except in the impact it has on other lives."
~ Jackie Robinson

The Independence basketball players knew each other outside of school even though half of them attended Whites Tower and the other half attended Kenton Elementary.

Sean Dougherty and Greg Ponzer saw each other nearly every day. "I would ride my bike from Roselawn over to Mayflower. The Doughertys had a built-in swimming pool. Troy McKinley lived down the road from Sean. We would always play together," Greg Ponzer recalls of his childhood. "We always competed against each other. We were friends, but when we got out there, we played as hard as we could against each other, especially for team tryouts."

"I can remember playing Billy Meier one day after grade school in one-on-one up at Bob Medley's house on Maple Tree. Billy took it to me pretty good. He drove to the basket one time and I literally drove him into the goal post and he swung at me. We nearly fought a full blown fistfight. But that's the way our relationship developed. Three minutes later, we played basketball laughing and giggling, then walked home on our merry way. We simply competed hard. All the guys were competitive," Greg Ponzer remembers of the competitiveness.

The boys learned to compete hard and take no quarter in part from their fathers. Greg Kordenbrock played baseball in a summer league with the future Simon Kenton basketball players. "One game we played Cottage AC down in Covington. The opposing team's parents went after the umpire. Our parents intervened. A mom from the other team pounded Bob Medley with a purse. Vic Ponzer beat the hell out of a man from an old fashioned boxing stance. It was a crazy scene," Greg Kordenbrock laughing recollects of the baseball melee.

The fathers of the boys, led by Bob Medley, took the gang every year on a fabulous road trip from Northern Kentucky down Interstate 71 to Louisville, a one hour and half drive, to watch the annual Kentucky Sweet Sixteen Tournament.

The Sweet Sixteen tournament is the culmination of the Kentucky High School basketball season. The sanctioning body for the Sweet Sixteen is the Kentucky High School Athletic Association. The Association divides the state into sixteen regions. Each region contains districts. Based upon record, each district in February plays a seeded tournament. The two fortunate teams who reach the district finals win a bid to the regional tournament. Each winning regional team reaches the state tournament played in March.

In the entire sixty plus years of the tournament, when the 1980-1981 basketball season began, no team from the 9th Region of Northern Kentucky ever won the state tournament. 61 teams tried and 61 teams desperately died in the elusive quest.

Bob Medley and the other fathers packed the boys up and drove them to the Sweet Sixteen as an annual ritual. Bob Medley led the yearly basketball expedition. All the boys didn't necessarily make the trip each year and not all the fathers joined them. The exception was Bob Medley who never missed a trip.

Sean Dougherty recalls his parents removing him from school on Thursday and Friday to go to Louisville for the state games. The tournament is held Wednesday evening to Saturday evening. A team is required to win four games over a few days to win the State Tournament. "We'd watch every game. We stayed in the same hotel," Sean remembers. He recalls Dave Medley giving him the wrong time to meet at the car at the hotel one year resulting in Sean and Greg Ponzer missing the ride from the hotel to the final session.

Ron Coleman, the Simon Kenton Booster President and Public Address Announcer for 1980 - 1981, recalls trips involving four men sleeping cramped in two twin beds and five boys sacked out on the floor. Ron also recalls Bob Medley predictably waking him up with his loud snoring. Ron Coleman, whose daughter Shawna would also be a graduate of Simon Kenton in 1981, became the president of the Simon Kenton Boosters in 1981. Ron remembers the years taking the group of young players to the state tournament as his fondest basketball memory.

"Bob Medley was the ringleader. He would take eight to ten kids. We would go with two or three of the parents. My dad would go. Bob Medley would go. I think Sean's dad went a couple times and the Ponzers too. My gosh, my first experience at a state tournament was at Freedom Hall, '75, when Darrell Griffith played. He was unbelievable," Alan Mullins recalls of the trips.

Dave Dixon appreciated the support and encouragement the parents provided he and his friends. "A major impression on me was when we were in the fifth grade and sixth grade, a group of adult leaders, the men involved in taking us down to the State Tournament to see State Tournament games showed great interest in us. It was one of the best choices they made in preparing us to play. They knew it at the time too. From the sixth grade, every year, they bought us new uniforms. They always took care of us. They planned our future," Dave Dixon recalls of the parent's impact on the boys lives.

Dave Medley remembers the trip to Lexington with his family accounted for the annual family vacation. "We went every year for every game," Dave Medley recalls. "In middle school, dad started taking the team down in the Suburban. There would be seven, eight, even ten of us piled in the Suburban. We'd drive down usually for the quarterfinals on Friday. Sometimes, we spent the night and stayed for the semis and the finals the next day. The Suburban totaled over 250,000 miles before the end of its time. It was a beautiful two tone-yellow and orange machine."

"Bill Dougherty went. Alan's dad went. It was the fathers and the team. We were exposed to the environment and the thrill for many years. It was a big deal to our fathers. It was a great big deal to my Dad. My Dad attended every Sweet Sixteen since 1954. Dad may be one of the biggest basketball fans in Kentucky ever," Dave Medley respectfully recalls.

"My Dad would be sitting by a guy from a county two hours away and in ten minutes he's trading stories with the man as if he's known him all his life. Dad possessed extreme knowledge of the game," explains Dave Medley of his father's memory. Ron Coleman recalls Bob Medley remembered every horse, jockey and trainer for every horse which won the Kentucky Derby in the Derby's entire illustrative history.

"He came to every game he could which I played. My senior year, thanks to a rule the railroad used, he was paid days for not working. The reserve board is what the railroad called it. He made almost every game my senior year," Dave Medley remembers.

Greg Ponzer also recalls the trips to the state tournament. Trips he now takes every year with his wife and children. "I attended the Sweet Sixteen since grade school. Bob Medley always took us," Greg says.

PIONEER SPIRIT

Fidgeting in their seats at Rupp Arena, the seven boys ate hot dogs and popcorn, drank soft drinks, teased each other, watched the games and dreamed. Their fathers, proudly sitting behind them, dreamed with them.

CHAPTER 10
Twenhofel

"Don't ignore the small things. The kite flies because of its tail."
~ Hawaiian Proverb

Built in 1962, Twenhofel, in the 1970's as it is now, is the middle school or junior high, for all the students living in southern Kenton County including Independence. The Twenhofel Thoroughbreds, like Kenton Elementary, also adopted as their school colors Kentucky's blue and white. Three boys from Kenton Elementary and three boys from Whites Tower Elementary arrived at Twenhofel in 1975 to play basketball for the first time together on a school team rather than against each other. The years 1975 - 1978 proved to be the formative years of an outstanding basketball team. It really began in 1975 when Gay Best, Twenhofel's principal, hired a couple promising coaches named Pelfrey.

In 1975, Bill Pelfrey, Sr. coached the seventh grade basketball team at Twenhofel. Coach Pelfrey focused entirely on teaching fundamentals to his players. He ran drills. He repeated the drills. He repeated the drills again. Bill's plans remained simple. He emphasized execution and repetition. Stern, but fair, Coach Pelfrey always dressed in his suit and tie for games. The Twenhofel gym with its poor lighting and cramped space never deterred the focused Coach Pelfrey from his mission. Parents and fans crammed into the Twenhofel stands and gym which were smaller than an elementary school. It didn't matter. Coach Pelfrey would have conducted his practices and drills in a garage or a living room.

Bones McKinley appreciated the fundamentals Bill Pelfrey, Sr. taught his son Troy. "Everybody was scared to death of him because he yelled and screamed, but the kids knew why he was yelling and screaming. Also, it wasn't a mean yell and scream. His first year with the boys they lost one game in double overtime to Newport. The next year, eighth grade, they never lost," Bones proudly boasts.

Greg Ponzer remembers Coach Pelfrey, Sr. as a tough coach. "Some coaches you could get away with a little bantering back and forth, but you never tried that with him," Greg recalls with respect.

"He never cared about the score," Troy McKinley said. "If you made a mistake, he called you immediately over to the bench and pointed out your mistake and then he sent you back to play. He focused on skills and learning skills. He wanted each of us to play basketball the right way from dribbling, passing and rebounding."

"I remember playing against Newport. They stole the ball from me and a player headed down court with a break away. Coach yelled for me to come over to the bench. I had to let the guy go and make a lay-up because Coach preferred to tell me about my mistake than run back to defend," Troy McKinley laughs of the incident. Coach Pelfrey's attitude after a turnover against his team also applied for his own team causing a turnover.

"You could be on a breakaway fast break with an open goal, and, if you made Coach Pelfrey angry about something on the defensive end, he'd call you over to the bench. If you were ready to make a lay up, you still dribbled over to receive an earful from him," Dave Medley explains regarding the discipline from the coach.

At Twenhofel, Coach Pelfrey coached Troy McKinley, Dave Dixon, Bill Meier, Greg Ponzer, Dave Medley and Sean Dougherty in the seventh grade, together on the same team for the first time. Coach Pelfrey began to mold these eager and talented six players as a team. Along with their other team-mates, the six lost only one game as seventh graders. They still won the middle school championship. Mike Sebastian coached the team in their eighth grade year. The team was undefeated and won another championship.

Bill Pelfrey, Jr. coached the team in their ninth grade year. In the ninth grade, the Thoroughbreds lost only one game by one point to Holmes. "We had to play in the Holmes senior gym which had heaters sticking out of the low ceiling. Troy's shot at the buzzer hit the heater and we lost," Sean Dougherty recalls. Sean remains convinced Troy's shot was headed through the basket. Despite the loss, the Twenhofel Thoroughbreds won an unprecedented third straight middle school championship in the 9th Region.

Assistant Head Coach at Simon Kenton, Dave Schadler, recognized the potential for the Twenhofel team. He recalls attempting to convince Bill Pelfrey, Sr. to play Dave Dixon more.

"I told Larry Miller that David Dixon and Billy Meier were going to be solid basketball players. I told him they could be great basketball players. I told him 'Hell, we could win the region with these guys. We'd have more size than anybody,'" recalls Dave Schadler with enthusiasm.

"Dixon was really starting to improve. He possessed great quickness for a six-six guy. He also had a good head on him. Great quickness and he could jump. He also developed a nice touch around the basket. Billy never was a scoring machine, but he was a great athlete. When he was a sophomore, Billy was about six-four, big and lanky with a huge wing span. On defense, I'd put Billy on the point during junior varsity games. No team could get the ball past half court. Billy was quick enough to get his foot out of bounds before they could dribble around him and he blocked every pass they made. I played my five starters for a quarter, then substituted the second five. I didn't care. We focused on giving them experience," explains Dave Schadler of the talent he helped develop.

Troy McKinley played more basketball his freshman year than he ever played in his life. Troy started for the freshman and junior varsity teams. He also played varsity. "I played freshman and I started junior varsity. Coach Miller wanted the Twenhofel team to stay together. Despite my playing varsity and junior varsity, he wanted me to play with the guys my age too," Troy remembers.

"It was Larry Miller's belief the freshmen at Twenhofel should remain together to allow them to continue to win together. Troy came up and started junior varsity and also played varsity. But freshmen came first to Larry. Troy lacked one quarter of playing enough varsity to letter as a four-year basketball player. The reason he missed it was during a couple of the away varsity games, the freshmen played at home and Troy stayed with the freshmen. Larry recognized the importance of their remaining together. The players were buddies and a close-knit group. They were very motivated and very competitive on the basketball court," Bones McKinley recalls of the team.

Coach Miller in his first year as Simon Kenton varsity coach in 1978 instinctively reached out to the Twenhofel coaches and players.

"Bill Pelfrey, Jr. was 9th grade coach and his dad was the 7th grade coach. I asked Junior to come over and sit on the bench with us at Simon Kenton because I wanted a good relationship with our middle school. I drove over and watched them practice. Days they had trouble using their gym, they'd come over and work out with the varsity," Coach Miller remembers.

"Troy stood 6-3 as a freshman. Billy was a project with raw talent. Dave Dixon looked thin, but I saw the potential. Greg Ponzer was a strong kid.

Dave Medley and Sean Dougherty were good basketball players," Coach Miller assesses.

Alan Mullins never received the opportunity to play with his future high school teammates at Twenhofel. The rule at the time required a student to be in the same grade as the team.

"I always looked up to them because they were so good," Alan said. "They went through three years at Twenhofel and lost only two games in three years. We usually played our games before their game so we hung out and watched them play."

Dave Dixon remembers making the seventh grade team, but never receiving an opportunity to play. He recalls a funny conversation he held with Coach Pelfrey, Sr. on the playing time issue. "I asked him one day after practice, 'What do I have to do to play for you?' And he replied, 'Nothing.'" Fortunately for the future of Simon Kenton basketball, Dave Dixon never allowed Coach Pelfrey's decision to inhibit him from playing eighth grade basketball the following year.

After sitting the bench for Bill Pelfrey, Sr. in the seventh grade, Dave Dixon never played in games in the eighth grade either under Coach Sebastian. In Dave's ninth grade year, the Simon Kenton coaches asked players from Twenhofel's ninth grade team to play junior varsity and varsity. "They asked all the guys except for Brett Butler and me," laughs Dixon. Dixon finally received his chance. The coaches asked Dave to join them for practice one day . "In my first practice I faced Todd Penick, one ornery guy. Todd Penick pushed up against me. He's elbowing me while telling me he's going to kick my ass. I looked at him said, 'You're going to have to do it.' After I stood up to him, I never had a bit of problem," Dixon recalls.

"During practice, it was cut throat. You had to earn your way. You weren't going to get to walk. The challenge for us was time. We woke up at 5:00 a.m. in the morning to practice at 6:00 a.m. at Simon Kenton. Then after our shower, we went to school at Twenhofel. After school, we practiced freshman basketball. We left the house by 5:30 a.m. and returned at 8:30 p.m. every day. If we played a game, we got home even later. We played a lot of basketball. If it snowed, Bill Bromback opened up the Twenhofel gym and we'd play pickup games with anybody and everybody who came up to play," Sean Dougherty remembers of practice.

Dave Medley is convinced the team's junior high experience molded the team into winners. "Especially in junior high, but even back to the days of playing for Bob Wells in boosters and in grade school, we were always part of winning teams. This included basketball, baseball in the summer and fall booster football. We were exposed to winning," Dave Medley explains.

One of the funniest highlights of their junior high years was a fight on the court between players, Dave Medley and Dave Moore, while their fathers pounded each other at the same time. "It was at practice and during a jump ball situation. I tried to grab the ball first. I crossed over my leg in front of Moore's. I stepped on his foot too. I really wanted to beat him to the ball," Dave Medley recalls. "I remember Dave Moore's dad running out on the floor and yelling at my dad, 'Your son is doing dirty tricks.' Then my father came out on the floor and all hell broke loose."

"I think Coach Pelfrey chastised David Moore more than David Medley. Bill Moore took exception. Parents were there to pick everybody up and Bill Moore heard Coach Pelfrey yell at Dave Moore. Bob Medley and Dave Moore bickered back and forth over whose son started the ruckus. They both ended up going out on the court," Greg Ponzer recalled.

"Bob Medley grabbed Bill Moore in a headlock and began hitting him boom, boom, boom. Old Bill Pelfrey, Sr., ran over to try to break it up. He wasn't any bigger than a minnow. Bob Medley probably weighed 250 or 275 at the time and Bill Moore was tall and skinny. It was funny to watch. Coach Pelfrey yelled at us 'Boys, go in the locker room, go in the locker room,'" Billy Meier laughs recalling the players/parent fight.

Greg Ponzer gradually grew frustrated his freshman year at Twenhofel. "I played, but became frustrated with sitting on the bench too much. I didn't like it. I sat there thinking the hell with this, I don't want to be here," Greg Ponzer recalled. Greg's competitive fires burnt too hot to simply watch a contest. He needed to be in the action.

Bill Pelfrey, Jr. remembers the coaches attempting to develop the team from middle school. "We scheduled tournaments everywhere. We took the kids to Mt. Washington outside of Louisville. Steve Small who later coached the girls basketball team at Western Kentucky University coached an undefeated team down in Louisville. Our freshman and eighth graders played his kids on their court and beat them," Bill Pelfrey, Jr. recalls.

"We played games with the eighth and ninth grade together. Troy's eighth grade year and Mike Medley's ninth grade year played together. We sensed when Mike Medley and Danny Mullins were seniors and Troy and those guys were juniors we could have a good team," Bill Pelfrey, Jr. remembers.

Bill Pelfrey, Jr. developed a complete basketball program at Twenhofel. "When I moved up as the freshman coach at Twenhofel, I told the principal,

Gay Best, I would work for nothing to coach. He made me athletic director on the spot. I told him he didn't need to give us any money from the athletic budget. Just allow me to spend on my kids what we make. He enthusiastically agreed. We were practicing with rubber balls, wooden backboards and an old clock with the second hand going around. I felt I owed the kids in exchange for their playing first-class that they receive first-class treatment. We bought sanknit uniforms. Sanknit at the time was the Cadillac for uniforms. Keep in mind, this is for a junior high school team. We bought identical shoes. I contracted with a sporting goods company to discount shoes to the kids so they all owned the same shoe and looked like a team. We practiced with leather Rawlings game balls. We put up fiberglass backboards. We put side goals up. We refinished the gym floor and repainted the gym. Everything about the Twenhofel program became first class and it didn't cost the school a penny. We held dances. We brought in Coke machines. The coaching staff raised money on their own and we put all the money back into the basketball program. My coaching staff's philosophical goal was no other program in Northern Kentucky was going to look, act or play better than our kids," Bill Pelfrey, Jr. explains of the program.

Bill Pelfrey, Jr. also recruited his father, Bill Pelfrey, Sr., to the basketball program. "Dad coached at Ryland Heights and a vacancy opened up at Twenhofel for the seventh grade. As the ninth grade coach and athletic director, the principal asked me for suggestions on coaches. I said, 'Well, my dad expressed an interest in coming over from Ryland. He never suffered a losing season at New Haven or Ryland. He's interested.' The principal asked me, 'How do you feel about working with your father?' And I replied, 'He's an excellent basketball coach. He has the credentials. The fact our name's the same doesn't bother either of us.' Gay Best then hired my dad to coach seventh grade. Dad recognized our group as special. Everybody in the program knew they were special," explains Bill Pelfrey, Jr.

"Larry Miller looked to build a middle school program which would enhance the high school program. Rather than having two programs, he preferred one program. Larry embraced the idea and brought us all together. He wanted us to teach fundamentals at middle school so by the time players reached high school he didn't need to teach them how to dribble, block out, rebound and play defense," explains Bill Pelfrey, Jr. of the plan Larry Miller set in motion.

One day, Larry Miller arrived to watch a practice at Twenhofel. Bill Pelfrey, Jr. walked Miller around practice. Larry witnessed Troy McKinley shooting for the first time. Troy shot straight out from his forehead. Larry saw Troy shoot in this unconventional manner and said to Bill Pelfrey, 'Oh, Coach, we need to change his shot.' Bill Pelfrey, Jr. asked Larry to hold his thought. Troy continued to shoot from several spots around the floor and swished every shot. Coach Miller turned to Bill Pelfrey, Jr. and remarked, "Well, maybe we won't worry about that right now." Coach Miller would never need to worry about Troy McKinley's shot again.

In 1978, the Twenhofel boys basketball team finished a remarkable three year record of 55-2. Friendships formed during these Twenhofel years which would last a lifetime. Along with the boys, many of the cheerleaders who later attended Simon Kenton High School also attended Twenhofel. Jill Brueckner and Mary Zimmerer not only lived next to each other on Pelly Road in Independence, they attended Kenton Elementary and Twenhofel together. Growing up, the two became inseparable. Jill's father, Lloyd Brueckner, actually starred at Simon Kenton in basketball in the 1950's. One of Jill's and Mary's summer pasttimes included riding horses on the Brueckner family farm. They also rode their bikes up to downtown Independence to buy a hand dipped ice cream cone or penny candy from Riley's or Roxie's. During the winter, they rode sleds over the same hill they rode the horses. Another friend, Tami Elliott, would have Jill, Mary and the other girls over to her farm where they would fish and swim in the lake.

The April 1978 Twenhofel yearbook, *Thoroughbred Express*, reported the popularity of the future Simon Kenton Pioneers. Tami Elliott and Billy Meier won "Most Attractive" by the vote of their classmates. Dave Medley won "Most Talented". Greg Ponzer won "Most Popular". Jill Brueckner won "Most Athletic". Sean Dougherty and Mary Zimmerer were crowned "Mr. and Miss Twenhofel". Accolades would continue to follow the group through high school.

CHAPTER 11
"Exploding"

*"I returned and saw under the sun, that the race is
not to the swift, nor the battle to the strong, neither
yet riches to men of understanding, nor yet favour
to men of skill; but time and chance happeneth to
them all."*
~ Ecclesiastes 9:11

In 1978, after three successful years at Twenhofel, the Class of 1981 arrived at Simon Kenton High School as wide-eyed sophomores. Their sophomore and junior years would be full of accomplishment and the typical high school fun. Their senior year (1980-1981) proved to be as dramatic a year as any senior class could possibly experience.

Debbie Lockard served as the 1980 yearbook editor for the Simon Kenton Pioneers. For the 1980 yearbook theme, the staff chose the theme "Exploding." Not only would the word "Exploding" appear splattered across the dark blue cover of the yearbook diagonally from the lower left corner to the upper right corner, but the theme carried forward through the entire yearbook. Someone on the staff suggested the "Exploding" theme based on the ongoing construction on the school and the increased enrollment during the 1978-79 school year. Someone also recalls Western Hills High School in Cincinnati, Ohio, alma mater of Pete Rose, once using the theme. The staff's theme choice would prove eerily prophetic.

The following year, in 1981, the yearbook staff, led by Editor Michelle Sorrell, chose a rainbow cover with the theme, "No Stopping Us Now." Mary Zimmerer, art director for the yearbook, designed the cover. "We picked the theme before anything happened that year," Michelle Sorrell recalls of the choice. Shawna Cartwright and Connie Beach provided the teacher support for the yearbook. Connie supervised the work and Shawna served as the arbitrator of disputes over any decisions. The yearbook won first place with special merit from the Columbia Scholastic Press Association.

In 1980 - 1981, the entire world was filled with uncertainty, fear and a general discontent. The American public feared nuclear holocaust. Mark Chapman shot and killed a portrait of peace, the former Beatle, John Lennon. Iranian militants finally freed fifty-two American hostages after 444 days of captivity. Ronald Reagan won the presidency. Later, John Hinckley, Jr. tried to assassinate President Reagan. Also, in 1981, NASA launched the first space shuttle Columbia and Calvin Klein jeans became the fashion rage among the fashion conscious of the same year.

Top songs during 1980-1981 were "Call Me" by Blondie, "Lady" by Kenny Rogers, "Another One Bites the Dust" and "Crazy Little Thing Called Love" by Queen. "The Rose" by Bette Midler produced goose bumps on listeners. "Funky Town" gave everyone a dance in their step. "Celebration" by Kool and the Gang developed into an anthem to victory. Abba inspired its audiences with "The Winner Takes It All" and Styx released "The Best of Times." The King of Pop, Michael Jackson, shot up the charts with "Rock with You."

At the box office in 1980, "The Empire Strikes Back" led sales. The "Blues Brothers" became a cult classic the same year. In 1981, "Raiders of the Lost Ark" grabbed the sales top slot and the high school movie, "Porky's" made audiences laugh at disgusting adolescent humor. On the television, audiences watched "Charlie's Angels," "Chips," "Happy Days," "Mork & Mindy," "Magnum P.I.," "Dukes of Hazzard," "Dallas" and "Dynasty." The "Waltons" and "Little House on the Prairie" still drew an audience.

In country music, Barbara Mandrell won Entertainer of the Year in 1980 and 1981. George Jones won Male Vocalist both years.

In 1980, AMC introduced the first SUV, the Eagle. In 1980-1981, a Big Mac at McDonalds cost $1.25, french fries 45¢ and a Coke 40¢. A movie ticket cost $3.75 and gas was $1.30 a gallon. A young couple could take in dinner and a movie for $20.00.

In 1980, the United States at the direction of President Carter boycotted the Olympic Games in Moscow. Mt. St. Helens erupted causing a natural disaster. CNN began broadcasting on June 1, 1980. In 1981, Pope John Paul II also survived an assassination attempt. Prince Charles married Lady Diana. President Reagan appointed Sandra Day O'Connor as the first woman to the U.S. Supreme Court. MTV aired for the first time in 1981. A new house cost $78,220 and average income was $21,073.

Meanwhile interest rates and unemployment rates skyrocketed. The country found itself in severe economic crisis. Despite the national and world problems, the students at Simon Kenton High School were simply enjoying pleasant autumn weather and the excitement of the football season in full swing. In the middle of all the entire political and economic strife, the country found hope with a "Miracle on Ice." On Friday, January 22, 1980, the United States' mens hockey team unexpectedly and dramatically defeated the Russians during the Lake Placid Winter Olympics. The U.S. hockey team won their next game to capture the gold medal. The U.S. hockey team proved sports transcended politics. Al Michaels, while calling the end of the Russian game, rhetorically and appropriately asked, "Do you believe in miracles?" The win proved once again in sports the improbable sometimes happens. A group of young boys from Simon Kenton, along with the rest of the nation, took note of the hockey team's accomplishment.

CHAPTER 12
Explosion

"The grass must bend when the wind blows across it."
    ~ Confucius

October 9, 1980 fell on a Thursday. The school buses dropped off students at Simon Kenton High School before the first bell rang at 8:10 a.m. Seniors and juniors lucky enough to drive to school parked in their assigned spaces in the front and side parking lots. The mood of the faculty and student body was upbeat. Everyone saw Friday in sight. Many looked forward to the football game with Lloyd Memorial High School. This included Greg Ponzer, Sean Dougherty, Billy Meier and Alan Mullins, all football players. The weather added to everyone's spirit. Under clear skies, the temperature rose as high as 81 degrees. A slight breeze blew. It was a beautiful fall day.

Every school has one or two, maybe more, female teachers whom the young male students believe are hot. The rock band Van Halen commemorated the experience with a song "Hot for Teacher." Linda Whittenburg was a hot young teacher. A self-described hippie, Linda loved Led Zeppelin, Woodstock and the peace sign. She wore her dark hair in an eighties perm. Her slim figure reflected her health consciousness. Attractive inside and out; the students loved Linda Whittenburg.

Born in Owensboro, Kentucky, in 1961, Linda moved to Florence when only eight years old. In that year, her father, a terminal superintendent for Standard Oil, now Chevron, transferred to the Northern Kentucky area. Linda received much of her artistic talent from her mother, a seamstress. Her mother taught Linda to quilt, and Linda sewed her first quilt when she was only five years old. In 1970, she graduated from Boone County High School. Linda next attended Morehead State in the eastern mountains of Kentucky before attending Northern Kentucky University where she obtained three degrees.

In 1978, Linda graduated from Northern Kentucky University, and like many college graduates at times, couldn't find a job. Desperate, she reluctantly accepted a job substitute teaching at Boone County High School. Paul Hogan, in charge of substitute teachers at Boone County, was a friend of Bob Abel, the Simon Kenton principal. Paul Hogan suggested Bob Abel consider Linda for a full-time teaching position.

As Linda recalls the events, Bob Abel called Linda from a football game on a Friday night from Simon Kenton and informed her he needed an art teacher. Linda immediately accepted the offer and began her promising teaching career at Simon Kenton in 1978 in the middle of the year. Linda taught all grade levels of art in her first year.

The second art teacher at Simon Kenton was Jan Sulkis. According to Linda Whittenburg, Simon Kenton at the time boasted the only high school in Kenton County with two art teachers. Jan soon focused on beginning and introductory art courses and Linda taught advanced students. "While at Simon Kenton, I instituted the advanced placement art program," Linda recalls.

Anyone who ever attended high school or any school understands the difference between a humdrum class with a boring teacher and a dynamic class with an inspirational instructor. As a teacher, Linda possessed the talent to transfer her enthusiasm to her eager students. A self-professed free spirit, Linda encouraged the same in her students. She allowed the students to play WEBN on a radio while they painted in class. WEBN remains the hard rock station broadcasting out of Cincinnati, Ohio into Northern Kentucky and the surrounding area. Led by characters like Gene Kavanaugh who received the vote of the 1981 class as Most Humorous, Linda's students enjoyed their art class. The students not only excelled in their individual work, they also painted many school projects. Linda's class painted backdrops for freshman and sophomore dance pictures and paper hoops for the players to jump through prior to home basketball games. Martha Zimmerer and her sister Mary painted the ceiling and walls of the front lobby of Simon Kenton in the 1970's. The work would remain for over 25 years until the 2006 remodeling of the high school. Linda Whittenburg rewarded her class with outdoor pizza parties. They returned her generosity by good naturedly playing tricks on her. Moments before noon on October 9, 1980, twenty-eight-year-old Linda Whittenburg was teaching her advanced art class in the first floor art room in the northeastern corner of the building.

The windows to the room fell just below the room's ceiling. Five to six feet of wall from

the ground met the window glass at its bottom. The windows compared to the windows of the first floor of a bi-level home. To paint the windows required students to stand on a chair or ladder. For several days, Linda Whittenburg permitted her students to paint seasonal Halloween scenes. Ghosts, goblins, witches and pumpkins would cover the glass. The in class assignment was a reward for the students hard work on their art portfolios. Because they painted glass, the students used tempera paint. As the students painted, Linda stood at a sink giving student aide Glen Bridges a difficult time. She good naturedly fussed at Glen to scrub harder as he cleaned the sink.

The students divided themselves in teams of two to paint the series of windows along the wall. On October 9, the two girls who painted the first window nearest the wall to the boiler room were not in class. Scott Wallin and Robert Williams, two juniors, painted the next window over from the wall. A fan of rock-n-roll, Scott Wallin chose a more elaborate and contemporary subject than ghosts or pumpkins for the window he and Robert Williams chose to paint. As Glen Bridges recalls, the two talented junior artists chose the back of the Black Sabbath album "Sabbath Bloody Sabbath" to paint on their window. Appropriate for Halloween, the back of the album of this hard rock group which in March, 2005 was voted into the Rock-N-Roll Hall of Fame, consisted of a four poster bed with a satanic figure struggling against being tied down. The satanic numbers 666 marked the baseboard of the bed. The lead singer of Black Sabbath was no other than the current pop culture icon, Ozzy Osborne. As the students painted, WEBN blasted from a nearby radio.

As the class progressed, a former Simon Kenton art student who previously graduated, Curtis Huser, stopped by to visit Linda Whittenburg. As Curtis smiled and walked toward Linda to greet her, a loud hissing sound slipped out from behind the concrete block wall which separated the art room from the boiler room. "We each turned toward the wall where the sound came from. I was probably twenty feet away," Linda Whittenburg recalls of the sound.

Scott Wallin stood on a stool near Robert Williams. Scott remembers at the time he "saw smoke coming out at the corners and underneath the wall." As soon as Scott turned around to look, the wall blew out. Scott saw Robert Williams fall. Because Robert stood on the floor, the concrete covered him. The explosion blew Scott clear. "I didn't know what was going on, but I saw the wall fall and knew we had to get out of the art room fast," Kenny Kleisinger remembers at the time.

"The kids were standing along the windows perpendicular to the wall where the sound came from. The door to the room was up right next to that wall. As we all turned toward the wall it exploded. It completely filled the room with dust and dirt. It threw everybody to the ground. We were shocked," Linda Whittenburg recalls of the explosion.

"I couldn't see the kids. I couldn't see anyone else. Curtis and Glen ended up beside of me on the floor next to an overturned table. We crawled behind the table and immediately realized we couldn't remain in the room. Flames rolled past us as the room temperature elevated to an incinerator," Linda explains.

"It happened so fast. We knew we couldn't leave by the door because the blown out wall blocked it. We couldn't crawl out the windows because the flames rolled down the wall below the windows. The flames shot straight at us like a blow torch. We pulled each other up and scrambled away from the blown wall. Someone led us to the door to the storage room which connected with Jan Sulkis' room. Our rooms were connected by a walk-in closet with shelves. We made it to the closet and I thought this could be like Beverly Hills Supper Club fire where they found people stacked up against the locked exits trapped to die. The Beverly Hills tragedy occurred a few years earlier so it was fresh in my mind. I knew I needed to get the students off that door in order to get it opened. It opened into our room. Somehow, I got the door open," Linda remembers.

Bob Abel, the Simon Kenton Principal, explained that the summer before the 1980 - 1981 school year, the closet did not exist. During the summer, the school created the passageway. Fortunately, it served as an emergency exit for Linda Whittenburg's class. If the explosion had happened a year earlier, the class would have died a horrible death trapped inside the burning room. Glen Bridges also recalls the door to Ms. Sulkis' class was supposed to be locked. Fortunately again, the door remained unlocked permitting the students to find safety.

"We made it through the closet and into another room. We worked together to open the door and we succeeded. We spilled into Jan's room which was also below ground. We actually crawled out her windows. It was a three foot drop to the ground, but we climbed out. Outside, I looked around for all the kids. I tried to take a count of heads, but once we escaped they scattered. I'm supposed to have my teacher class list in my hand so I can check off names, but I obviously left it in the panic," Linda Whittenburg recalls of the events. Glen Bridges recalls Gene Kavanaugh going back in to look for his girlfriend at the time, Charlotte Woods. He also recalls Scott Wallin climbing out later than everyone else and being covered in black oil.

As Linda counted heads, she saw Bert Bennett and Neil Steigelmeyer, the superintendent and assistant superintendent respectively, outside of the front of the building. She ran over and informed them she thought at least one student was missing. They asked her what happened and she tried to explain it the best she could in her shaken state. Linda then left and found everyone in her class except young Robert Williams. The seat of Gene Kavanaugh's blue jeans actually blew off in the explosion. Red paint covered Scott Wallen and Linda at first feared it was blood. The students had held their pallets of paint prior to the explosion, so each of them suffered a splattering from their paint.

Hope came from word someone saw Robert Williams outside the building, but Linda Whittenburg continued her search. She walked over the entire high school campus. She even ran over to Kenton Elementary where evacuated students waited. She searched and searched. Dazed, she sat down in the fall grass to rest. She laid back for a moment. One of the recently arrived EMS members ran over to check on her. She assured the good Samaritan she simply needed to rest.

After a short rest, Linda walked over to a house immediately across the street from Simon Kenton. She knocked on the front door and a kind elderly lady answered. Linda asked to use the phone and the lady readily consented. A long line had already formed to use the lady's phone. Fellow teacher, Mike Collins, held the phone. Linda walked over to Collins and, as fate would have it, Collins had already called Linda's husband for her. Linda accepted the phone from Collins and asked her husband to please call her parents to ease their fears.

"Then Mike and I walked back outside and across to the school. We stood in the front parking lot. As we stood there to speak, another explosion rocked the school. The power of the explosion knocked us both to the ground. For a while, we remained on the ground in disbelief. As we stumbled to our feet, the television news crews began showing up. They later interviewed me." Linda Whittenburg recalls.

The fire consumed Linda Whittenburg's purse and driver's license. Despite all which happened, Linda still worried about driving home without her license. She approached a Kentucky State Police trooper on the scene and asked if she could drive home without a license. He assured her that under the circumstances, she could. As the day's ordeal ended for Linda, it only began for others.

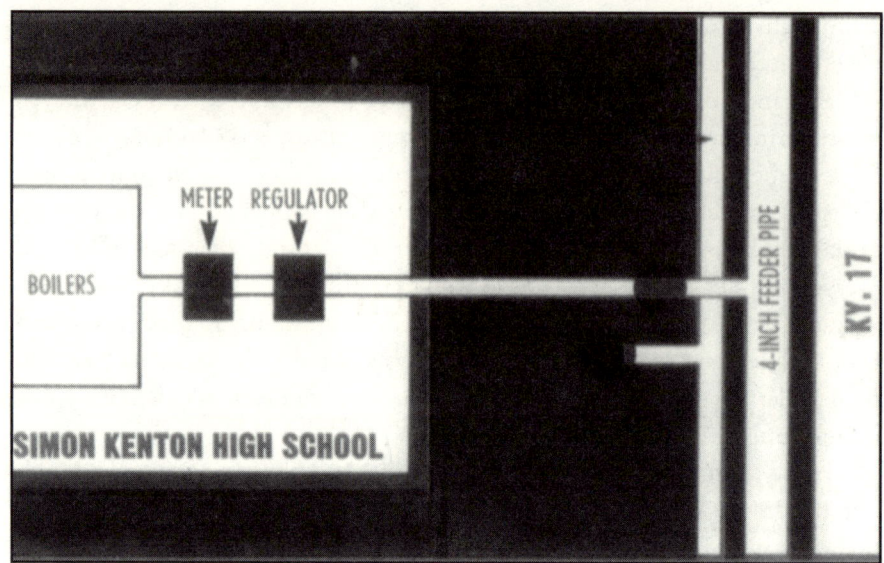

Diagram of the gas lines from the road to the boiler room. (Courtesy of The Kentucky Enquirer*)*

CHAPTER 13
Firemen

"Men are dependent on circumstances, not circumstances on men."
~ Herodotus

In 1980, the Independence Fire Department consisted entirely of volunteers. The department owned three stations covering the central, eastern and western parts of the town. The department operated three fire engines and a life squad. Approximately fifty-five volunteers supported the department with boundless time and energy. The department also boasted a ladies auxiliary. The department's revenue came from a tax on fire district property, a contract with the City of Independence, and an annual fundraiser called the Independence Firemen's Picnic. Over the years, the picnic grew into the social event of the year in Independence. Held the final weekend in July every year, the firemen took over the Courthouse grounds adjacent to their firehouse. The festival provided rides for kids, gambling games, music, dancing, a beer booth and fried fish for everyone. Everyone in the area looked forward to this annual event. If you failed to see someone during the past year, you came to the picnic to catch up with them.

In 1980, according to the Assistant Chief then, Rick Messingschlager, a dozen firemen reported to a scene for a normal fire during the day. On October 9, 1980, the Independence Fire Department's Chief, Terry Barnes, happened to be enjoying the initial days of an annual hunting trip to Colorado with his brother-in-law, Bob Young. Rick Messingschlager, the Assistant Chief, worked the day shift at Cincinnati Milicron at the time.

Every volunteer fireman kept a radio receiving device called a plectron in their homes. The men also kept portable radios in their cars and trucks. In the event of a fire, the volunteers would listen for their specific tone on their radios and respond if their circumstances allowed. How many volunteers made it to a fire scene was always uncertain. In 1980, the department had no paid men or women. The volunteers placed red emergency lights on top of their cars or trucks or their dashboards which they activated when rushing to a scene. The men usually kept their equipment with them. The volunteers became the Minutemen for fires in the community volunteer spirit of Ethan Allen. These community minded men often joined the department at an early age and the department consumed their free time. Training. Meetings. Runs. Their social lives also circulated around the department. Wives shared their husbands with the cause of the community. Ponzer's Tavern, across the street from the Courthouse and firehouse, served as the off-duty gathering place. Vic Ponzer, the owner of the Tavern, also volunteered. The Bach family boasted over ten members to the department: Bobby, Wayne, Kenny, Eugene, Tony (all brothers), their cousins, Tommy and Jerry, and numerous other cousins by another name including several Scherders. Most of the Bach wives or sisters served in the auxiliary.

In 1971, Ron Dennis joined the department at age thirty-one. Like Rick Messingschlager, Ron worked for Cincinnati Milicron. "I'd been around the department all my life because my dad joined when it was started. I didn't join as soon as I could. I waited quite a few years. I thought it was one of the best in the state. It was run well and everyone worked together. We also maintained good discipline," Ron recalls.

The department always kept a hierarchy of leadership based upon experience. In the 1970's, Warner Cox, Herbie Elbert, Roy Holten and Don Messingschlager, Rick's older brother, served as chiefs at various times. The men always elected their own officers. Charles Deters, who lived in the area, served as the department's attorney and guided them through any legal issues. He rarely, if ever, sent a bill.

A little before noon on October 9, 1980, Ron Dennis enjoyed his vacation without leaving town. Ron hung out at Harney's Service Station simply passing time. He left Harney's to go home, driving north on Madison Pike. Driving home, he passed by Simon Kenton High School. "I heard this awful roar which sounded like a jet plane. I looked all around. Then I saw all the kids coming out of Simon Kenton. I wondered what was going on. Why were they conducting a fire drill this time of morning? Then I saw blue flames shooting up the north eastern front side of the building. I accidentally became the first fireman on the scene," explains Ron Dennis of his unexpected report to duty.

Taylor Mill Athletic Boosters Boy's Basketball Team, Troy McKinnley is #8. (Courtesy of Medley Family)

Kenton Elementary Gym where Billy Meier, Greg Ponzer, Dave Medley, and Alan Mullins played in grade school. (Courtesy of the author)

Kenton Elementary's 5th and 6th grade teams

Live action in Twenhofel days. (Courtesy of Medley Family)

1977 8th grade boys basketball team

1977 8th grade basketball team in action

1978 freshmen basketball team

The undefeated Twenhofel 9th grade boys' team and cheerleaders 1977-78. **Back Row:** *5th from left #23 David Dixon, #31 Troy McKinley, #35 Dave Medley,* **Middle Row:** *from right, #11 Greg Ponzer, and Sean Daugherty. Mary Zimmerer is second from right in the front row.*

1978 boys basketball game

1978 Regional Champion Team Pic

MR. & MISS TWENHOFEL
SEAN DOUGHERTY
MARY ZIMMERER

SUPERLATIVES

MOST POPULAR
GREG PONZER
ROBIN GARRETT

MOST ATTRACTIVE
BILLY MEIER
TAMI ELLIOTT

MOST TALENTED
DAVE MEDLEY
MISSY NOLAND

BEST DRESSED
BILLY SHERRARD
ANGIE PARKER

White Tower Gym where Troy McKinley, Dave Dixon, and Sean Dougherty played in grade school. (Courtesy of the author)

69

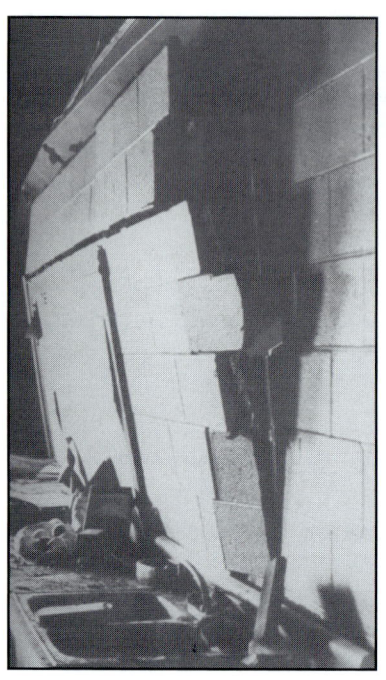

Mr. Jan Sulkes' art room after explosion

Lockers in empty north wing of school

Firemen soak Simon Kenton High School after explosion. (Courtesy of The Kentucky Post)

Damage from the explosion (Courtesy of The Kentucky Enquirer*)*

Damaged car owned by Tina Alsip

Creater dug in search for the gas cut off
(Courtesy of The Kentucky Enquirer*)*

Art room after the explosion (Courtesy of The Kentucky Post*)*

Following the explosion the high school smolderd for hours

Rubble and 6 inches of water in Mr. Shadlers math room

![Debris from explosion and flag]

Debris from explosion and flag

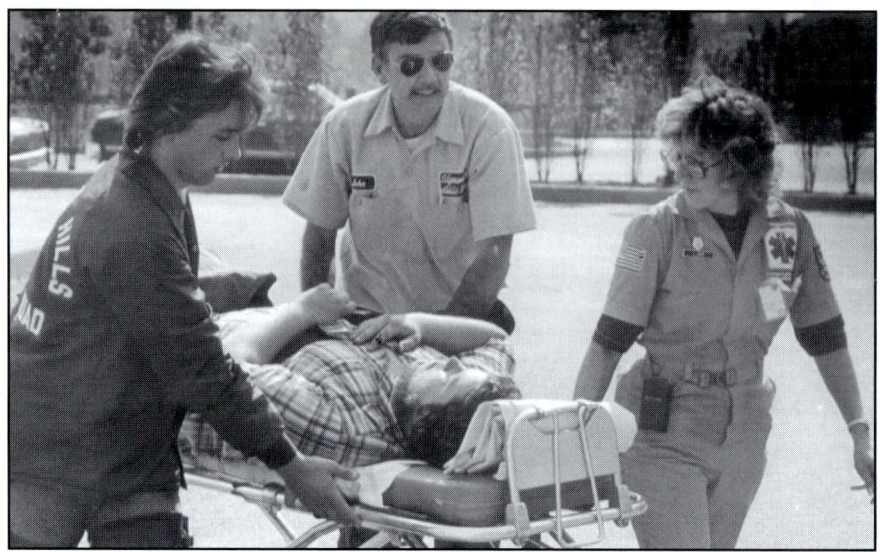

Life Squad members and a volunteer carry a fireman away from battling the fire for medical help on a stretcher. (Courtesy of The Kentucky Enquirer*)*

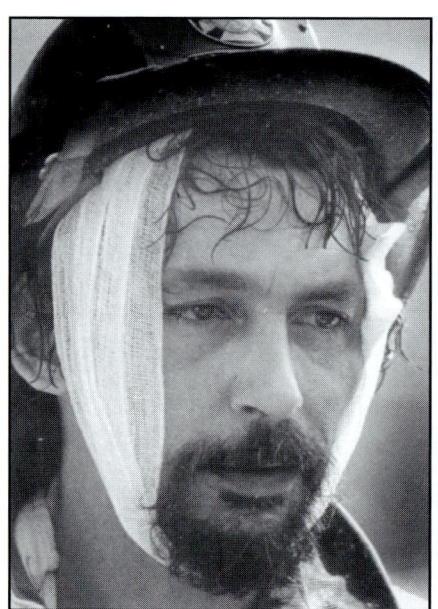

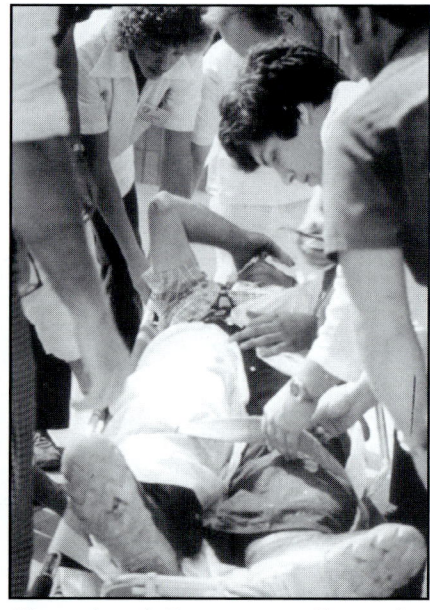

Injured Fireman (Courtesy of The Kentucky Enquirer*)*

Hospital and Emergency staff attend to an injured firemen (Courtesy of The Kentucky Enquirer*)*

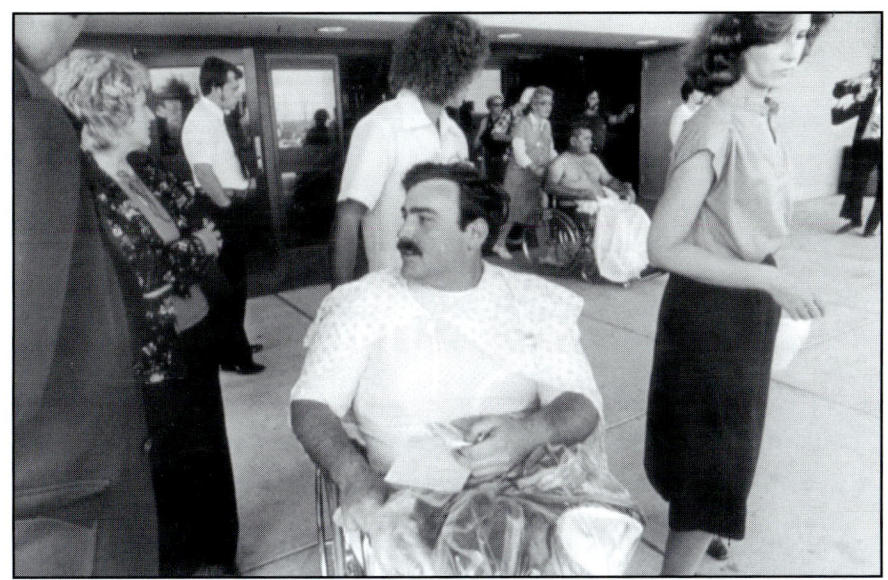

Firemen leaving St. Elizabeth Hospital after treatment of injuries sustained from the Simon Kenton High School blaze. (Courtesy of The Kentucky Enquirer*)*

Fireman remove Robert Williams' body from the building. This photo poignantly marks the greatest tragedy of the SKHS explosion, the loss of a talented young man's life. A life that would provide much inspiration to both the team and the whole student body in the coming school year. (Courtesy of The Kentucky Enquirer*)*

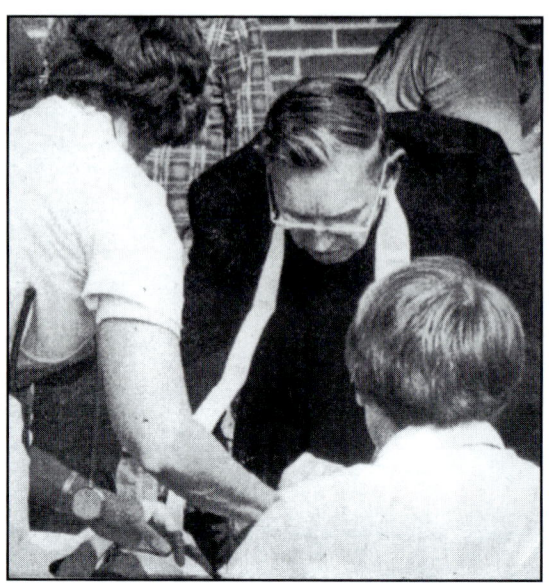

This SKHS clock's hands were frozen in time, chronicling the very moment of the horrific explosion.

Father James Rachford, St. Cecilia Catholic Church in Independence administers Last Rites to Vic Ponzer, owner of Ponzer's Tavern, as medical attention is given to him at the scene before being taken to the hospital. (Courtesy of The Kentucky Post)

Aerial view of the section of SKHS that exploded (Courtesy of The Kentucky Enquirer)

Front of school with flag at half mass   *Warning Signs*

Independence Fire Truck at the scene of the explosion

Worker hauls debris from school (Courtesy of The Kentucky Post*)*

National Transportation Safety Board conducted hearings into the cause and ramifications of the explosion. (Courtesy of The Kentucky Enquirer*)*

These paintings were created by SKHS senior Robert Williams, the only student to perish in the explosion.

R. W. Williams

Robert Williams was a Simon Kenton junior at the time of his death. His special interest and special talent was art. These paintings are a sample.

The Tiger is an example of one of Robbie's favorite subjects, wildlife.

Brenda and the Baby is a portrait of Robbie's cousin and her newborn child. In 1980 the portrait was judged best in show at the Simon Kenton Art Show and received first place honors at the 80 Boone, Grant and Kenton County Fairs.

Myrtle Beach is Robbie's last completed painting and was done in August 1980 following a family vacation.

The Clipper Ship is painted entirely in shades of purple. It received honorable mention at the 1977 Kenton County Fair and first place at the '77 Boone County Fair.

The Elvis portrait received first place from judges at the 1978 Grant and Kenton County Fairs. At the '78 Boone County Fair, it was judged first place, best in show and received the first Grand Champion ribbon awarded for art in the history of the fair. Robbie was 14 when he painted Elvis as a gift to his father.

Elvis

Art courtesy of Mr. and Mrs. R. W. Williams.

Robert Williams

School district administrators had already called the Kenton County Police, Independence Police, Independence Fire Department and the utility ULH&P. Three county and one city cruiser also arrived after the dispatch. The police who arrived first radioed the dispatcher to summon all available fire and emergency units in Northern Kentucky. Everyone feared the worst. The dispatch activated the tones to the volunteer firemen of Independence and firemen began arriving. The ULH&P workers in the area arrived to search for a gas cutoff valve in light of the strong natural gas odor outside the school building. The police dispatcher also called Dr. David Suetholtz, Deputy Kenton County Coroner, in anticipation of casualties. Later, the state arson investigator, James Stephens, asked the Kenton County Police dispatcher to call in the federal Alcohol, Tobacco and Firearms explosion experts to the scene.

Seconds after the explosion at Simon Kenton High School, Kenton County Police dispatcher Pam Siffel's switchboard exploded. "Get us help down here at Simon Kenton right away. We've had an explosion," Sharon Hesselman, receptionist at the Kenton County School Board office, told Ms. Siffel. From that moment forward, circumstances caught dispatcher Siffel in a communications crossfire. She activated alert units in the homes of volunteer firemen throughout Kenton County. She located and dispatched every available fire and life squad unit while fielding telephone calls from hundreds of parents frantic about their children's safety. "The phones went berserk. Everyone called. It got so busy. I was extremely upset because I didn't know if my nephew, a junior at Simon Kenton, was safe. I didn't want to ask, but it did bother me. It was just a thing that you have to lay everything else aside and do your job," explained Pam Siffel at the time.

Listening to the dispatch tape provides an accurate report of the emergency personnel reporting to the scene. Countless departments call in and Ms. Siffel tries her best to respond. After the initial call, Ms. Siffel called all Northern Kentucky units to the scene as directed. After realizing casualties were not as high as expected, a disregard is sent to all departments with the exception of water tankers. The anxiety and fear in all the voices is evident. Then there is a radio calm. However, after a second explosion hits, all hell breaks lose again. It's clear many, many firemen are injured in the second explosion. Those who moments earlier were told to disregard are called hurriedly back to the scene. This includes the Airport's unit with a capacity to accommodate 200 casualties. Units coming from different counties ask directions. Through the noise and heavy radio traffic, Ms. Siffel gives them directions. Requests come in from ambulances to call relatives. Ms. Siffel explains she doesn't have time for that responsibility. Quite simply, she performed extremely well under the pressure. Police secretary, Carol Callis, along with police Chief James Callahan and Patrolman Steve McCoy, also helped man the phones with Pam Siffel. Ms. Siffel's voice is the only one heard on the dispatch tape.

Every police officer on Kenton County's police force responded to Simon Kenton High School. Miami Township (Ohio) and Cincinnati police called to offer help. Neighboring Boone County units hurried frantically to the scene. At the scene, fire trucks and life squads arrived in overwhelming force. The vehicles surrounded the building, filled the parking lot in front of the school and lined both sides of Madison Pike north and south of the school. Fire fighting units responded from neighboring counties to the south, Gallatin County and Grant County. St. Luke Hospital in Ft. Thomas in Campbell County dispatched its disaster van. The Greater Cincinnati International Airport's emergency command post van also was called to the scene. The American Red Cross and Salvation Army set up canteen operations with hot coffee, soft drinks and sandwiches.

"I kept an adjustable wrench in my Jeep and I had my equipment. I put on my coat and helmet, walked to the plug (the only one in front of the school), took the caps off and started loosening things so when our truck arrived, I'd be ready. The first truck pulled up and I hooked him up. About the time I finished hooking him up, someone over the radio asked us to move the truck. So I unhooked him," Ron Dennis recalls of his first actions on the scene.

Independence volunteer Tommy Bach also grabbed a hose line. Tommy arrived on the scene ten minutes after the explosion from his mechanics job at the Rockcastle Auto Dealer in Florence, Kentucky. His future wife, Barb Hensley, a member of the Independence auxiliary also rushed to the scene and triaged patients. Tommy remembers the chaos from all the departments "doing their own thing" which resulted in one department putting out the gas fire over instructions to allow the gas to burn. Ron Dennis asked Tommy if Tommy preferred Ron to take Tommy's line. Tommy handed the hose to Ron because, at the time, Tommy ranked the highest on the scene from Independence and the department needed Tommy elsewhere. Ron methodically watered down the fire through the blown out windows. Ron saw and smelled natural gas spewing from the building. He doused the books and desks he saw burning and searched for a young student everyone confirmed missing. Then, with overwhelming force, a second explosion struck at approximately 12:20 p.m.

"I recall flying through the air and hitting the ground. I heard my hair sizzling as it burned. When my hair hit the water, it just sizzled. I laid there unable to move a muscle. The force knocked me out. When I awoke, two or three men attempted to pick me up. They took off with me, but then dropped me. I probably weighed 250 pounds. I also couldn't see. Being blind scared the hell out of me. I just saw gray. I thought, oh, man, I have small kids. What will I do if I'm blind? Some men covered up my face with bandages and drove off with me in an ambulance. I asked, 'Where you boys from?' They responded, 'Florence'. I replied, 'Boy, I'm glad some of my neighbors got me.' They drove me to the hospital where my bandages were removed. I thanked God because I could see. I was so happy I could see them. I suffered cuts and burns all over my face and hands. We didn't have the equipment we have today. I burned third degree in places," Ron Dennis explained his condition. After the second explosion, a freshman, Carolyn Perry, recalls Cheryl Dennis, a student and Ron Dennis's daughter, saw her father blown back from her vantage point near the school. Carolyn recalls Cheryl yelling in horror, "Dad, that's my Dad!" Cheryl began to run toward the school when Carolyn's mother grabbed her. Carolyn's mother told Cheryl she may be mistaken and should not jump to conclusions. The three sank to the ground and prayed in silence.

Bill Eggleston is a member of one of the largest Independence area families. His mother, Loretta Schoborg, was a member of probably the Independence area's largest family. Loretta's brother, Norb Schoborg, served as Mayor of Independence for a brief time. Loretta married Howard Eggleston and populated Independence with two sons and nine daughters. Bill's sisters, Rita and Barbara, proudly hold several women's basketball records at Simon Kenton High School. In 1980, Bill worked for a trucking company, C W Transport. At noon on October 9, 1980, Bill found himself at the Independence firehouse drilling. When the call came in for Simon Kenton, Bill leaped in the first available truck and drove as fast as possible to the scene with all the truck's lights flashing and sirens wailing. Bill Stambaugh brought the second truck from the station. Stan Kahrs and John Piper would soon join Eggleston and Stambaugh on the scene.

"Smoke and flames shot out of the bottom of the windows. People scrambling everywhere. I grabbed the radio after arriving and called the county dispatch. I spoke to Pam Siffel and yelled - 'Send me all the ambulances you can get. I don't have time to talk. I've got a bad fire here.' I had no clue how bad it was, but it didn't look good. I started setting up the truck. I was in charge until Tommy Bach came. I never left the truck. I stayed as a pump operator. Finally, the third truck came up and we sent it to the lake for more water because we sucked the plugs dry. We hurried to the lake and laid a line. At that time, the second explosion blew and I was thrown flat against the truck. I witnessed more firemen blown in the air. It was a hell of an explosion," Bill Eggleston recalls of the second explosion.

As the firemen and utility company workers searched desperately to no avail for the gas cutoff valve to the school, Russell England, a Kenton County Sheriff Deputy, hurriedly blocked ongoing traffic at the intersection of Walton-Nicholson and Madison Pike two miles south of Simon Kenton. Nearly all the parents he stopped from driving their cars up Madison Pike, stopped, parked their cars on the side of the road and ran the two miles to Simon Kenton. Russell's son, an Independence Policeman at the time, Rusty, Jr., could operate a back hoe and knew his father kept one at his home less than a mile north from the school. Rusty sped to his father's, rushed the backhoe up to Simon Kenton and began frantically digging for the gas cutoff which appeared covered over with grass and dirt. This was about 1:00 p.m. In his desperate search, Rusty dug a hole large and deep enough for a crater created by a celestial meteor. The architect for the school, Robert Hayes, arrived about 1:00 p.m. too. Hayes' plans indicated the location of the valve. At about 1:40 p.m., the men located the valve and finally turned off the gas entering the school. By 2:00 p.m. the firefighters extinguished the fire and entered the building to conduct the unpleasant assignment of searching for bodies.

"CG& E didn't know the location of the valve and we couldn't find it until the architect for the school showed up," Rusty England said at the time. Rusty England said Robert Hayes directed him to "within about 10 feet of the line". A section of ground, twenty by twenty feet wide and ten feet deep, was turned over with the backhoe in the effort to locate the valve. Rick Messingschlager believed the second explosion could have been prevented if the gas had been shut off sooner. "There was no question gas fed the second fire," Messingschlager explained. Superintendent Bert Bennett later attested the furnace boiler for the north wing's water heating system had been inspected two and a half weeks earlier by Lewis Farmer, an insurance company inspector, who certified the boiler for state officials. Bennett said Farmer found no defects in the boiler. "The boiler did not explode," arson inspector Stephens reported.

Southern Hills Fire Chief Joseph A. Messmer's units also came to the scene. "When we pulled up to the front, the building was fully involved in fire, but the windows were still intact," Messmer said at the time. "We needed water because the lack of pressure. I ordered the men on the trucks to lay a five inch line to the nearby lake." Messmer supervised the lake operation when the second blast occurred. At various times during the afternoon, Kenton County Police called for three water trucks to supplement the fire pumpers.

Meanwhile, other firefighters in addition to Ron Dennis suffered injuries in the second explosion including former Independence Chief, Herbie Elbert. Vic Ponzer, staring through a window when the second explosion occurred, was thrust back against a fire truck and injured so severely the local Catholic priest from St. Cecilia, Father James Rachford, administered the last rites. Witnesses reported the second explosion blew firefighter helmets higher than the three-story school.

"Our foreman at Milacron walked by and asked me if I had kids in the school. 'No, why, what's going on?' I said. He informed me of the explosion. I grabbed the phone and called the firehouse, but naturally nobody was there. They were already at the scene. Then I called Ponzer's Tavern. Sue Ponzer answered the phone crying and told me Vic was involved in the second explosion. That's when I left work," Rick Messingschlager recalls.

Stan Kahrs is also a former Chief of the Independence Fire Department. His trademark is a cigar eternally meshed between his teeth on the side of his mouth. He looks like Brutus from Popeye with his rough beard and his cigar hanging out. On October 9, he took advantage of the fair weather to toil in his garden on Belle Drive in the heart of Independence. By 1980, no longer the Chief, Stan served as the department's arson investigator. As he tilled his garden, Stan heard his plectron sound off inside his house. Stan dropped his hoe to rush to the high school. Jumping in his truck, Stan activated his emergency lights on his dash and sped south down Madison Pike. Stan reached Simon Kenton behind the first firetruck driven by Bill Eggleston.

Stan Kahrs parked his truck and checked first on the back of the high school between the library and new gym down the hall from the fire. He then helped set up a line from the truck Bill Eggleston drove to the scene.

Next, Stan walked to the front of the building with the Assistant Chief of Covington. Stan instructed the men on the water lines not to put the fire out due to the gas, but simply wet the area around the fire to prevent it from spreading. Stan then bumped into the Wilder Fire Chief, who also worked for the utility company. They held a short discussion regarding the shut-off valve problem. Standing ten feet from the window where flames shot out is where Stan found himself when the second explosion rocked the area. It launched Stan off his feet and in the air and abruptly dropped him in the driveway between the grass and parking lot. His face burned and his ears packed with sand and mud, Stan slowly rose to his feet and struggled to Ron Dennis laying on the ground nearby. Stan dragged Ron back from danger with the assistance of several Florence firemen. Stan didn't realize it at the time, but his back was marked from flying debris and he would later require medical attention at the hospital.

After extinguishing the fire around 2:00 p.m., firefighters found Robert Williams' unrecognizable body beneath the rubble in the art room. It took the firemen over an hour by hand to dig Robert out of the debris and secure his body. They brought Robert's body out of the school at about 3:15 p.m. A photograph in the local newspaper depicted the ghastly scene. "I was in the art room when they placed him on the stretcher and carried him out. My brother Donnie helped carry him. It was one of those sights you don't want to see again," Rick Messingschlager recalls.

They brought Robert's plain silver cross necklace to Linda Whittenburg and she identified the necklace. The realization that she had lost a student crushed her. Robert Williams' body was taken to the Hamilton County, Ohio, coroner's office. Deputy Kenton County Coroner David Suetholz reported Williams was burned extensively and suffered severe skull fractures. He never suffered the pain of the burning. He died in the first explosion from head trauma. "He was the best art student Simon Kenton ever had," reported Linda Whittenburg at the time. "Robert knew he was good because everybody told him. But it never made him uppity toward others. The kids all adored him. I'm just at a loss what to say." Prior to the death confirmation, Mr. and Mrs. Robert Williams reported their son missing to the school board office. They soon learned the worst news any parent could ever hear. They had lost their child.

Steve Sierveld worked as an insurance agent at the Heritage International office complex in Erlanger, Kentucky. A burly young man with beard and glasses, Steve also volunteered with the Southern Hills fire department the three years prior to October 9, 1980. A little before noon, Steve received the radio transmission for Southern Hills to respond to Simon Kenton High School. Steve sped in his car from his office with his partner, Jim Fulcher, to the Southern Hills fire station off Dudley Road which intersects with Madison Pike seven miles north of Simon Kenton High School. The trip to the firehouse took Steve less than five minutes. Four other volunteers also dutifully reported.

As the six Southern Hills volunteers made their way to Simon Kenton, they pondered the ghastly site which lay ahead. As they approached the intersection of Harris Pike and Madison Pike, a hundred yards north of Simon Kenton, Steve Sierveld recalls he had never seen so many police cars. "There were so many police cars, we had difficulty maneuvering around them," Steve recalls.

As the two trucks from Southern Hills pulled into the Simon Kenton High School driveway, Steve saw the flames coming out of the north end of the building and other firefighters already spraying water into the fire. After the Southern Hills crew parked and jumped off their trucks, a Covington Assistant Chief recruited them to use their oxygen tanks and enter the building for a search for students. Dutifully following orders, Steve and Jim entered the burning building from the front entrance on the second floor to the left of the fire. Breathing their oxygen, the two men turned right and headed directly down the hall towards the fire. In less than the time it took for them to walk ten feet inside the building, the second explosion struck. Steve Sierveld recalls Jim Fulcher being thrown back to the front door, while Steve flew to the ceiling. Steve will never forget the surreal sensation of slowly slipping down a slide as the floor beneath him gave way beneath him. In seconds, he passed out.

Steve Sierveld awoke to Jim Fulcher and others pulling on his legs. The pain was excruciating. Steve had fractured his right leg at both the tibia and fibula. Firemen placed Steve on a short backboard and his legs dangled over the side. The men slipped him in the Southern Hills ambulance which had arrived after their trucks. Steve Sierveld calculated only fifteen minutes passed from the time he arrived at Simon Kenton until he left in an ambulance. He would spend twenty days in the hospital and fully recovered from his injuries. On October 9, 1980, Steve's wife, Mary Sierveld taught school at Kenton Elementary adjacent to Simon Kenton. After Mary learned of the fire and explosion at Simon Kenton and not knowing Steve's plight, she called her husband's office and left a message for him that he might want to come to the school and help out. She didn't realize he was already there, had broken his leg and was headed to the hospital.

Leslie Leeke, seventeen at the time, showed up to the scene as a volunteer member of Walton's department. "I was standing by the boiler room vent with the hose when this guy in a yellow helmet tried to reach in and turn the gas off. He tried to put a wrench on it and it went up. I just heard boom and I was lying on the road fifteen to twenty feet away," he recalls. Remarkably, Leeke only suffered burns.

In the Cincinnati/Northern Kentucky area in 1980, no radio station could top the ratings of Q102, a pop/rock radio station. Their top disc jockey was Mark Sebastian. Obnoxious, loud and crazy, Sebastian enjoyed his job. Years later before leaving the station, he lost it one night and played Billy Squire's "Everybody Wants You" nearly a hundred times in a row. He ended each of his radio broadcasts informing his listeners he hoped to see them "completely, and I do mean completely, naked." Sebastian also adopted the habit of making fun of Simon Kenton High School from time to time for being a "hick" school. A little after noon on October 9, 1980, Mark Sebastian came on the radio and announced: "This is not a joke. There has been an explosion at Simon Kenton High School. All available fire departments are to report to the scene." He repeated this ominous message several times. It became perfectly clear this time, Mark Sebastian was serious, dead serious.

Parents, friends, grandparents, everyone who heard Sebastian's broadcast and others on other radio and television stations, felt their blood grow cold. What tragedy had befallen the school? Who and how many must be dead? Horror and terror filled the hearts and minds of everyone as they pictured a completely leveled school with over a thousand students, teachers and staff trapped inside.

Kenny Bach, my brother Thad and I were building fence near a creek on the back of the family farm on Green Road off Walton-Nicholson when we heard Mark Sebastian's radio broadcast. We sprang into a pick up truck and with Kenny driving, we went the five to six miles to the school as fast as possible. We beat Russell England's roadblock at Madison Pike. We feared the sight we might witness. We weren't alone. Hundreds, maybe thousands, dropped everything. Their jobs. Their work. Their plans. Many, their cars blocked, fled on foot running in a panic, hoping to find their loved ones. It was complete chaos. Relief took hold only once everyone learned their loved ones were safe.

In response to the Mark Sebastian and other media announcements, as well as Pam Siffel's dispatches, fourteen fire departments reported to the scene. Every single fire department in Kenton County came. Florence from Boone County brought their aerial truck. Fortunately, no one died in the second explosion.

CHAPTER 14
Players' Experiences of Explosion

"If you're going through hell, keep going."
~ Winston Churchill

Varsity cheerleader Pam Meenach focused on her classwork in math class above the boiler room before noon on October 9, 1980. After the explosion, Pam recalls believing another country had bombed her school. Considering the times, her reaction wasn't too unreasonable. Today, Pam's amused that she discovered outside the building she alone held the "bombing" opinion.

Sean Dougherty helped direct others out of the building.

"The new gym, which is the current basketball gym, wasn't completed. It was under construction. I was a teacher's aide my senior year that hour. I walked down the hallway outside where the new gym is and I was in the middle of the hallway. All of a sudden I heard and felt a loud boom. The doors at both ends blew open and all the ceiling tiles went up. My first thought was that something had blown up in Mr. Keith's shop class. Mr. Keith came down and I saw him shoving people out of the school. I remember stepping out the doors and looking out and seeing nothing but black smoke bellowing out from the front left corner. We helped direct students out the doors and out to the parking lot and then just sat there. I started worrying about my friends and sister. An hour later, I found my sister. Kelly's classroom was right near where it blew up. Ricky Grimes had stopped her class from walking down to that hole. She was pretty shook," recalls Sean Dougherty of his concerns.

The explosion would bust Dave Medley skipping class to leave school.

"I was skipping band to go home and eat lunch. I was walking around to get into the Suburban to drive home, eat lunch and come back. I was on the side where the explosion hit. I was walking through the parking lot when all hell broke loose. The explosion shook the ground and I fell to the ground. When the explosion hit, things moved in slow motion. I didn't know what it was. There was glass all over the place. The band was starting to go out on the football field. Students were pouring out of the school. I kind of got into a crowd there and went through the new gymnasium. I was standing over at Kenton Elementary when the second explosion hit. I felt a concussion, like they all describe, from over there," Dave Medley recalls of his experience.

Greg Ponzer escaped the explosion much better than his father.

"I was actually in the new building right above the boiler room and art room. I was on the third floor. I was an aide for Mr. Tom Hamilton. I was in one room grading papers and Mr. Hamilton was in the other."

"At the time of the explosion, we heard a loud thud. We looked around and the windows shattered. I thought what the hell was that. I walked out and looked in the room where Mr. Hamilton was and all these freshman students were on the floor under the desks crying and screaming. Simultaneously, the fire alarms went off. Mr. Hamilton went and looked out the window and saw flames and yelled 'Everybody get the hell out of here'."

"As kids, we didn't really respect what was going on. We reached the top of the third floor stairwell and smoke and heat were already up to the third floor. We didn't touch many of those steps on the way down. We ran down those steps and out the back. Everybody was outside. We were on the side of the building. We could see smoke bellowing out of the building and we could see fire. It was pretty upsetting, but we also thought great, the school is on fire, we probably won't have school tomorrow."

"I do remember teachers asking for Robert Williams. Then they moved us over to Kenton Elementary. We were all there and still pretty jovial. Then the second blast hit. I could feel the percussion from over at Kenton Elementary on my face. That's when we learned the firemen had trouble. We could feel the explosion on our faces and we were probably three hundred yards away. We started realizing it was a pretty serious situation. The city was flooded with cars. Parents ran to the site from two miles because they couldn't get through."

"I didn't realize it, but my dad responded. I didn't know he was hurt until later in the evening. Initially, they thought my father was dead. We were fortunate to keep him."

Billy Meier describes his recollection of the school explosion. "I was on the opposite end of the school near the cafeteria. It was lunchtime and I was in Mr. Hillard's criminal justice class. All of a sudden, we heard a loud rumble. The old radiators were real loose and we heard those rattle and then the alarms went off. We were close to the cafeteria and we exited out the rear door. We looked up and saw all the smoke coming over the roof of the school. Everybody thought, what's going on. Then everybody saw the flames. That's when it hit us. My mom was substituting teaching that day. Also, my brother John was a sophomore. I found out later my mother was walking around crying because she didn't know where we were. I was on the Kenton Elementary side, underneath the tall trees. I felt the second explosion there. In fact, I remember when it happened, I looked up and saw a fireman's helmet blown higher than the building. I thought oh, my God. Then all hell broke loose," recalls Billy Meier of seeing the aftermath of the explosion.

Dave Dixon, like many students, first thought the idea of their school burning down was an event to be celebrated.

"I was registering for classes before the school year and I wanted to take Ms. Wittenburg's class. She was a cute teacher and I thought it would probably be a good thing for me to take her class," David explains with a sheepish grin.

A photograph in the 1981 yearbook actually shows Dave Dixon drawing in Ms. Sulkas beginners class. Dave regretfully didn't receive his wish to attend Ms. Whittenburg's advanced class.

"I didn't have any experience with art so they assigned me to the other art class. Our art room went to lunch before Ms. Whittenburg's. We were in the lunchroom when the explosion occurred. When we walked out of the cafeteria, we were behind the school. We thought it was another false alarm. We were all joking and jabbing each other in the side. 'Burn, baby, burn,' is what we were saying. When we saw smoke and flames, we thought it might be more serious. They made us walk over to Kenton Elementary. We were standing on a ridge over there talking when we could see the smoke. Then we heard an explosion and a huge shock wave hit us," Dave Dixon recalls of his experience.

Alan Mullins found himself in close proximity to the first explosion. "I was actually in Phyllis Lonneman's chemistry class, two floors above the explosion. We were in the middle of a class when we heard a loud boom. It was glass breaking."

"Then the alarms went off and there was a little bit of panic. However everybody stayed calm. We walked fifteen to twenty yards to the corner of the building to the stairwell. By the time we started down the first flight of stairs, the smoke began coming up the stairwell from the bottom floor.

That's when kids began panicking. Everybody made it from the top floor to outside. We still had no idea how significant the damage was or the extent of what happened," Alan Mullins recalls.

"I was above the explosion. The explosion happened in the basement in the boiler room and I was two floors up in biology class. The explosion lifted our chairs up off the floor. We all looked at each other. The fire alarm went off. We realized it was not a false alarm. We started walking down the stairway. The smoke hit us in the face as we made our way down. We knew we had to get out of there," Troy McKinley remembers.

"We exited the building on the side where the room exploded. Smoke and flames were coming out of the art room. We saw Mr. Tolliver, the assistant principal, go back through the window. He stayed for a while and came back out."

"They evacuated Kenton Elementary too. They told me and another student to run over to Kenton Elementary and make sure everybody's out. We ran across the field to Kenton Elementary and then ran through the elementary school screaming to make sure everybody was out," Troy McKinley recalls.

Bones McKinley remembers it was the principal, Charlie Miller, who sent Troy through the school. "He said, 'Troy, you're long-legged and you're fast, go through the school and make sure everybody's out,'" recalls Bones. Bones shakes his head and grins at the idea of his son being sent back into an evacuated building.

CHAPTER 15
Coaches Explosion Experience

"When it is dark enough, you can see the stars."
~ Emerson

L arry Miller's initial thought when the fire alarm went off was "just another false alarm."

"The explosion happened a few minutes before noon and my class was at lunch. The old road ran right down beside the building back to the bus garage. It was dry that fall and they kept blowing up dust and it would set off the fire alarm. One false alarm after another."

"We were sitting down in the cafeteria. The alarm went off. I looked around and I said, 'I'm not going out. We've done this ten times in the last week.' Then Walter Bowen came running in and said, 'This one's for real. Get out. Get 'em all out.' So we rushed all the kids out. I went out to the front and I saw the fire coming out of the building. The firemen were there. It looked like only a little fire down in the hole. I didn't realize a wall had been blown over on Robert Williams."

"They put the fire out, but the gas was not shut off. The building filled with gas and another spark hit and I mean Boom! Those firemen blew out of there; it looked like a bad cartoon," Larry Miller recalls.

Dave Schadler references October 9, 1980 as the "longest day of my life."

"I was in my classroom on the second floor. The bell rang and it was lunchtime. We had to wait about twenty minutes and they would call us for lunch. All of a sudden, I heard a noise. The first thought which ran through my head was a delivery truck had backed into the building. That's what it sounded like."

"The fire alarm went off. We shut the windows, grabbed my grade book, and we rushed out. As soon as I made it out the door, I saw smoke around the front of the building and I asked one of the teachers to stay with my students. I walked around to the side of the building, and I saw Eugene Keith and other teachers. I remember Eugene saying 'Hell, we've got to find the gas lines so we can turn the gas off.' I tried to help Eugene, but I knew I didn't know where that daggone shut off valve was. I walked over and saw Linda Whittenburg and she told us Robert never made it out."

"I was between Simon Kenton and Kenton Elementary when the second explosion occurred. I saw the roof of the school go up a couple of floors and come down. Never saw anything like it. I ran to the building and the fire was worse than ever. They were pulling people out of there. We didn't know how many of them were hurt. Some of those guys were unconscious. We thought Vic Ponzer might be dead."

"I'm a bus driver so I started to load kids to take them home. It didn't matter where they lived. I don't know how many runs I made. By about 9:00 p.m. that night, well after dark, I finally didn't have any more kids to take home. I drove back to school. I parked the bus. I knew we're not going to have school for a while."

"I drove to Larry's house. I was dating my wife then and she had been trying to reach me. You couldn't obtain a phone line because everything was locked up. Finally, I reached her and told her I was all right. She thought I had gone back into the building."

"I arrived at Larry's house, and he gave me the news about Robert Williams. Everyone was devastated. After talking a long while about Robert, we refocused on our problem with basketball practice set to start in a week. Larry said, 'I'm going to work on a place and you reach the kids. Tell them we're going to try to keep everything as normal as we can and we're still practicing. You can drive the bus and we'll take them wherever we find a court.' We began making phone calls to organize practice. The first place we found was Walton-Verona. We started practicing over there. I'll never forget how exhausted I was at the end of the day of the explosion," Dave Schadler recalls. Despite the explosion, Larry Miller remained focused on his responsibility to coach the basketball team. Losing the gym and half a school failed to throw him off track.

CHAPTER 16
Administration and Community Response

*"Patience and perseverence have a magical effect
before which difficulties disappear and obstacles
vanish."*
~ John Quincy Adams

On October 9, before noon, Principal Bob Abel was standing in the middle of the school cafeteria. He felt a slight shudder, followed by fire alarms sounding. "Mr. Abel do we have to leave?" students asked him. Before he could reply yes, Walter Bowen, director of the school district's facilities, burst into a full cafeteria and screamed for everyone to leave. In response, Bob Abel calmly walked up the hallway to his office where he saw smoke and flame. He bumped into Tom Hatley, the Dean of Boys and a biology teacher. Hatley reported everyone was leaving the building in an orderly fashion. Together Abel and Hatley walked out the main front door. Only 39 years old at the time, Abel served as principal at Simon Kenton from 1971 to 1988. His philosophy of administration involved hiring a good staff and teachers and allowing them to do their jobs. As Bob Abel stood in front of the building in the parking lot, he experienced the full wrath of the second explosion. Bob Abel recalls watching a firefighter running out of the building with severe burns on his hands and elbows.

Pam Barnes, school receptionist and secretary to Assistant Principal Mike Tolliver, recalls many teachers believing an earthquake caused the building to shake. She personally thought a kiln from the art room blew. Few could claim greater connection to Simon Kenton and the Independence community than Pam Barnes. Her sister, Marilyn Young, worked as Bob Abel's secretary and bookkeeper. Her son, Danny was a freshman at Simon Kenton on October 9, 1980. Marilyn's daughters, Mischelle and Kim, were juniors and freshman respectively. Pam's other son, David was a fourth grader at Kenton Elementary. David and Danny Barnes would later be decorated wrestlers at Simon Kenton. David won a Kentucky state wrestling championship and attended college on a wrestling scholarship. Pam is also the cousin to David Schadler, the Coach. Pam recalls the week of the explosion was ironically "Fire Prevention Week."

In 1966, Mike Tolliver graduated from Simon Kenton High School. He moved on to the University of Kentucky, where he received a degree in education. Mike returned to his high school alma mater for his first teaching position. He later became Simon Kenton's assistant principal in 1978. In 1989, he became principal at Simon Kenton and served in that position until 2003. His daughter, Chelsea, is a current star on Simon Kenton's girls varsity basketball team. His wife, Tammy, graduated from Simon Kenton in 1981 where she also played basketball. A talented athlete himself, Mike passed for a dark haired and bearded Paul Bunyan, towering over everyone. He played catcher and first base for the professional softball teams, the Cincinnati Suds and Cincinnati Rivermen.

Before noon on October 9, Mike Tolliver sat in his office talking with a student. The assistant principal's office was on the right immediately inside the main front door. From his office, Mike heard a noise he knew was out of the ordinary. Mike stood up from his desk and walked down the hall from his office toward the art room. The double doors in the hall automatically closed as a result of the fire alarm.

Unable to advance further down the hall, Mike used the stairwell to move to the lower level. As he reached the lower level, Mike saw smoke seeping through the cracks of a classroom door. Feeling the heat through the door, Mike chose not to open it. He continued down the hall and exited to the outside. Along the way, Mike encountered Bill Boyle, a physical education teacher and wrestling coach. They walked to one classroom to look in the window. They discovered the room was clear of students. They stared into another and saw no signs of students. Next, they came to Jan Sulkes' art room.

Bill Boyle worked as the wrestling coach and physical education teacher at Simon Kenton. With a host of talented young wrestlers, in the 1980's Bill turned Simon Kenton into a state powerhouse for wrestling. Today, Bill, of all places, is the superintendent of Walton-Verona schools. His wrestling team, as a result of the damage to the school he now surveyed, was forced to practice in the old cafeteria all winter with no heat.

Mike Tolliver describes what happened next. "We couldn't see in Ms. Sulkes' room. My instincts told me somebody may be in there. Smoke hovered thick in the room. Bill decided to join me in entering the room. We both carefully crawled through the window. As soon as we made it to the floor, heavy smoke bellowed about us. We crouched down on our knees and felt around the best we could. We also yelled and received no response. After a few minutes, we both decided we should leave. We climbed out the same way we had come in. We saw the flames coming out of the next room. By the time we climbed out, the first firemen arrived. Bill left in another direction and I walked around to the back of the building to the courtyard area. I was standing behind a huge oak tree in the courtyard when the second explosion erupted. I heard and felt the rush. The tree saved my life," Mike Tolliver recalls gratefully.

Patsy Wagner, taught first grade at Kenton Elementary. Now retired, in 1980 she was, as she is today, a beautiful petite lady who always carries herself with elegance. She remembers the explosion from the vantage point of Kenton Elementary. "They informed us there was an explosion. I saw the smoke and the debris flying through the air from Kenton Elementary. We calmly walked the children to the back of the school. Parents ran from every which way. All the children became frightened. We tried to distract them, but it was awful," Patsy Wagner recalls.

Miskel Whitaker worked as Kenton Elementary's secretary. Her son, Greg, was a senior at Simon Kenton and a member of the Class of 1981. From Kenton Elementary, Miskel saw the band out on the football field. Knowing Greg played in the band, Miskel breathed a sigh of relief.

Bones McKinley remembers the explosion from Ponzer's tavern.

"After we heard an explosion occurred at the school, I couldn't eat. I had a knot in my stomach. I walked back to my office and tried calling my wife, Mary. All the lines were busy. I finally reached Mary. As a mother of two students at Simon Kenton, Mary grew hysterical. We heard on the radio and television that buses were taking students to Twenhofel. I drove over there looking for our children. I drove the back way to avoid the traffic. I also ran into Bob Williams at Twenhofel. He frantically looked for Robert. I said, 'Bob, he must be here somewhere.' I had talked to a fireman and I told Bob he told me everyone made it out. Bob managed the K-Mart in Erlanger and after he heard about the explosion, he rushed to Simon Kenton. I thought I was comforting him. I didn't know Robert's fate," Bones expresses with empathy and sympathy.

Neil Stiegelmeyer exemplified the calm, tough and orderly school administrator. Neil received an undergraduate degree in chemical engineering. He followed this degree with a masters in industrial administration. He worked for the Cincinnati based consumer products giant Proctor & Gamble, makers of Tide detergent and countless other products. After being active in the Big Brothers program and finding work with children appealed to him, Neil decided to shift to education administration. The same precise mind who applied principles of chemical engineering applied his talents to the efficient running of a school district. In 1970, he first taught chemistry, physics and science. He then became assistant principal at Beechwood High School in Ft. Mitchell, Kentucky in 1973 and followed that position with that of principal from 1976-1979. Neil joined Kenton County as assistant superintendent the following year in 1980.

Neil recalls his personal experience which led to his realization that sports played a critical role in high school. Beechwood High School received the Sportsmanship Award at a conference awards program in the 1970's. He asked those seated next to him why his school had won the award. "In fact one of the two people who answered the question was Simon Kenton's Athletic Director, Joe Stark. I was sitting between Joe Stark and Stan Steidel. They are both the same size. Huge. I am sitting at this banquet and I am thinking, this is nice receiving this award. I said to Joe and Stan, why did we receive this. Both of them, in a chorus, said, 'It's because you have the worst records'. That's when I went back to school and told the staff if the reason we win the awared is for losing, I don't want it."

Beechwood, through the hiring of a series of great coaches and player and parent commitment, became and remains a Kentucky state powerhouse in IA football.

Despite holding a well-deserved reputation as an academic, Neil realized the importance of winning athletic programs. "Everybody feels better. So whether or not you are winning in the school is important. I would like to say it's equally important for academics and other extra curriculars to go well within the school, but there is not a separate section in the newspaper for them. The publishers reserve an entire section of the paper for sports. The same is true for the television news. Sports affects how students feel about themselves and their school. It also engenders a spirit of cooperation within a school and makes the environment one of "we" as opposed to "us and them."

"It's interesting how schools cultivate the spirit. It results from success. They wear more school shirts and sweatshirts. Students attend more events. More kids desire to participate in athletics. It carries over. It's a part of society we created. You must recognize the reality."

On October 9, 1980, Neil Stiegelmeyer served as Assistant Superintendent for Kenton County Schools. His office, as all the District offices at the time was located one hundred feet from Simon Kenton High School on Madison Pike. "I was in the office at the front of the building. We heard a loud noise, but we couldn't determine the source. I walked outside the door of the office when I heard the noise," recalls Neil of the initial commotion. "Bernice Terry used a little cubicle across from my office. I was standing there by her cubicle the same time Richard Day, elementary supervisor, ran in the back door and yelled, 'This is for real.' I walked over to the door and intercepted him. We saw flames spewing from the vent by the boiler room and rising up the side of the building."

"I told Bernice to call the police and inform them we had a fire at Simon Kenton and then I walked over to the school. I entered through the main door of Simon Kenton because flames were coming out near the other entrance. At that point, we simply got everybody out and away from the building. I walked back outside to insure everyone went far enough away from the building. Within a matter of minutes, the teachers accounted for everybody in the building, except Robert."

"I was in front of the school when the second explosion hit. I was down by the doors so it didn't knock me down. The person I remember most at the time was Gerry Scaringi, a Simon Kenton track coach and teacher. The man constantly looked to see if anybody else remained in the building. We became concerned about Kenton Elementary. I contacted Bob Walter, the bus director, and he in turn found a whole fleet of drivers to drive buses to begin hauling kids home. We drove many of them from Kenton Elementary to Twenhofel. I needed a safe place to put them. Many bus drivers drove students straight home. I didn't know if we were going to have a problem at Kenton Elementary," explains Neil of the decision.

At noon on October 9, Vic Ponzer, age 50 at the time, served his customers behind his bar. Vic heard the fire alarm call via a fire department radio monitor he routinely kept in the tavern. Vic also heard and watched the trucks leave the firehouse across from his place of business. He soon joined others who headed to the scene a mile south on Madison Pike.

"I just ran out of the tavern and headed south. I left my wife Sue behind to watch the place," recalls Vic of his jaunt on foot.

Vic always kept the radio as a courtesy to the volunteer firemen who frequented his establishment. Vic also drove the ambulance when no other volunteer was available. He occasionally responded to scenes. On October 9, Vic worried about his son, Greg, a student at Simon Kenton. Vic's hurried trip to the school nearly cost him his life. Standing near the building gazing in a window with no fire equipment, Vic exposed himself to danger. The second explosion rocked the grounds and a section of aluminum grating from the boiler room vent struck Vic in the chest blowing him into a firetruck.

Mike Ponzer, Vic's son and Greg's brother, worked third shift at Johnson & Johnson in Cincinnati. A phone call to the Ponzer home woke Mike up a little after noon. When Mike answered the phone, he had on a pair of jeans, no shirt and no shoes.

"Mr. Ponzer," the voice on the other end of the phone said. "This is Channel 5 News. We know your family lives in Independence and we wanted to know what you could tell us about the explosion at Simon Kenton High School."

"What explosion?" Mike managed in his half asleep and disoriented state.

"There was an explosion at the school and we are trying to find out how bad it is," came the response.

Mike never took the time for a verbal reply. He slammed down the phone, disconnecting the call. Mike broke to and through the door without bothering with shoes or shirt. He also didn't bother to drive his car. He wasted no time sprinting up the street in his bare feet as fast as he could in his panicked state. Mike finished the quarter mile up Roselawn to Madison Pike in short time and stopped at the intersection to pause. Roselawn sloped up hill to Madison Pike so Mike found himself slightly winded. Directly across where Mike stood, gathered a sea of people between Kenton Elementary and Simon Kenton.

In remarkable fortune, the first face Mike identified from the crowd was his little brother Greg's. Relieved at knowing Greg was safe, Mike next jogged over to Simon Kenton. He reached the middle of the front parking lot when a large percussion slammed him to the ground. In a daze, Mike slowly regained his feet. As Mike struggled to stand, a firefighter reached him and suggested he check on his father. When asked why, the volunteer informed Mike his father remained unconscious from being thrown into a firetruck. Mike jogged toward the trucks and stumbled upon his father lying lifeless on the ground. Standing above his father, Mike found Father James Rachford, parish priest of nearby St. Cecilia, giving the Catholic sacrament of last rites. As anxiety overcame Mike, another fireman requested Mike search for his father's shoes. Vic lay barefoot as he received his blessing. Mike couldn't care less about the shoes, but in his frightened state, walked around to the front of the school searching for the shoes as directed. There in the grass, a small distance from the building, Mike found his father's two shoes pointed in the direction of the building with the shoe laces still tied. The explosion literally blew his father out of his shoes without disturbing the shoes.

Later in the evening, long after the life squad had transported his father to the hospital earlier in the day, Mike drove over to Cherokee Bowl on Taylor Mill Road in Independence. A typical noisy and smokey bowling alley and bar, Mike entered the bowling alley and to his amazement, the entire place grew silent. A few patrons walked over to him and expressed their condolences regarding his father dying. In a state of shock and disbelief, Mike ran to a payphone to call the hospital. To Mike's relief, his father was not dead. Mike learned later a television news show had mistakenly reported his father had been killed in the explosion.

Joe Stark carried a lot of weight on his enormous six foot plus frame, but Joe had a bigger heart. He looked the part of the legendary Sheriff Buford Pusser who inspired the *Walking Tall* movie. Joe served as the Athletic Director at Simon Kenton for over a decade including the 1981 season. The Simon Kenton basketball gym is named after the man whom everyone called "Big Joe". It's aptly named "The Joe Stark Memorial Gymnasium." During home basketball games, Joe always guarded the boys' locker room from any would-be thieves. An enthusiastic basketball fan, Joe attended the Kentucky state boys' basketball tournament each year. On October 9, the date of the explosion, Joe's wife, Billie, lay in a Jewish Hospital bed in Cincinnati giving birth to their son, Michael.

CHAPTER 17
Aftermath

"Character cannot be developed in ease and quiet.
Only through experience of trial and suffering can
the soul be strengthened, ambition inspired and
success achieved.
    ~ Helen Keller

Radio and television newscasts innocently and inadvertently created the traffic jam as parents rushed to the scene on the reports. By 1 p.m. on October 9, 1980, cars clogged the parking lot of Twenhofel, as parents of Simon Kenton High School students arrived to pick up their children. Countless parents cried, while many others sat and waited in stunned silence. By three p.m., only three buses arrived at Twenhofel with children on board. The majority of the students never showed up at Twenhofel because several school officials instructed the bus drivers to take the students directly home. Most of the 1,100 Simon Kenton students caught rides home with other students who drove to school and who were able to drive their cars out of the Simon Kenton parking lot.

A water shortage severely hampered firefighting efforts at the school after the explosion. In September, 1978, school officials applied for approval of plans to build a new gymnasium with lockers and showers, music room and industrial arts room at Simon Kenton. As required, school officials submitted plans for the addition to the Northern Kentucky Area Planning Commission for review. Water pressure tests at Simon Kenton at the time revealed hydrants in the area supplied only 1,000 gallons of water per minute. This was less than half of the 2,850 gallons per minute as recommended for schools by the Insurance Service Office in Frankfort at the time. Confronted with the obvious water shortage near a county school, commission members voted against construction of the school addition. Despite the negative recommendation, the school board moved forward with their plans for the addition.

When water pressure at Simon Kenton faltered, a pumper placed a line into the lake near Simon Kenton to refresh vanishing supply. Victor Fender, general manager of Kenton County Water District No.1, said at the time that the plans drawn up by fire departments for emergencies at Simon Kenton called for using water from the lake. "That would be the only reason to keep a lake at the school property," Fender said at the time. "Otherwise it would just be a nuisance. The lake used to be the only water supply to the school before a public water system was built. It was pretty common for schools built in rural areas to have lakes nearby."

A state fire inspector inspected all of the Kenton County School District buildings after the explosion. "We place emphasis on school general inspections," Carl Smoak, Deputy State Fire Commissioner said at the time. "We require one each year. They are our first priority." In addition to general inspections, schools are subject to inspections of their boiler systems once every two years. Insurance companies inspect the boilers and submit a report on findings of the inspections to the state. State records reflect the eight to ten boilers at Simon Kenton were inspected and approved during the late summer and fall of 1979. Bert Bennett, county school superintendent, maintained the boilers had been inspected again two weeks prior to the explosion by the insurance company responsible for the inspection.

Everyone injured at Simon Kenton High School suffered injuries from minor to critical. A volunteer firefighter for Piner, Dexter LaFollette, was working on his family farm in Piner when he heard the news of the explosion at Simon Kenton. He rushed to the scene in minutes. "I was up in front shooting water into the boiler room when a guy asked me to back up. I was out by the sidewalk when all of a sudden ... BOOM," recalls Dexter LaFollette at the time. The explosion lifted LaFollette thirty yards east of the building and dropped him flat on his back. When he awoke, LaFollette witnessed another fireman lying next to him with his head split open. LaFollette suffered minor burns on his face and an injury to his right side.

Covington firemen Mike Cioffe, Al Angelini and Ted Owens meticulously rummaged around the second floor inside the school scouting for possible casualties when the second explosion occurred. "They thought they had it under control and we went in to search for people inside. We saw a flash. In most explosions it's the debris that blows around and hurts guys. But it was the heat from the flash that burnt us," recalled Angelini at the time of his burn injury.

"I was just down the hall from where the second explosion occurred," said Walton Deputy Chief Bobby Glenn at the time. "It threw us up against the ceiling. The floor buckled up about three feet."

Despite thirty being injured, miraculously all the firefighters escaped with their lives.

Steve Brauch held his job as Community Relations Director at St. Elizabeth Medical Center for only two months prior to October 9, 1980. The explosion at Simon Kenton would be Steve's first disaster. Nursing supervisor Patricia Steuver issued a code "yellow" pursuant to hospital policy indicating the possibility of many incoming patients. The majority of patients injured at Simon Kenton were transported to the Medical Center's South Unit at Edgewood, Kentucky, the closest hospital. St. Elizabeth called in twenty to twenty-five doctors to treat patients. "Generally, most of our beds are full during our regular operations. Thursday, we called in doctors early to check out patients to make room for the injured," explained Assistant Hospital Administrator, Wiley Carr at the time. Inside the hospital, social services created an information center in the main lobby and issued updated information to anxious family members and friends. By 2:35 p.m., the "yellow" code ended as the hospital treated, released or admitted the last of the patients.

The National Transportation Board conducted a thorough investigation and interviewed everyone remotely connected to the explosion and gas valve issue, including the firemen. Rick Messingschlager of the Independence department testified his men received limited training with natural gas fires, but acted appropriately by not extinguishing the natural gas fire. Rick testified many Independence firemen were trained in procedures for battling natural gas fires in initial training at the state firefighters' school in Lexington. Ronald Dennis, the first Independence fireman on the scene, testified he had little or no knowledge of the proper technique for dealing with natural gas-fed fires. However, he testified he was instructed by Herbie Elbert, his former chief, not to douse the flame, but merely to try to control the spread of the fire. This is the proper technique and the strategy is designed to curb the gas flow to prevent further explosions until the main valve is shut off. However, many departments on the scene acted on their own at the scene and Rick Messingschlager believes one of the departments put out the natural gas fire. This led to the natural gas build up and a single spark set off the second massive explosion.

As evening came and night fell on October 9, 1980, the Independence and Simon Kenton community faced a paradox of feelings. Collectively, they carried heavy hearts from the death of a student and injuries to so may firemen and others, yet they breathed the sigh of relief knowing they had escaped what easily could have been a more lethal and fatal day.

CHAPTER 18
Robert Williams

"God's Finger Touched Him, and He Slept"
~ Tennyson

The Simon Kenton 1981 yearbook chose the moving quote above in their section honoring Robert Williams. His life tragically shortened, it is surreal that a promising artist would die prematurely in art class.

Robert Wilson Williams, II will unfortunately be remembered forever as the sole fatality in the Simon Kenton High School explosion. Born February 3, 1964, to Sandra and Robert Williams, Robert was generously blessed with an unmatched artistic ability. Anneliese Wahrenburg taught art in Walton, Kentucky, a town adjacent to the east from Independence. At age eleven in 1975, Robert began taking art lessons from Mrs. Wahrenburg.

"He was really outstanding, my best student in school," said Mrs. Wahrenburg at the time. "I visited with his parents and his father pulled out every drawing Robert had completed from childhood. I saw how he developed."

Mrs. Wahrenburg described Robert as a kind loveable person. "He sensed when a person was troubled and could smile it away. I held high hopes for him. His death is such a loss. It is a shame he didn't capture a bit of his fame while he was alive," Mrs. Wahrenburg explained Robert's loss at the time. She recalled telling a visitor to her art gallery that the world would hear from Robert Williams. "I loved him," Mrs. Wahrenburg added, explaining that she and Robert were alike. "I was always running around with a pencil in my hand and so was he."

"He was so promising. He had so much gold in his hand. He was a natural artist. He didn't have to work at it. His brain made his hand work. Most people have to work so hard," Ms. Wahrenburg explained. She said she could point out a stream and a beautiful sunset and Robert's remarkable talent allowed him to sit down and draw the scene without looking again.

Dwight Searcy taught Robert Williams and Scott Wallen sociology immediately prior to Ms. Whittenburg's art class on October 9, 1980.

"I always stopped a few minutes before the end of class and walked around to talk to kids. The day of the explosion I walked to the desk rows next to the heaters, back by the window, and I sat there on the heater. Robert and Scott sat at the back desks. I sat there and held a five or seven minute conversation with them. We talked about their art. If I had known, I would have grabbed them and held onto them," Dwight Searcy recalls in a choked voice.

Robert and Sandra Williams, Robert's parents and a younger sister, Stacy, fourteen at the time, survived Robert. Robert's best friend was his cousin, Jeff Williams. "Friends really isn't a strong enough word. We were a team. We shared secrets. You know the kinds of things you don't talk to anyone else about. We always joked around. We made other people laugh. We cheered each other up," Jeff Williams said at the time. Jeff and Robert played racquetball together, double dated, looked forward to attending college together and working as commercial artists. "We were different in that I'm excitable and he was always very calm. He would calm me down," Jeff reflected at the time. The cousins also optimistically dreamed about the future.

Robert's natural talent exceeded his years. The 1981 Simon Kenton yearbook honored Robert posthumously with five outstanding samples of his artwork. They included "Tiger" which captures the face of a tiger so perfectly it could pass as a photograph. One of Robert's favorite subjects was wildlife. "Myrtle Beach" would be Robert's last completed painting. Robert completed it in August 1980 following a family vacation. "Clipper Ship" is a haunting rendition of a ship and sails at sea. Robert painted it entirely in shades of purple. "Clipper Ship" received honorable mention at the 1977 Kenton County Fair and first place in the 1977 Boone County Fair. "Brenda and the Baby" is a portrait of Robert's cousin and her newborn child. In 1980, this portrait won Best in Show at the Simon Kenton Art Show and received first place honors at the 1980 Boone, Grant and Kenton County Fairs. The final portrait shown in the yearbook is a painting of Elvis Presley. It is a four foot tall, full figure of Elvis. Robert painted it as a gift to his father, an Elvis fan, when Robert was only fourteen. It too won first place in the 1978 Grant and Kenton County Fairs. The same year, Boone County judged the Elvis painting first, Best in Show and it received the first Grand Champion ribbon awarded for art in the history of the fair. After his untimely death, Pam Barnes believes Robert's family repurchased and reacquired as much of Robert's art as possible.

Linda Whittenburg still painfully misses Robert Williams and his talent. "He was just the sweetest boy. I never thought of him as anything other than just a sweet boy because he was kind to everyone. He always volunteered to help. Polite to all the kids, too. His classmates loved him. If they came over and asked him how to develop a color or where should a line be drawn, he would help them. There was nothing egotistical or self-indulgent about him," Linda reflects with admiration of Robert.

"He'd been taking art lessons since the age eleven. He painted realism. He involved himself in his paintings. He projected emotion in his work when many artists his age are simply trying their best to learn the basics. At his age, he was able to go even further and bring in the emotional aspect. That's a trait which usually comes with an advanced age in art," explained Linda.

"He painted primarily in oils. However, he could draw with anything. He drew with pen and ink. He drew in pencil. He used acrylics. He worked in any medium, but he preferred oil.

I think he was not quite ready to begin to pursue college. He hadn't started researching colleges. His big goal was simply his driver's license. He was a kid with this phenomenal talent. He understood it and he understood how important it was. He was willing to work and improve it. He wasn't going to let it lie. He also was having a good time dating girls and hanging out with his friends," recalls Linda Whittenburg of Robert's other interests and versatility in art.

Mrs. Whittenburg enrolled Robert in an honors program for high school students at the Cincinnati Art Academy and Robert had attended two classes.

"There was not a mean bone in his body. He never said bad things about other students or other people," remembers Linda Whittenburg of a trait lacking in many teenagers.

Melissa Morgan, a classmate and friend of Robert Williams, wrote the following poem in tribute:

Angel Named Robert
I know an angel named Robert
Who had to be sent from above
And now I know he'll return there
To be greeted by God with love.

He was taken so early in his life,
He was just coming into his prime,
But I think God knows when we must go,
He knows when it comes our time.

His talent was loved by many,
His paintings of birds flying free,
His expression on canvas pleased everyone,
And his honesty made blind men see.

It's hard sometimes not to question
My faith in God, though it's strong,
Especially when an angel is taken,
And the pain seems to last so long.

But I know once again I'll see him
In the place they call heaven above
Because God won't separate friends
When He knows that between them is love.

The Williams family appropriately pursued a claim for wrongful death against ULH&P, the utility company. The family received a settlement of an undisclosed amount. The family used a portion of the settlement to generously establish a scholarship fund at Simon Kenton in Robert's memory. Bryan Hamlin, a 1982 Simon Kenton senior who built models in paper mache, plexiglass, wood and cardboard, won the first Robert Williams II scholarship.

"I think it's a really good way to remember Robert," said Linda Whittenburg of the scholarship. "Robert will always be remembered by the kids who win it."

Chambers and Grubbs, one of the two funeral homes in Independence, handled the services for Robert Williams on Sunday, October 12 from 5 to 7 p.m. in the evening. Prior to the visitation, the art students held an exclusive memorial service at the funeral home. Linda Whittenburg remembers the event being extremely loving and emotional as everyone present exchanged stories resulting in both painful tears and cheerful smiles.

"I remember they invited us to come early. I took the art students and a couple of the other teachers. We sat in a circle. I don't remember there being anyone there, but us at that time. We sat around and talked. It was a sad, but lovely evening. They held the funeral the next day. I know several kids met with counselors. That evening was very, very inspiring, and I believe it's how we made it through the funeral the next day," explains Linda Whittenburg of the memorial service.

Reverend Steven Pettit, associate pastor of Ashland Avenue Baptist Church, Covington, Kentucky led the services at Chambers and Grubbs. "Steve Williams, Robert's cousin, spoke about how he threw me in the creek when we were with his family at Pioneer Park over Memorial Day," said Carol Roth, Robert's girlfriend for nearly a year at the time. "It was a beautiful service. Everyone loved him. There was a lot to say about him."

David Medley barely knew Robert Williams. "Somehow I knew he was an Elvis fan. I was always an Elvis fan too. I barely knew him enough to say hi to him in the hallway though," recalls Dave Medley of his relationship with Robert.

"Jimmy Grubbs, when they held the memorial service for him at the funeral home for kids from the school, asked me to attend the memorial service and play "Love Me Tender" on my guitar. I couldn't say no. I mean, how could I say no?" Dave Medley explained. "I didn't make it through the song. I'm sitting there and I start into a verse and everybody's just sobbing. I got choked up too and stopped. I said, 'Listen, I didn't know Robert like you guys did so why don't you tell me about him. Okay?' After a few moments, everyone began opening up and talking and laughing and telling funny stories and the mood lightened. The entire experience for me seemed surreal," recalls Dave Medley of his struggle to make it through the song.

Greg Ponzer didn't personally know Robert Williams either, but succinctly summed up how Robert's death moved the student body. "He was an art student and we never talked, but it made no difference. We were all connected by attending the same school. Sometimes people forget certain common bonds. His death was unsettling to everyone," Greg explains.

Months after Robert died in the explosion, Linda Whittenburg's dark hair turned gray. Linda dyed her hair until she reached forty before capitulating to the reality of her hair color. The Junior Class at Simon Kenton paid tribute to Robert Williams by choosing the Elvis Presley song, "If I Could Dream," as their class theme song. Alan Mullins, the only basketball player who knew Robert Williams from being in the same grade level, recalls Simon Kenton flying the flag at half mast in honor of Robert.

"It's a pretty feeble effort, but I'm asking the schools to fly their flags at half-mast," said Superintendent Bert Bennett at the time. At the school board's direction, a moment of silence was observed in honor of Robert Williams at the Dixie Heights and Scott High School football games the Friday after his death.

The Williams family held the funeral for Robert at 10:00 a.m. Monday morning on October 13 at the venerable Hickory Grove Baptist Church in Independence. The family requested the playing of Elvis Presley's recording of "How Great Thou Art" at the service. Reverend Robert Pugh, Robert's second cousin and pastor of Asbury Methodist Church, Highland Heights, delivered the sermon. The following is a brief passage:

"Day after day, we expect our lives to be the same. No one in this community realized last Thursday would become a day that would be long remembered. Many of you may never have known the joy your children's voices could bring until last Thursday. On last Thursday, there was great joy in every home in the community - every home except one. Maybe out of this, there will be a revitalization of the family in this busy contest we call living."

Hickory Grove Baptist Pastor Rev. Colburn Hooten read from St. John's Gospel, Chapter 14, "Let not your heart be troubled: ye believe in God, believe also in me. In my Father's house are many mansions: if it were not so, I would have told you. I go to prepare a place for you."

The Williams family lay their beloved Robert to rest at Carter's Chapel Cemetery, Gardnersville, Kentucky. High atop a ridge off a country road, Robert's gravesite eternally embraces the morning sunrise. A sturdy maple tree once stood nearby. The gravestone includes an artist pallet and the following biblical reference: "Our dear son with whom we are pleased." A sea shell is placed at the foot of the stone.

I knew Robert's father, Robert, as a realtor in the same office building where I once practiced law. One day in 1997 at noon time, I drove up the hill of Madison Pike toward Independence to eat lunch with my children at Kenton Elementary. The small size pick up truck directly in front of me ran off the road and struck a tree. I parked my Blazer, ran to the truck and called 911 from my cellphone. The driver, a bearded man with glasses, slumped over in the seat. I failed to recognize him. As I held his head in my hands, I spotted a medicine bottle. I looked at the label. It read - "Robert Williams." I held Robert Williams' father as he took his last breath and joined his son.

CHAPTER 19
Blame

"Don't find fault, find a remedy."
~ Henry Ford

After the initial assessment of the total damage, school officials thought Simon Kenton would remain closed for the remainder of the school year. Both Ray Giltner, Chairman of the School Board and Bert Bennett, Superintendent, believed little chance existed to hold school at Simon Kenton until the following year. Contractors later represented to the Board the building could be repaired by the end of 1980 in time for the second half of the school year. Klensch Construction handled the reconstruction effort. Original estimates for $200,000 to $300,000 worth of damage to the middle and southern ends of the building proved low. Martin Walsh, executive vice president of KZF Inc., provided the estimate, but the estimate failed to include damage to the north end of the school where the explosion occurred. Access to the middle and southern portions of the building could be in six weeks. Walsh believed it would probably be the summer before the remainder of the building could be reopened. "This could have been America's second or third worst disaster," Walsh speculated at the time.

State arson investigators completed their investigation the Monday after the explosion. It fell to the Kenton County Commonwealth Attorney, Frank Trusty, to decide whether to file any criminal charges. R.C. Richardson, Assistant Kenton County Police Chief, wanted Trusty to file charges in connection with the death of Robert Williams. "I've read a lot about what police are doing in the newspaper and seen a lot on television, but so far I haven't received a call from anybody," Trusty reported at the time.

Jim Stephens, state police arson investigator, reported his agency withdrew from actively probing the explosion following a meeting with representatives from the state fire marshal office, National Transportation Safety Board and Kentucky Energy Regulatory Commission. "It now comes under the jurisdiction of the fire marshal, since the nature of it was a gas explosion," Stephens said at the time. "State police only investigate intentional crime." R.C. Richardson still insisted someone should be prosecuted. "It had to be gross negligence on somebody's part," R. C. Richardson stressed. "Somebody's responsible for the death of that boy. It was unsafe to begin with." R.C. Richardson, a big hearted old school police officer, could be passionate about his work. He appropriately knew when circumstances dictated he should look the other way and when he should lower the boom. A charmer, he called every woman or girl "Hon" not in a chauvinistic manner, but with southern respect. R.C.'s massive big heart sought justice in some forum for the Williams family.

Officials from the National Transportation Safety Board reported records shown to them by Union Light, Heat and Power Co. (ULH&P) indicated the utility thought the line was correctly connected. ULH&P officials admitted a high-pressure test of the four-inch line coupled with the improper hookup contributed to the explosion. CG&E was the parent company of ULH&P

Initially, the utility company blamed the delay on the groundskeeper for Simon Kenton. "Someone covered up the shutoff valve with sod," claimed a CG&E representative at the time. "We don't know who did it or when they did it." Walter Bowen, director of maintenance and grounds at Simon Kenton, denied covering up anything. "The only problem we had was getting the gas to cut off," said Bowen at the time. "I feel like Cincinnati Gas and Electric is at fault because they put the valve three feet below ground." The state arson investigator claimed he had never known a shutoff to be buried so deep. School district business administrator John Engle phoned the utility from his office in the board of education building next to Simon Kenton moments after the initial explosion. According to Engle, the boiler in the north unit was the only boiler which used natural gas. The other two boilers in the main building burned oil. CG&E admitted the control box for gas lines is normally visible. Insurance inspectors checked the boiler and gas furnace two weeks prior to the explosion and two school employees also inspected the furnace the Monday before the explosion.

"This is something that happens very often, unfortunately," said CG&E spokesman Bruce Stoecklin at the time. "We have a whole crew who does nothing but go around and uncover these valves that have been paved over. It's a common practice that we pave over them (valves/utilities), and then it's up to the owner to bring them up to grade," explained Charles White, district engineer for the Northern Kentucky highway office at the time. "We notify the utility companies of the upcoming project, and then they have the opportunity of raising the manhole or utilities."

Henry Shepherd, chief of the safety board pipeline accident division for the National Transportation Safety Board, flew to Cincinnati from Washington, D.C. to help in the investigation. To his credit, ULH&P President William Dickhoner quickly admitted the increased test pressure to the larger line contributed to the explosion. ULH&P offered no explanation how the line to the school boilers became improperly connected to the gas main. Michael Cushing, counsel to the chairman of the National Transportation Safety Board, said the board wanted to know whether CG&E followed proper operating procedures in conducting the high-pressure tests that led to the first explosion.

Other unanswered questions included:

· What equipment gave way in the boiler room before the first blast?
· What caused the second blast? How could it have been prevented?
· Why was the gas shut-off valve buried under the ground?

The natural gas was not turned off until 1:40 p.m., almost two hours after the first explosion.

ULH&P radio transmissions of utility workers testing pressures in the pipeline north of the school on October 9, included this remarkable verbal exchange over the radio:

"I've got 150."

"So do I."

"So do I. Step it up."

"I've got 160."

"We've got an explosion. Cut it! Cut it! Dammit!"

The utility claimed the improper hookup went unnoticed for years because ULH&P ran gas through the larger feeder pipe at barely greater pressure than through the parallel 2-inch distribution line. When the larger main was tested for high pressures required to serve new customers, it blew. The utility suspended testing. Paul Herking, a vice president for gas at CG&E/ULH&P, suspended his Florida vacation to oversee the utility's response to the accident.

The State Fire Marshall, Gayle Horn, and the National Transportation Board investigated the explosion and made the following conclusions:

"The stage for this tragedy was set ten years ago when through error oversight, the school was attached to the wrong type gas pipeline.

"The school's boiler was tapped directly into a gas transmission line rather than a distribution line. Transmission lines, twice the size of distribution lines, carry gas under higher pressure than distribution lines. CG&E didn't know of the tap-in and when pressure tests were run the pressure was tripled. The reasons for the explosion were many."

"First, the connection of the school's pipeline to a gas supply line larger than necessary. The second was the inability to locate the cutoff valve. Third was the testing being done by ULH&P. Fourth was the questionable functioning of a gas system pressure-reducing device. Last came the failure of the coupler inside the school."

Horn said the coupling device used to connect two pipes inside the boiler room of the school was blown off by the pressure increases of the testing. The boiler itself never blew up. The hissing noise students heard shortly before the first explosion was natural gas filling the building after the coupler broke. The gas ignited, probably by a pilot light, causing an explosion. The first explosion blew out a twelve foot long cinder block wall. The second explosion happened at about 12:20 p.m. Superintendent Bert Bennett stated the natural gas cutoff valves at other county schools after October 9 were found and painted bright yellow. Principals at each school were notified of their location.

John Smithers, Chief of Engineering Division, Kentucky Energy Regulatory Commission stated: "As I read the regulations, the burden of inspection rests with the utility. They are required to inspect and keep adequate records. We, in turn, are to do spot checking. You know it would take a force of five thousand to keep track of all that's going on with every connection that is made. A preliminary search of the company records failed to reveal when the error was made or by whom. Sometimes we did it. We don't allow anyone else to do it. Utility employees never suspected school boilers were hooked mistakenly to that feeder line rather than a two-inch distribution line running in the same trench."

"They had a lot of customers going south, all the way to Piner. They were increasing pressure. They had another line they put in that was a four inch. That was a main feeder line to get it out further. They were increasing the pressure on that line. With Simon Kenton being on the wrong one, it was on the four inch and they were putting it up to, I'm guessing, two hundred pounds," explained Rick Messingschlager, Independence Assistant Fire Chief.

Gas at 165 pounds per square inch hit the regulator inside the school, rather than a volume at 50 pounds pressure for which the device was designed.

"There were four houses and a church that should have blown up at the same time. The Church of Christ Nicholson and four houses down the street were all hooked up to the same line," remembers Rick Messingschlager of the other buildings exposed to the danger.

Linda Whittenburg would be subpoenaed to the hearing of the National Transportation Board. She received $39.00 for her trouble.

The Kentucky Energy Regulatory Commission (ERC) fined Union Light, Heat and Power Co. $100,000 in connection with the explosions at Simon Kenton High School.

The Commission cited the utility for six violations of state regulations following an ERC investigation of the incident. In a hearing before the agency, the utility admitted it violated state regulations.

The Commission found the following violations of state regulations:

1.   The utility's maps and records failed to show the high school's gas service line connected directly to the four-inch transmission line instead of a two-inch distribution line.

2.   The service lines to the high school, a church and two private residences had no primary regulator for reducing gas pressure from the four-inch line.

3.   The service line into the high school included a compression coupling not properly strapped or braced.

4.   The curb cutoff valve on the high school's service line was covered, concealing its location.

5.   The company's written emergency plan did not contain any provisions for emergency shutdown and pressure reduction.

6.   They failed to check the curb valve for accessibility within a period of a year before the explosion.

The Commission failed to find any willful violations of regulations.

The factors for assessing penalties used by the Board were the appropriateness of the penalty to the size of the business, the gravity of the violation and the good faith of the company in attempting to achieve compliance once it has been notified of the violations.

"In this case, the gravity of the violation (i.e., the death of one person and serious personal injuries to many others) must be weighed heavily against the other factors considered," the commission reported in its Order.

The Order disallowed the utility company from passing the cost of the fine along to its customers as an increase in rate. Money from the fine is paid to the state's general revenue fund, not to the school or the injured. The commission also ordered Union Light, Heat and Power to file a method to verify the accuracy of its records, a schedule of compliance of curb box accessibility and a revised emergency plan that meets regulatory requirements. The commission also ordered the utility to research its piping system in Northern Kentucky to determine whether any primary regulators are omitted from the high-pressure lines and to survey all systems to insure there are no unrestrained compression couplings. The utility had to submit confirmation employees conducting public building inspections have been provided adequate training.

"Evidence of a great number of witnesses supports the conclusion that the curb valve was so buried that this condition must have existed for a considerable period of time," the commission stated in its Order. "The second explosion at the high school occurred while utility company employees were searching for the cutoff valve. If the gas was turned off after the first explosion, there would have never been a second explosion."

The attorney for both the Kenton County School Board and ULH&P in 1980 was Robert Ruberg, a well respected attorney in Northern Kentucky. Due to a possible conflict of interest as it related to responsibility for the explosion, the Board hired special counsel, Charles Deters. Charles Deters claims he will never forget the settlement of the insurance claim.

"The Board's recently purchased insurance policy was a replacement value policy, not a straight value policy. This meant the Board could rebuild the school and regardless of the cost to replace, it would be covered. The claim exceeded a million dollars in property damage. The big shot insurance company representatives and their big city lawyers flew in from their home office for a meeting to negotiate. After preliminary discussions indicating they wanted off the hook on the total claim, I simply leaned across the table and said, 'Look, here's what we are going to do. We'll fix our school and send you the bill.' That was the end of that and that's what we did," Charles Deters proudly explains of his handling of the issue for the School Board.

Gene Kavanaugh, 1981 senior superlative winner "Most Humorous" and football "Mr. Hustle" winner, lost his track medals in the explosion. Gene would be one of 118 students to later receive checks for personal property which they lost. Students, teachers and staff who lost property completed personal loss claims. Charles Deters presented the checks to the students at a special assembly in the new gym fourteen days before the end of the 1981 school year. Basketball player Alan Mullins received $40 for a calculator, sweatshirt and shoes. "Right after the explosion a lot of us were feeling sorry for ourselves. "It's nice to receive some compensation," said Alan Mullins of his check.

The October 9 explosion fell on a Thursday. Simon Kenton was scheduled to play football the following night on October 10. School officials canceled the game as a result of the circumstances surrounding the explosion.

"Tonight's Simon Kenton at Lloyd football game has been canceled and may not be able to be rescheduled," announced Simon Kenton athletic director Joe Stark at the time. "The fire and blast were down in the area where all our football equipment was stored. We won't know until late Friday or Saturday just what we have left. We'll do our best to get back into action for next week. It wouldn't be fair to the kids not to. I'm optimistic that we can."

Dwight Searcy remembers the sensitivity of the Pioneer students, parents, faculty and staff at basketball games, football games and in general after the explosion.

"When we traveled to Erlanger Lloyd to play basketball later in the year, the student cheering section for Lloyd made signs which said, 'Blow Up the Pioneers,' 'Burn the Pioneers,' 'Fry the Pioneers.' The signs hung on the walls. Our school's parents were infuriated," Dwight Searcy recalls of the sign incident. "I didn't like it much either. Principal Abel visited their principal and tried to have them removed. They wouldn't do it. They left them up. Their principal said, 'Oh, they're just kids, you know, let them have their fun.' So the signs stayed up."

"The very first football game we played after the fire and explosion of all places was at Highlands. (Highlands wins Kentucky 3A state football titles year after year.) We canceled the Friday night game with Lloyd. Dan Daniels and the band suffered damage in the band room. They lost instruments. They lost uniforms. The band played at Highlands in street clothes. Other school districts loaned us instruments so the band could get on the field. When our band took the field to march, even the Highlands crowd gave a standing ovation. Highlands stomped us as always in the football game. When Highlands scored their first touchdown, the cannon they shoot every time they score went off. I mean to tell you, I thought the Simon Kenton student section, the teachers and everybody there were going to have to be taken to the hospital. It scared us to death," Dwight Searcy laughs of the cannon explosion at Highlands.

In a year where Simon Kenton suffered the tragedy of an explosion at their school, another setback occurred in the form of a car accident. Butch Hays, the girls' varsity basketball coach, believed he had the talent in 1980-1981 to go to State. After the girls' varsity basketball team began the year 7 and 1, five varsity girls basketball players including four starters suffered serious injuries in a car accident. The accident occurred on Friday, December 19, 1980, two months following the gas explosion. Tina Schadler, the sixteen year old driver, lost control of her station wagon. Also riding in the car were Jo Ellen Freeman, Tammy Ashcraft, Rita Eggleston and Barb Dorgan. The girls destination was Scott High School for the last day of night school before the holidays. Tina Schadler suffered a fractured leg and injured hip in the crash. Tammy Ashcraft suffered a dislocated hip and face lacerations. Jo Ellen Freeman suffered leg injuries and face lacerations. The accident broke Rita Eggleston's nose. Two other players, Laura Whaley and Kelly Dougherty, were supposed to be with the girls at the time of the crash. "The explosion and now this. You kind of can't help but feel like the school's jinxed," Joan Ashcraft, Tammy's mother said at the time. Three of the girls failed to finish the season. Butch Hays tried his best, but the team struggled and finished 10-12, losing in the District opener. Donna Voges, Troy McKinley's girlfriend and future wife, played on the team. Sophomore Rita Eggleston is the little sister to Bill Eggleston, the first fire truck driver on the scene of the explosion. Butch Hays recalls weeks after the first car accident, a second car accident injured more girls on the team. Considering the year a bad omen, the next year Butch Hays quit as the girls varsity coach and left Simon Kenton.

CHAPTER 20
Night School

"One of the most important things in life is simply showing up."
~ Keanu Reeves in the movie *Sandlot*

Bert Bennett, Kenton County Superintendent, wasted little time communicating to the students and staff of Simon Kenton to inform them of his plan moving forward. He wrote a letter to the editor to the daily evening newspaper, *The Kentucky Post*, October 10, the day after the explosion:

We are all deeply saddened by the explosion and fire at the Simon Kenton High School yesterday that claimed the life of Robert Williams and injured 33 firemen.

At the same time, it is hard to find the words to express our gratitude to the many emergency units that responded. The valiant efforts of the faculty and staff of Simon Kenton High School, along with the firemen, police and emergency medical units, kept this from becoming an even greater disaster.

We have a lot of work before us now. We have been, and will be, exploring our options to find the best way to continue the education of the Simon Kenton students. We are, however, confident for the future.

The administration of three high schools and Twenhofel Junior High of the Kenton County District met with central office administrative staff to consider several alternatives. Committees have been appointed to investigate the several possibilities before any decision is made.

The following will be in effect until such time as other decisions can be made:

1. Simon Kenton will not be in session during the week of October 13-17.

2. Simon Kenton vocational students choosing to attend the Kenton County Vocational School and the Northern Kentucky Regional Vocational School may do so at their regularly scheduled time. Students so choosing to attend must provide their own transportation.

3. All other Kenton County Schools will be in session on their regular schedules.

4. We will have an announcement later regarding picking up personal property at Simon Kenton. At present, we have not been permitted to enter the building.

Bert A. Bennett, Superintendent
Kenton County Schools

Kenton County school administrators and principals met to begin drafting a plan to send Simon Kenton's 1100 students to Scott High School.

Junior Kelly Dougherty, Sean's sister, summed up the circumstances well from the students' perspective. "Everybody hated school, but now that it's gone, everybody wants it back," said Kelly at the time. However, split sessions posed not only tremendous scheduling problems, but also emotional ones according to Bert Bennett. Bennett remembered during construction of Scott High School, split sessions at Dixie Heights for Scott and Dixie students created unusual tension. Both Bert Bennett and school board members hoped that under the emergency situation, tension would be reduced. "I think the Scott people felt they were outsiders and the Dixie people felt they were being intruded upon," Bert Bennett explained at the time. But Simon Kenton and Scott students questioned the possibilities. "I don't want it because they'll probably tear up the school and tear up the carpet. They don't like the school," accused Scott junior Billy Stamm at the time. "Nights wouldn't be good. We had to do that at Dixie," agreed Scott junior David Overley at the time. Simon Kenton senior Dave Moore only wanted split sessions at Scott if it was in the morning for them "because a lot of us work at night, and you got sports (at night)." "We don't get along," Kelly Dougherty stated bluntly, referencing Scott and Simon Kenton.

Scott High School administrators met in assembly with their entire student body to discuss possible double sessions at their school. "We made it quite clear to our students that if Simon Kenton students come out here, they're to treat them as first-class people because they are first class," said Bill Storer, Scott's vice principal at the time. During the completion of Scott High School in 1978, Scott students attended Dixie Heights High School from 2-8 p.m. and Dixie students attended early sessions. "Our faculty likes their faculty and many of the students are very close friends," Bob Storer said at the time. Storer offered his office to the Simon Kenton principal and assistant principal.

While the school district planned split sessions at Scott High School, the school district retained an engineer to determine the extent of damage caused by the explosion. The district also reviewed their insurance coverage. "We don't intend to use the building at all until we obtain a structural engineer to tell us if it's capable of being used," Bert Bennett reported at the time. "But we will use the school again." Bert Bennett informed Ray Giltner, Chairman of the Kenton County Board of Education that the school lost the science-library wing for the rest of the school year. "It sounds callous, but this is all behind us now," Giltner stated at the time. "We have a responsibility to have school Monday. We don't know how, but we have a responsibility. If something can be fixed, it will be. The buses will still have to pick the students up at the same places," Giltner explained further. "But Bob Walter (Transportation Director) needs to know where to take them before he can put the buses on the road. And he needs to know by Monday morning. It's going to be a long weekend for a lot of people."

The district immediately, as reflected in Bert Bennett's public letter, canceled classes for Simon Kenton students for the five days following the explosion. During those days, school administrators worked out bus schedules, room assignments and plans for split sessions at Scott High School. Students and teachers feverishly arranged for library privileges, lockers, office space, storage areas, posted maps of the school and welcome signs.

Neil Stiegelmeyer explained the process of split sessions at Scott High School. "Once we dealt with the catastrophe of the day, we needed to return the students to school as soon as possible. The longer you have them out, the more difficult it is. We needed to address the needs of kids coming back. We knew, relatively soon, we lost a child."

"Sometimes we forget when you have a traumatic situation, your staff has as much difficulty as young people dealing with the situation."

"We also needed to be sensitive to where we took the Simon Kenton students for school. We looked at different alternatives. Keeping them together was the main factor. We considered our space availability and how we could best accommodate the monumental problem."

"We needed to address Scott's concerns. Split sessions disrupted their day. It helped that Bob Konerman served as principal at Scott after serving as the assistant principal to Bob Abel at Simon Kenton. Also, Mike Tulliver and Bob Storer, Assistant Principal at Scott, knew each other. Mutual respect existed. They liked one another. We created two schools in one. Walls reflected Scott and Simon Kenton spirit."

"First, we submitted a plan to the state for approval because we reduced the school day. Requirements on time must be met. We drew up a new master schedule of the buildings in terms of utilization of classrooms. Some of them made sense. You place the science people in the science classrooms and so forth. But you still had to find ways to work in other schedules. The Scott students served willingly as guides to Simon Kenton students. The Scott teachers met cooperatively with the Simon Kenton teachers. It required the cooperation of many people."

"We rerouted buses. We picked up on the same route. We simply took them to a different school. You didn't change the bus driver. You simply drove children to a different school. The principals became cheerleaders and motivators to create the necessary environment."

"We considered physiological factors. We could schedule high school late because teenagers require more sleep and different sleep at different times. With after school athletics and work, sleep patterns become disrupted."

"Teachers lost their second jobs. But everybody recognized the welfare of the children first. Everyone pitched in together and made it all work," explained Neil Stiegelmeyer of all the challenges facing the schools and the teachers.

At Simon Kenton, faculty members urgently took book inventories, boxed materials and moved supplies to Scott High School or to their homes. Staff tagged student property from classrooms and lockers and sent the items to Kenton Elementary's gym where PTA members supervised a pick-up station. Teachers began the task of completing insurance forms and reordering materials. The school librarian, Pat Slusher, salvaged the card catalog. Science department chemicals needed to be disposed of due to heat exposure. Football equipment required reconditioning and repair. Many students assisted their teachers in the move. Students sporadically arrived at Kenton Elementary to claim purses, coats, notebooks and term papers. Athletic team members and band members continued to attend practices, but constantly worried whether or not their seasons would really continue.

In the end, the Kenton County School Administrators decided to completely close Simon Kenton High School while they focused on its reconstruction. The school suffered damage severe enough to affect the function of the entire school. In addition, everyone knew the building, now an investigation scene, required scrutiny by the appropriate experts to determine safety and security. Simon Kenton canceled all extracurriculars, not simply football, the first week after the explosion.

Built in 1978, Scott High School made a natural geographical choice. Simon Kenton, Scott and Dixie comprised the three high schools in the Kenton County Board of Education system. Simon Kenton teacher, Mike Collins, remembers the Scott personnel and teachers always being kind and helpful to the Simon Kenton teachers.

The monumental logistical effort to pull off the split sessions began immediately. "The teachers hauled their own books and materials to Scott and back again," said Bob Abel at the time. The Duro Bag Company donated bags to hold items from cleaned out lockers. The district dealt with coordination of bus routes, cafeteria services, classroom use, scheduling, practices, clubs, every conceivable facet of a school operations. Scott students would attend 7 a.m. to 1 p.m. Simon Kenton students would attend from 1:30 p.m. to 7:10 p.m. Shortened classes consisted of forty-five minute periods. Simon Kenton students ate at 4:15 p.m. Four students shared a locker. Vocational school students attended vocational school 8:30 to 11:30 a.m. or 1:30 to 4:00 p.m. Since both schools kept a shorter school day, the school district requested approvals from the State Board of Education to insure students met all accreditation. Considering the emergency, the State Board granted approval. The move to Scott added one extra-curricular for the students of Simon Kenton. When the district built Scott High School, they included an indoor swimming pool.

The split sessions inconvenienced the Scott students as much as the Simon Kenton students. Rather than waking up to make it to school at eight a.m., Scott students set their alarms earlier. Students who relied upon parents dropping them off on the way to work adjusted. Parents simply left for work earlier. The same problems arose for the students return trip home. "I heard our students complain they couldn't make car payments because they couldn't work after school," recalls Mike Collins of one of the problems.

Simon Kenton students began their adjustment to starting school at 1:30 p.m. Normally, the final bell sounded at 2:30 p.m.. Students now concluded class at 7:10 p.m. when they usually would be attending a practice, working, studying or sleeping. Simon Kenton students had one advantage. They could sleep in. However, Simon Kenton parents who drove their children to and from school would be inconvenienced. Many of the high school students still had younger brothers and sisters on the regular schedules at elementary school and junior high.

"I always taught high school in the day and college at night. Now I taught college in the day and high school at night. Northern Kentucky University accommodated me and two of the professors there traded classes with me so that I could still teach both," explained Mike Collins of the switch he made.

Conveniently, both Scott High School and Simon Kenton High School used blue and white as school colors. The Scott High Eagles also included a tinge of silver in their triumvirate of colors. Allegedly, Scott chose the colors popular with the time of the 1970's Dallas Cowboys NFL team. The drive from Scott High School to Simon Kenton covered seven miles. Scott's students arrived at school at 7:30 a.m. Monday, October 20 and were dismissed at 1:10 p.m. to make room for the 1,125 Simon Kenton students arriving. Simon Kenton students attended classes from 1:30 p.m. until 7:10 p.m. Continuing the insanity following Simon Kenton, the school received a bomb threat at 4:30 p.m. the first day of split sessions which forced school officials to evacuate the building for a half hour while police searched the building. Thankfully, the threat amounted to a cruel and misguided prank.

After the first day of split sessions, Scott Principal Robert Konerman reported parking as the primary issue. "We need to have our students drive out earlier so the Simon Kenton students who drive can find a place to park," Konerman said at the time. The schools set up tables at the main doors on both levels of the building for passing out schedules and maps. "At the end of my day, I'll throw everything in my box, and at the end of his day, he'll do the same," Konerman said of sharing his office with Bob Abel. "He has his desk drawers and I have mine. Both assistant principals, the teachers, the secretaries, everybody has to share everything." In addition, the custodians cleaned up after more than twice the normal student population at the building. Restroom and cafeteria facilities served double duty.

Scott students shared lockers with Simon Kenton students. Simon Kenton reversed class schedules to accommodate Simon Kenton students who attended vocational school in the morning. The Pioneer students' days began with their sixth period classes and concluded with their normal first period classes. Scott's junior and senior classes served as guides. The thirty guides remained at school until the dismissal of Simon Kenton classes the first day.

Robert Walter, director of transportation for the school district, and George Lonnemann directed traffic in the parking lot as eighteen busloads of Scott students departed and fourteen buses filled with Simon Kenton students arrived. "We knew it was going to be a mess getting all these buses in and out in fifteen minutes," Lonnemann said at the time. "But we'll get it done and we'll get better at it as the days go by."

Simon Kenton's librarians, guidance counselors and cafeteria workers all worked at Scott too. Several janitorial employees from Simon Kenton worked with Scott's staff. "So far, so good," said Principal Bob Abell at the time. "Things went as smooth as could be expected. Everybody was terrific and it can only get better from here. For me it went pretty good," said Simon Kenton junior, Lori Richardson at the time. Lori and her brother Eric, a senior, both worked after school. Lori could now only work weekends. Eric's employer, Cherokee IGA, modified his schedule so that Eric could work more hours. Eric Richardson's education never missed a beat. He later became a doctor.

On October 24, 1980, four days after the beginning of split sessions, Governor John Y. Brown, Jr. traveled from Kentucky's capital in Frankfort to Scott High School to speak words of encouragement to the Simon Kenton student body. At the time, a young Simon Kenton graduate, Bruce Lunsford, served on the Governor's staff as Commerce Secretary. An outstanding basketball player at Simon Kenton, as a young boy growing up in Piner, Betty Sue Cook drove Bruce to ball games. Probably the most financially successful Simon Kenton graduate, Bruce Lunsford later founded Vencor, a long-term respiratory care facility, which after a public stock offering made Bruce extremely wealthy.

The Simon Kenton student body screamed and applauded as the Governor walked into the packed gymnasium at Scott High School. When speaking to the Simon Kenton students, the Governor offered this advice:

"We just have to understand that these things happen in life. I just want you to treat this as an experience in life, and learn from it. I very specially wanted to stop by and pay my respects, and my regrets, and express the affection and love for Robert Williams from throughout the state."

Many of Simon Kenton's athletic teams moved practices to the morning. Others held practice after school, resulting in players' days concluding as late as midnight. Coaches for the football and basketball teams juggled practice. Basketball practice was scheduled to begin one week after the explosion before the explosion. The practice start for basketball was delayed for a week. "We practiced football at night. We practiced after school at Simon Kenton. We practiced on the game field with the lights. The weather turned awful. We should have competed for state, but under the circumstances, we came up short. Practices became disjointed. Plus, we missed several weeks of practice," Greg Ponzer recalls of the football practice and season. Many seniors, having secured enough credit hours, received an early dismissal from school. As a result of split sessions, Simon Kenton flip flopped times and early dismissal became late arrival. Greg Ponzer remembers showing up for school at 2:30 or 3:00 p.m.

"It was difficult for everybody. We never made it back into the flow of school again," Greg Ponzer explains of the schedule change. "We also knew kids from Scott from our Twenhofel days, but we never ran into them at school though because they already left the building when we came to school."

Sean Dougherty remembers the practice problems. "The explosion left devastation in its wake. When we returned later to Simon Kenton, the school reeked of burned plastic and smoke. We couldn't practice basketball at Simon Kenton after the explosion. All the water used to extinguish the fire ran into the new gym. Construction crews tore up the entire new floor and replaced it before we even played one game or practice in there. We thought we'd never have a chance to play in our new gym as seniors. We attended school at night and practiced during the day wherever we found an open gym. Practicing football under the lights was neat, but we were getting home at 11:00 p.m. We never developed a smooth routine," Sean explains of the team's predicament. Sean remembers teachers practicing leniency on school work. "I sensed they were more understanding. I don't believe they reduced the testing, but they reduced workloads," Sean remembers of the classwork.

To aid in Simon Kenton's comfort level, the Pioneers placed Pioneer banners up at Scott and treated the school as their own when they attended. Many teachers at Scott and Simon Kenton knew each other from teaching together at Simon Kenton before Scott opened. The district built Scott High School to alleviate student body increases at Dixie and Simon Kenton. Therefore, Scott's student body, for the most part, attended middle schools attended by Dixie and Simon Kenton students. This meant students at the three schools of Dixie, Simon Kenton and Scott knew each other. To initially staff Scott, the district plucked teachers from Dixie and Simon Kenton.

"As far as time deadlines and issues which often put pressure on students we made allowances. We all had too much pressure on us already and we needed to avoid more. We avoided placing additional pressure on anyone. I taught math. We attempted to keep our students focused," remembers Mike Collins of his handling the situation. Many parents of students believe their children lost a quality year of education as a result of the explosion. Margie Dirr is still shocked her daughter, Lisa, still became a surgical nurse. "They lost their chemistry lab, so her entire senior year, she never had a lab," recalls Margie Dirr of the problem of lost lab space.

Several players who played basketball with the Simon Kenton players at Twenhofel attended Scott High School. "We lost Jimmy Ryder, Jeff List, Billy Sherrard and Robbie Shell to Scott. Those four guys played on our Twenhofel teams, but chose to be part of the first graduating class at Scott," Sean Dougherty explains of the class schism.

Troy McKinley thought the Scott High School experiment went as well as could be expected. "It was different because they used open classrooms and three or four of us shared a locker. Scott students made the sacrifice of getting up at 5:00 a.m. to go to school," Troy explains of the experience.

Linda Whittenburg's class shared the art room at Scott High School. "I enjoyed using a brand new room, but I lost all of my teaching materials. Mike Tolliver snuck into Simon Kenton and found a box full of tempera paint and a few brushes for me. The district required us to requisition new supplies. Lynn Acres, whose room I shared at Scott, graciously gave me supplies from her ample stash. She flung open her closets and said 'use what you want,'" Linda recalls gratefully.

Besides sharing an art class, Linda's cheerleaders faced the exact problem as the basketball team in finding practice times and locations. "It was tough. We held cheerleading practice after we left school at night. We managed to use Kenton Elementary's gym sometimes. We couldn't use it in the day because they were having school. Occasionally, after the holidays, we used undamaged sections at Simon Kenton. We occasionally used the new gym at Simon Kenton. Water and smoke destroyed the old gym. I also believe they used the old gym as the staging area for the reconstruction. I was just in a daze. I would arrive back home exhausted after 11 p.m. every night," Linda Whittenburg recalls of her marathon days.

"The School Board required teachers to complete requisition forms for insurance recovery. I couldn't remember everything I lost. I lost my personal college work which I brought in for show-and-tell for the students," recalls Linda Whittenburg of the losses . Linda became flexible in her demands of the students. "They lost their work too. What was I going to do? They were doing their best to catch up. Because so many of them planned to study art in college, they needed their senior portfolios. I helped any way I could. I simply gave them grades because I had nothing to grade anymore. It was all lost," Linda Whittenburg explains of her grading predicament.

Dave Medley is shocked at the amount of basketball practice the coaches held. "School became secondary because we practiced in the morning, practiced at night, and we still felt the fog from the explosion. Practice in the morning would be an hour. Practice at night usually two hours. Heck, we held two-a-days in basketball," Dave Medley laughs of the exhaustive practices.

"I didn't have a problem with going to Scott," said Billy Meier of his new school. "It was something different. Other than having to go to basketball practice before school, I stayed up late and slept late. It was different, but in ways pretty cool. Plus, it was a different school. You saw how they did things. It was also a newer school. It was kind of neat, I thought."

Cheerleader Tami Elliott remembers everyone believing a chair in a classroom at Scott being possessed. "We suffered more deaths that year than Robert Williams. I forget the teacher and class, but I believe two people who sat in that exact chair died in car crashes. One was Orville Bush. (It is believed Bennie Dyer was the other.) I remember nobody would sit in the chair," Tami explains of the students' superstition.

Signs throughout Scott High School show the Simon Kenton students' appreciation for the warm welcome they received.

CHAPTER 21
Back to Simon Kenton

"All greatness comes from loss."
    ~ Philip of Macedonia, father of Alexander the
Great

Robert T. Klensch Contractors, general contractor, worked desperately and nearly around the clock to reconstruct the demolished sections of Simon Kenton High School. Numerous subcontractors aided in the effort. The school district, in collaboration with the architects, engineers and contractors, adopted what the district labeled a "fast track" program following the explosion. Debris clearing, damage assessment, design and reconstruction moved forward simultaneously rather than sequentially. The contractor removed the buckled concrete floors and replaced them with new flooring. All the broken and stained ceiling tiles required replacement. Steel metal framed doors violently ripped off during the explosion also needed to be discarded. Entire stairwells, holding on precariously by a few metal bolts, needed reattachment. The reconstructed school received new tile floors, carpet, fresh paint and a complete re-wiring of the electrical system. The Klensch construction crew of thirty employees finished the $1,200,000 project in forty working days. However, a few classrooms and the ravaged library remained unavailable after the Pioneers returned to their home.

On December 19, 1980, the final day of the school semester, the Simon Kenton community undertook the burdensome task of moving back to their reconstructed school. On January 4, the school held an open house for parents. "It just looks like old Simon Kenton to me," said Vic Ponzer as he walked through the halls at the time. Vic stubbornly refused to view the photos of the explosion damage posted throughout the school as a 'before and after' display. On January 5, the students returned to classes at Simon

Kenton. A huge "Welcome Back" sign greeted the students inside the main front hall. "They used to complain all the time about being in school. I've never seen a bunch of kids so happy about coming back to classes," Linda Whittenburg said at the time of the reunion between students and building. "We've got everything in good shape, but it's like starting the year all over again," said Bob Abel as faculty and students walked the halls again. "We don't have any laboratories, so some things will have to suffer," said Neil Stiegelmeyer, assistant county school superintendent. "If there's anything we've learned from this experience it's flexibility."

The heavily damaged library wing would be the only section of the school not useable when school resumed in the building. Libraries represent the heart of learning. Early in antiquity, a library served as the only repository of knowledge. Even before books and the Gutenberg press, libraries existed. The library of Alexandria is believed to have contained countless scrolls of historians, mathematicians, scientists, poets and rhetoricians, both known and lost to the ages when enemies of civilization burned the library to oblivion. Simon Kenton's library, damaged by the explosion and the subsequent efforts to extinguish the fire, lay in ruin after the October 9 explosion. As Pat Slusher, the school's librarian at the time, viewed the destruction of the school's books and reference center she must have felt despair. An entire catalog of replacement books and materials needed to be ordered to replace that which fire and water destroyed.

Linda Whittenburg taught in a wholly different atmosphere and art room than the one destroyed in the explosion. The art room where Robert Williams died would not be renovated until the following fall. This forced Linda to teach her art classes in the wrestling weight room. Linda recalls the challenge of teaching art in a room filled with the smell of a sweaty locker room.

The next year, Linda returned to teach in her original room. She found the return both depressing and eerie. "One student, Nina Schoonover, on the first day of school the next year, was also with me the day of the explosion. She came back as a senior the following fall. She made it as far as the double doors into the new section and then sat down against the wall. She refused to go in the room. We spoke to her for a while. The school counselor walked down and we worked with her. We finally coaxed her down the hallway and into class. It was sad," Linda Whittenburg recalls of Nina's hesitation and apprehension.

Reconstruction continued on Simon Kenton after the students returned. Linda Whittenburg recalls how touchy the explosion made the students. "The contractors set up a chute coming out the back of the building. The workers used wheelbarrows during the ongoing demolition and dumped debris in the chute. They discarded old bricks and concrete blocks down the chute several times a day. The first time the workers cast them in, my kids nearly ran out the door. We didn't realize the source of the noise and the loud crashing scared the hell out of us."

Reflecting the overwhelming support of the community after the explosion, Simon Kenton's PTA membership leaped from 133 members to 310, the largest percentage increase in high school membership in the state.

A handmade sign welcoming back students

CHAPTER 22
The Players as Students

"There is only one good, knowledge; and only one evil, ignorance."
~ Socrates

D ave Medley claimed the last quarter of the school year found him tied for first in his class. "I took a break after basketball," Dave explains of his scholastic "dive." He still received an academic scholarship to Western Kentucky and finished fourth in the 1981 Simon Kenton graduating class. Greg Ponzer remembers hanging out at the Medley's house one day when Bob Medley, Dave's father, ripped into Dave regarding a B Dave had received on a test. Greg sat on the couch thinking "holy cow, I wish I had scored a B on the test." Dave Medley rarely scored a B. "I had one B and one C in junior high. Up until the last quarter in high school, I didn't have anything but A's. My brother Mike received straight A's and won valedictorian of his class in 1980," Dave Medley remembers. Jerry and Becky Zimmerer, recall Dave Medley and their daughter, Mary, being the valedictorian and salutatorian at Dave and Mary's kindergarten graduation at Kenton Elementary. Mary, who finished seventh in the class of 1981 at Simon Kenton, received only one grade less than an A, a B, from junior high at Twenhofel to graduation from Simon Kenton.

Dave Dixon asserted genuine pride in all his pursuits, including his school work. "I worked hard in the classroom and tried always to do my best. Earlier, I lacked motivation. Basketball changed my motivation. It provided a closer connection to school. Also, I always intended on attending college on a scholarship," Dave Dixon explained confidently.

The players, as all teenagers, enjoyed fun outside of their sports. As youngsters, each of them enjoyed riding their bikes to each other's houses.

Dave Dixon rode his yellow Schwinn ten speed as far as he could take it on Madison Pike. Similar to Troy McKinley's love of motorcycles, Dave Dixon also scooted around the farm on his Honda 70 and a mini-bike. Schwinn, a leader in bike sales at the time, was the bike of choice for the players as kids. Alan Mullins sported a light blue one. Sean Dougherty pedaled his blue Schwinn with a high bar and banana seat over ramps to score "sweet jumps." Baseball cards stuck in the spokes provided audio for Sean's bike.

When the boys graduated to cars, the Schwinns were cast off for an assortment of wheels. Alan Mullins drove what he describes as a hideous green 1970 Chevrolet station wagon. However, as the saying goes, "it got him there and back." For a while, Dave Dixon folded himself into a 1976 Volkswagon Rabbit. The car suffered carburetor and major wiring problems. When Dave turned on the turn signals, the tail lights and license plate light blinked on and off. Dave claims the Volkswagon repair manual at Auto Zone declares "don't purchase a 1976 Rabbit." Dave junked the Rabbit for a 1976 orange Firebird he later painted royal blue.

"We had a lot of fun playing sports, but we had plenty of other fun. Roxie Hellman owned her old store in Independence. Being so old, Roxie couldn't see too well. We'd walk in there for a quart of beer every once in a while as high school seniors," Greg Ponzer laughs of his escapade. "I also remember Dave Dixon and me flying down the road from Nie's Drug Store to Simon Kenton traveling about ninety in his car. He slid the car sideways into Simon Kenton like Starsky and Hutch. We played Dixie that night. We probably drank a quart of beer. I remember Dave standing on the free throw line. Stan Shockey played for Dixie, and he looked over and said 'Ponzer, you guys been drinking beer.' Dave and I just looked at each other and smiled. If it was during the afternoon, we couldn't sneak into Dad's place so we'd usually wait until later. My dad kept old cases of Bavarian beer in our basement at the house. We also kept a couple cases in Billy Arnold's car," Greg Ponzer confesses.

Dave Medley recalls a story concerning himself, his older brother Mike and Greg Ponzer driving around throwing wet snow on unsuspecting victims during a snowstorm. Two surprised off duty police officers became inadvertent victims of their prank. A car chase between the police and the boys ensued and concluded at the dead end of Peach Drive a half mile north of the high school. The police officers scared the boys with a few threats before cutting them a break.

During high school, Dave Medley pursued his musical talents. "I played in bars from fifteen or sixteen years of age," Dave recalled. "Rock bands and country bands. We played at dances. I played a dance at Walton my senior year. I played a dance at Scott meant to bring Scott and Simon Kenton students together. At the time, our band was called "Thin White Line". Donna Klotz, a classmate, sang lead." Dave's band also played at the graduation for the Class of 1981.

Music, as with all teenagers, played a part in the players' lives. Dave Medley, talented enough to play his own, enjoyed all types of music from country, jazz, to rock. However, the favorite album for most of the players, including Alan Mullins and Dave Dixon, was AC/DC's newly released "Back in Black." Dave Dixon used its thumping songs to fire him up before he left the house for basketball games. Billy Meier and Alan Mullins included "Back in Black" songs as part of their pregame ritual. Rock, in the late 1970's and early 1980's, found its zenith. Fleetwood Mac, Queen, Bob Seger, and countless others sold eight tracks and cassettes by the truck loads. Disco also arrived and the disco groups grabbed their share of the players' tape decks. As basketball teams warmed up in gyms prior to the games, there was no shortage of "fire them up" music blasting off the gymnasium walls.

In a rather odd sports twist, Dave Medley chose to focus on basketball his senior year and decided not to play football. "It was kind of strange not to play football. It meant I could be in the marching band," Dave Medley explains, as if marching band was his only option. There is no crying in baseball and no tuba players in football. At least not until Dave Medley marched out on the gridiron. Dave would march in the Simon Kenton band his sophomore and senior year. He played football his junior year. Dave recalls a funny story his senior year involving the marching band. "Mike Keirnan and Joe Keirnan played football at Newport Catholic. Joe was my age. I played against him. Mike, if I'm not mistaken, may have played football at Notre Dame University in South Bend a few years before Joe. Joe played opposite me in the Newport Catholic game my junior year when we beat them eight to seven. I got to know him a little bit after that game," recalls Dave Medley of his connection to the Kiernans.

"During my senior year, we played Newport Catholic at Simon Kenton. The Newport Catholic football team walked on the field. Our marching band prepared to take the field the same time. Here I stood in a ridiculous Pioneer band outfit with a tuba around me. I walked past Keirnan, but then we stopped right next to each other. He looked at me. I peered over at him. I had my tuba around me. He didn't say a word, but the look he gave me I'll never forget. Like, "what the hell are you doing in the marching band playing a tuba?"

Dave Medley backed up Billy Meier his entire high school sports career. It's a wonder Dave doesn't still dream about playing second fiddle to Billy Meier. "I played tight end on offense and defensive end on defense. As a junior, I played in the Newport Catholic game and caught the game-winning conversion because Billy suffered an injury in practice the week before. I played backup to him at both tight end and defensive end. I backed him up at forward in basketball. Baseball, too. He was always first in the pitching rotation and I was second," Dave Medley laughs without animosity.

The high school students at Simon Kenton, including the players and cheerleaders, enjoyed the same teenage fun as other high school students. They attended movies, dated, shopped at the new Florence Mall in Boone County and gathered at each others homes for parties. Mary Zimmerer recalls every Friday night the cheerleaders headed toward the same destination everyone at Simon Kenton drove or rode to - McDonald's in Florence, Kentucky. A weekly Friday night ritual, Boone County High School and Simon Kenton High School students shared the McDonald's on Dream Street in Florence as a public meeting place. Teenagers in cars and trucks slowly cruised around the parking lot again and again like a carnival carousel in a teenage social ritual designed to meet friends and potential dates. When the inevitable boredom set in from driving around the same lot twenty times, young drivers parked at the Red Lobster or strip center on either side of the McDonald's. On occasion, kids actually purchased food and ate inside or in their cars. Boone County and Simon Kenton boys engaged in an endless challenge and counter-challenge. Boys put on the tough act. Though rare, fights happened from time to time. (Shawn Alexander of the NFL's Seattle Seahawks played high school football at Boone County.)

McDonald's management tolerated the kids in varying degrees. McDonald's retained a security guard to watch after their lot. Those poor souls endured endless and countless taunts from disrespectful but harmless teens who shouted, 'Hey rent a cop?' 'Hey pig?' and other adolescent humor in self amusement. Soon, McDonald's required students to eat inside and disallowed them to sit on their cars and trucks on the lot. Then, the rules tightened so much, the ritual of driving around McDonald's a hundred times died like a cult whose time finally passed.

CHAPTER 23
Background of Larry Miller

"Look with favor upon a bold beginning."
~ Virgil

L arry Miller was born in White Mills, a small town in Hardin County in central/western Kentucky. "Not much of a town there anymore," Larry expresses with a little sorrow. He recalls White Mills once boasted a high school, Lynnvale High School. Consolidations closed the school. Larry's father farmed and drove a truck to support the family. Larry's mother managed the home until Larry reached high school. Then she accepted a job offer at a plant in Elizabethtown. Larry's one sibling, a brother five years younger, is now an accountant who works in the Sears Tower in Chicago despite the 9/11 threats. Larry attended West Hardin High School which is now consolidated into the school where he currently works as an assistant principal, Central Hardin High School. Larry and his wife, the former Joyce Thomas, both graduated from West Hardin. The 1968 yearbook at West Hardin, The Voyager, notes Larry Miller as the graduate "most likely to succeed."

Larry played high school basketball at West Hardin. After high school, he attended Elizabethtown Community College. Elizabethtown began a basketball program his sophomore year. However, Larry received a scholarship to Jacksonville State University in Alabama. Larry played basketball at Jacksonville State and the school once won their conference. Larry majored in mathematics. After Jacksonville, he attended Western Kentucky and earned a masters degree. Next, he attended the University of Louisville to earn a Rank I, thirty hours above a masters for education administration, to enable him to be a principal. Chronologically, Larry graduated from Jacksonville in 1972, Western in 1976 and Louisville later in 1988.

Larry married Joyce in 1972 and after 33 years they still thoroughly enjoy their life together. Larry began his promising coaching career at Drakesboro High School as an assistant. After working as an assistant for four years, he craved a head coaching position. "Thought I knew everything," he laughs. Drakesboro High School no longer exists from a consolidation with Muhlenburg South in Muhlenburg, Kentucky. Larry Miller describes Drakesboro as an old coal mining town. "Most of it was undermined and when they blasted, it shook every building in the place. But it was a neat town with a lot of nice people," Larry remembers fondly. At Drakesboro, the administration worked Larry half to death. "I was assistant coach, freshman coach, eighth grade coach, seventh grade coach, coached baseball in the spring and cross country in the fall. For all of which, they paid me $500.00," Larry grins regarding his versatility. Larry earned this 'large' sum from 1973-1975. Despite the low pay, the valuable experience gained at Drakesboro served as the formative years of Larry's coaching career and he rapidly discovered that he thoroughly enjoyed coaching.

When Larry was graduated from college, he never planned to teach. He labored at a factory in Elizabethtown as a quality control manager. "I enjoyed it," he said. "Then they fired my boss. He enjoyed a drink. He strolled in one day without recovering from the night before. They fired him on the spot. I expected they would offer me his job. I was only twenty-two, but I knew the business. We were developing urethane foam insulation. It is pretty common right now in roofs. They also spray it on the walls in homes. I was in on the ground floor of the company, the Celetex Corporation. Jim Walter Homes bought them out. I thought I should move up to the head position in the department since there were only two of us. In that situation, if they fire your boss, you feel like you ought to receive the position. They decided to bring in a chemist from another plant in Knoxville. It ticked me off. They offered me another position. I declined it in anger and enrolled at the University of Louisville and obtained my teaching certificate. My wife taught. Also, several of my friends from school taught in Hardin County. I really missed basketball. I played in an independent league after school, but I needed to coach. So I returned to school so I could teach and coach."

Larry applied for head coaching jobs after only his second year at Drakesboro. One job he sought was the Mason County, Kentucky, head varsity boys basketball coach position. The Mason County school district's superintendent never called Larry back after he sent in his resume, so Larry took the initiative and called him.

"I called him because he hadn't called me. I didn't realize how good Mason County was in basketball," Larry explains.

"Mason was a big-time program and here I was an assistant at little old Drakesboro. So I called the superintendent and he asked, 'Are you a head coach or an assistant?' I responded, 'I'm an assistant.' He replied, 'Son, I've got a stack on the side of my desk as high as the desk on assistants.' I confidently replied, 'Well, I'm the best one in that stack.' He replied, 'When do you want to come and interview?' I responded, 'You name the date.'"

"It took me a half a day to drive from Drakesboro to Maysville. I stopped by the gym enroute to my interview and discovered they have a 7,000-seat gym. I knew I was in the wrong place. I walk in for the interview and the first question addressed to me was where is Drakesboro? The question reaffirmed I wasn't going to land the job," Larry laughs of his overreaching.

"He was nice and drove me around town. He introduced me to the business people. He said, 'Now, when you come here we can't pay you what you're worth, but you can receive your clothing at this store; they'll take care of you.' I said, 'Okay.' 'You can pick up your groceries over at this store. They'll take care of you.' So I thought that'd be a pretty good. Allen Feldhaus ended up with the job. Allen played at the University of Kentucky," Larry Miller recalls. Larry and Alan would later meet on the side of a basketball court.

"I drove all the way back home. I still knew I needed to leave Drakesboro. I applied and won the job under Woody Neil down at Breckinridge County. Woody found success in Indiana as a head coach and then returned to the Breckinridge County job. I coached under him a year as a freshman coach and then received a job offer at Frankfort as an assistant under Charlie Strausburger. Charlie coached at David Lipscomb College down in Nashville. I thought Charlie would be a good mentor. Woody Neil was an excellent defensive coach and I learned from him. Strausburger knew how to run an entire program. Charlie could sell ice to Eskimos. I worked under some great coaches. After working with Charlie for a year, I started applying for more head coaching jobs and landed an interview at Simon Kenton," Larry Miller recalls. Principal Bob Abel and Athletic Director Joe Stark had possessed the good sense to hire the 29-year-old brash young man with Drakesboro on his resume. Bob Abel recalls Larry Miller coming to Bob's house and impressing Bob. "We also had a teaching position open. We knew we had a good group of basketball players coming. I thought by hiring a tall former inside player such as Larry, he could help mold the tall front line we had coming in Billy Meier, Dave Dixon and Troy McKinley into a winner." Bob Abell recalls.

"Larry Miller turned it around," recalls Randall Wagner. "There was a casual attitude toward basketball before Larry. Larry came along and the team practiced ten days a week and eight hours a day. You're not supposed to probably, but that's about the time Larry kept the boys in the gym. He was so competitive. He picked opposing teams up defensively all over the floor. He made opponents work for everything. He made you work to score any basket. You could see the fire in his eyes sitting on the bench." In the classic Johnny Cash song, "Boy Named Sue," the father explains to his angry and vengeful son that the son, rather than kill his father, should thank him for naming him "Sue" because the name gave him the "gravel in his guts and the spit in his eye." It wasn't his name, but somewhere along the line, Larry Miller developed "gravel in his guts and spit in his eye." It revealed itself as he coached in practice or games.

Assistant Head Coach Dave Schadler forged a strong relationship with Larry Miller. "Larry was a disciplinarian and a leader. My job was to keep the peace with everybody. I was the bridge with school board members, principals, parents and players. It was tough on me. My job, my unwritten job, was to keep the heat off of him as much as I could," Dave Schadler explains.

In 1966, Dave graduated from Simon Kenton. He played basketball there with a little success. Simon Kenton won their District one year, but lost in the Region. The reason Simon Kenton failed to win the region is that Newport Catholic's roster included a player named Dave Cowans who happened to play later for the Boston Celtics. After high school, Dave Schadler played a few years at Campbellsville College in Kentucky. Worn out from the travel to and from games all over the state, he summarily quit. After college, Dave worked for Ashland Oil, Kentucky's largest corporation, as a refinery salesman for asphalt sales. Dave would later introduce Greg Ponzer to Ashland. After college, Dave moved to Nashville for a while. He returned to Independence, obtained a teaching certificate and began teaching at Twenhofel. Dave also began coaching eighth grade basketball. When Larry Miller hired on at Simon Kenton, Larry reached out to the Twenhofel coaching staff.

"He came over to Twenhofel and I met him for the first time. At the time, freshmen still attended Twenhofel. We enjoyed a great group of kids at Twenhofel. We lost some of them to Scott," Dave recalls. "The freshmen coach was Bill Pelfrey, Jr. Larry asked me over to Simon Kenton to serve as assistant coach," explains Dave regarding his coming to Simon Kenton.

Bill Pelfrey, Jr. was born in Jackson, Kentucky, in Breathitt County, in the mountainous eastern part of the state. His mother was from Harlan County. Bill's father taught school and his mother ran the household. His father, Bill, Sr., also coached and Bill played basketball for him in grade school. Bill Pelfrey, Sr. never endured a losing season over decades of coaching. After the Pelfrey family moved to Northern Kentucky, Bill's sister, Sue Bradbury, attended Simon Kenton High School. Sue would later coach boys basketball at Piner Elementary in southern Kenton County. Bill attended Twenhofel Middle School and played high school basketball at Pendleton County.

"I attended college at Morehead State. I majored in physical education because of my coaching aspirations. After graduating in 1971 from Morehead, I applied to a couple school districts in the Northern Kentucky area. Bob Barnes, the superintendent at Kenton County, sent me over to Twenhofel because I had attended there. Fortunately, Gay Best hired me. During my first semester, I informed Gay Best if a coaching job opened, I'd really be interested. He said, 'Well, right now, I've got a full staff. I don't have any vacancies.' I told him, 'Mr. Best, I really want to coach and I'll coach for free.' He loved the sound of that because Mr. Best managed his school with a financial tight fist. The next year, a coach left and I received the opportunity to become the eight grade coach. I was only 22 years old," recalls Bill Pelfrey, Jr. of his opportunity to prove himself. He would make the most of it.

CHAPTER 24
Coach Miller Takes Over

"An army of deer led by a lion is more to be feared than an army of lions led by a deer."
~ Chabrias

In 1977, at age 27, Larry Miller arrived at Simon Kenton High School to coach the boys' varsity basketball team. He defied the stereotype "jock" coach. In addition to his responsibilities as coach, Larry taught both physical science and the challenging physics class.

"Physical science was a freshman course which meant every kid I taught failed it the last year. Many failed the class more than once. I also taught physics to the very top students of the school. I taught four classes of students who failed and I taught the brightest students in school. It was an unusual schedule," Larry explains of his teaching paradox. "But I really wanted to teach math. The next year I also landed in the math department. But, I taught physics as long as I worked at Simon Kenton."

Larry's wife, Joyce, joined him in the teaching profession. "Joyce taught at Walton-Verona High School the first year the Millers moved to the area. Then a job for her opened up at Simon Kenton," Mike Collins recalls. "The faculty at Simon Kenton was a fairly social group and everyone got along," Dwight Searcy said. "I actually remember first meeting Larry during the summer before he started coaching. Bob Abel invited several of us over to his house for a cookout in his backyard to meet the new coach and his wife."

"They never won anything in basketball at Simon Kenton. When I arrived, they had failed to win a district tournament game for eleven years. Not one game. They'd go to District, they'd lose and that was it. They accepted it as part of their mentality. Parents simply wanted their kid to play.

Board members wanted their friends' kids to play. With that attitude they would never be successful," Larry Miller explained.

Bones McKinley remembers Larry Miller's arrival to Independence. "We didn't know much about Larry, but Simon Kenton failed to have a winning season for five years. Losing was accepted. We hit it off with the Millers. The first time we met him was in the Medley's yard. Larry pulled in and stepped out of his car and into Medley's big orange Suburban. All the kids piled in there and they drove to Oakland University in Michigan for a basketball camp. The camp was Larry's first contact with the boys. Larry's wife also stepped out of the car. Joyce was as big as Mary. Both were expecting children at the time. The Millers would have Bart. Mary would have Jeff five days earlier than Joyce gave birth to Bart," Bones recalls.

Over the years, people said, 'Oh, Mary's over at Millers again', as if I was sucking up, but it wasn't because of Troy playing for Larry. It was because of Jeff and Bart. They became buddies," Mary McKinley explains.

Coach Miller recalls struggling with the team the first year at Simon Kenton. Four of the five seniors coming back quit before Coach Miller coached them a day. Senior Matt Garvey stuck around. "Nice kid. Real good shooter, and he loved to play," Miller said. "His mother played in the Louisiana Hoedown when that was a big deal," Larry Miller laughs. Coach Miller's first team at Simon Kenton won seven games and lost eighteen. In the middle of his first season in 1977-1978, the worst snow and ice storm in the history of Greater Cincinnati struck, closing Kenton County schools for an entire month. "We were off school forever, so all our game dates backed up. We played eight or nine games the last two weeks of the season. The season was disappointing, but my hopes and dreams came from the team I saw coming back," Miller explains.

CHAPTER 25
Coach Miller's Philosophy

"Success is not always attained by a single undivided effort and it rarely follows a halting vacillating course."
~ Robert E. Lee

Coach Miller, as all coaches, borrowed from others. "I attended clinics all over the map. The popular speaker during those days were Bobby Knight and around here, Joe B. Hall from Kentucky. Bobby Knight, an excellent defensive coach, taught all the drills. I borrowed from him," explains Coach Miller. "I chose to play man-to-man defense as much as possible. Joe B. Hall played a one-three-one zone, and we played a little one-three-one zone. On offense, the coaches I emulated didn't carbon copy. They worked an offense to meet their personnel. John Wooden topped the list of offensive coaches. I followed a general offensive philosophy from John Wooden."

Coach Miller would rarely implement the press on defense and when he did call for it, he remained in the press for only a short while. When Coach Miller pressed, he placed Greg Ponzer, Alan Mullins and Sean Dougherty in the game as a three-guard defense. The three became known as the 'bumblebees'. Everyone knows a bumblebee floats, moves, buzzes about and when ready, stings. "We put them in as a group of three and they pressed and aggravated everybody all over the floor. We began it when the three were juniors. They'd go at it full throttle for two or three minutes. We'd take 'em out and put our senior guards Greg Allender and Mike Medley back in. The three received necessary experience with this concept," Larry Miller explains of the tactic.

Troy McKinley remembers Coach Miller setting the tone from the beginning of his tenure. "You could tell right off the bat, he demanded physical

At 7:15, buses are lined up and filled with weary nightlifers.

SKHS students in 1980 had the unusual experience of attending high school at night as they were bussed to other facilities to continue classes after the explosion rendered their own school uninhabitable.

Students move books and supplies back into the school after it was rebuilt.

Practicing in a borrowed gym, Coach Shedler prepares Troy McKinley for future battles in the paint. (Courtesy of The Kentucky Enquirer*)*

Governor John B. Brown expresses his good wishes to SKHS students.

Ray Powers moving books

Old School Building

Students are welcomed back to Simon Kenton High School after having night classes at Scott. (Courtesy of The Kentucky Enquirer*)*

Superintendent Robert Barnes

Assistant Superintendent Charles Miller

Members of the 1938 team, Simon Kenton High's first, at the dedication of the new gym. Athletic Director R. C. Hinsdale, Truette DeMoisey, John Coleman, James Gregory, Chester Ballinger, Max Gray, Charles Williams, Dick McKinley, and Eugene Hartloff.

*Simon Kentons first boys basketball team 1938. **First Row**: James Gregory, Chester Ballinger, Robert Hinnell, Paul Rust, and Bryson Fisk. **Second Row**: Gene Hartloff, Daniel Schadler, Junior Rankin, Charles Williams. **Third Row**: Athletic Director G. K. Gregory, Jr., John Jennings, Coach B. P. DeMoisey, Franklin Hamilton, John Coleman, Principal G. K. Gregory, Sr..*

Troy McKinley dunks during warm-ups for the first game in new gym

Greg Ponzer watches the ball go through the net as he scores the first point in the new gym on a free throw 21 seconds into the game.

The game ball from the first game ball in the new gym

Richard Collins with the mascot

Jill Bruckner, 1980-81 SKHS Basketball Homecoming queen

Homcoming court

Bob Abel , Simon Kenton Principal

Mike Tolliver, Assintant Principal

Larry Miller, Head Coach

Dave Schadler, Assistant Coach

Coach Larry Miller

Coach Larry Miller holds the net

Dave Schadler coaching JV with Bill Pelfrey

Greg Kroth, team trainer, cuts down the net after winning the 9th Region tournament

Team shows off Regional Trophy

The Simon Kenton High School Varsity Cheerleaders in a build.

Reserve cheerleaders: Debbie Huesman, Tami Kelley, Michele Michael, Missy Chadwick, Lori Lauterwasser, Joy McKinley, Sandy Jackson. Not pictured: Sherry Matteoli.

Jody Cuzick, Dave Moore and Greg Pickett cheering

Varsity Cheerleaders take third place at the state competition. **Front Row:** *Deneen Reimer, Mary Zimmerer, Charlotte Woods, Tonya Hignite.* **Back Row:** *Pam Meenach, Captain Tami Elliott, Jill Brueckner and Krista Isler.*

SK-ettes. **Front row:** Pam Raleigh, Patty Kiely. **Back Row:** Karen Glacken, Laura Stein, Michelle Young, Chalee Lorenzen, Sheila Daly, Karen Figgins and Kim Young.

SK-ette Lori Glen

SKHS 1980-81 Girls Varsity Basketball Team. **Front Row:** Kelly Dougherty, Mary Lou Hasekoester. **Second Row:** Coach Gerry Scaringi, Mary Ashcraft, Barbi Dorgan, Sandy Ross, Jo Elle Freeman, Rita Eggleston, Laura Whaley, Donna Voges, Marie Ashcraft, Lisa Parker and Statistician Jenny Gadker.

play. He put me in a game to see if I would knock somebody down," laughs Troy. "It was against Holy Cross when I was a freshman, but it was in the junior varsity game. They put me in the game and said, 'We want you to knock somebody down.' They put me in, then took me back out. I didn't do it. Tried a second time. I didn't do it. Third time. Same result. I never started junior varsity again that year," laughs Troy of his failed 'physical' test. "Miller and Schadler were both big guys. Schadler is rough as a cob. The two implemented drills to beat us up with football pads. Everybody run to the basketball. Everybody in the paint. It worked. Practices were rougher than games," Troy McKinley recalls of the practice regimen.

Mary McKinley keeps a simple assessment of Larry Miller. "He was just an awesome coach. He really was," Mary states admiringly.

The McKinleys remember Larry Miller calling a meeting of the parents before the first season he coached. Coach Miller explained his philosophy of coaching to the parents. "This is the way I work. I don't know you and you don't know me. I'm a first year coach. Here's the way I look at it. I'm the boss. This is my team and what I say goes," the McKinleys recall Miller declaring.

"These guys are my workers. I tell them what to do. Now, if they don't like it, they need to come to me eye-to-eye and voice their opinion. I'll accept that. I would not do anything to them for that. Bottom line, it's still my team, I'm the boss. I'm going to do what I want to do. All of them can be fussing and cussing at me, but I'm still going to do what I want to do," Coach Miller continued.

"I might listen to them. They may be right, and I may change it. The worst thing you as parents can do, is if your child comes home and he's fussing about the coach, agree with him and then come up and jump on me. Or even if you don't come and say anything to me, but talk to him about me. Whether you realize it or not, you are the apple of that boy's eye, Mom and Dad, not Larry Miller, because I will work him to death," Coach Miller explained of his concept of the coach and player relationship.

Coach Miller expressed the same attitude regarding the classroom in his introductory speech to the parents. "If the kid's clowning in the classroom and you agree with him and jump on the teacher, you're not helping your son at all. Now, let me tell you what also can happen. Between two players, one is a little more talented than the other, but one simply plays and does not hustle. The other doesn't cause any grief to the coach and he works hard. One's wanting to complain. He doesn't want to work. He doesn't want to shoot extra baskets. Who do you think is going to play?" Coach Miller asked according to Bones McKinley. "I think you know the answer," the Coach answered.

Bill Pelfrey gave a personal insight on Coach Miller's philosophy. "When I interviewed with Larry for the junior varsity position, he impressed me as an individual who was focused, determined and organized. His organization for basketball practice is unmatched. He meticulously prepared the practice schedules out to a minute interval. At 6:45, we're going to do this. At 6:48, we're going to do that. It was all on paper. It is one of the traits that impressed me and I wanted to be a part of it. I learned as much coaching from Larry as I learned from my own father," Bill explains.

Coach Pelfrey saved the detailed written practice schedules Miller prepared. One example is the very first practice Coach Miller oversaw as Simon Kenton's coach on August 4, 1977. The form reads:

Practice No. 1:
7:00 - 7:05 Talk
7:05 - 7:15 Exercise, Piggyback, Tipping
7:15 - 7:25 Ball Handling
7:25 - 7:45 Defensive Quickness - Quarter turn
             Drill on Floor
             Slide LRLB
7:45 - 8:00 3 Man Break
8:00 - 8:10 Zig Zag
8:10 - 8:25 Meat Grinder
8:25 - 8:35 Loose Ball Drill
8:35 - 8:50 Winner Drill

Randall Wagner probably witnessed more Simon Kenton basketball games in the school's history than anyone. "He always developed a solid game plan for the kids," Wagner said. "He was organized."

Dave Schadler believed Larry Miller's strengths were his drive and his vision for the team. " Larry geared practices around a series of two-minute drills. We're one point down, two minutes to go. Or we're two points up and thirty seconds to go. What can happen to us? He forced everybody to fill their roles. Sometimes all the kids didn't like him, but all the time, they listened to him. I'll never forget, a perfect example is the Lloyd game and Alan Mullins. Lloyd dressed a good team and they beat the hell out of Alan Mullins up the floor every time. Alan runs over to the huddle and he actually has tears in his eyes. Alan never liked to screw up. He never wanted to make a mistake. Alan's nearly crying in the middle of the game. I'm thinking, 'Larry go ahead, put your arm around this kid'. Alan is quiet and sensitive. He's not Greg Ponzer or Billy Meier. I would have handled it completely different. Larry grabs Alan by the jersey and yells, 'What are you doing? Grow up. Be a man. You have to play. You're the leader out there.' It worked. He pushed the right button when not even I realized which button needed pushing. He would do it time after time. I guess its why he was the head coach and I was his assistant," Dave Schadler laughs of his backseat to Coach Miller.

CHAPTER 26
Parents

"He whose generals are able and not interfered with by the sovereign will be victorious."
~ Sun-Tzu

As with any coach, issues sprang up with parents of players from time to time. "The young men developed into a very different team than from middle school. It was an evolutionary process many parents resisted. We struggled with them at times," Dave Schadler remembers. "Bill Dougherty was friends with Vic Ponzer. They'd be in the Ponzer bar all the time. Nice guys. They were fun to talk to, but they had their own strong personal views. They weren't particularly happy with the coaching every day."

"Being single and running around every now and then, I'd stop in Ponzer's. I don't believe the fathers who hung out there ever thought that matters were the way they ought to be. It usually involved either wins and losses or playing time. I learned you're not going to keep all the parents happy all the time. I stopped going into Ponzer's to even eat their famous fish sandwich because Vic would wear me out," Dave Schadler chuckles regarding his response to the pressure.

Dave Medley offered his father's opinion on Coach Miller. "He liked Coach Miller and he always expressed Coach Miller was one of the most intelligent basketball coaches he'd ever seen, high school or college level. Here's a coach who didn't teach physical education. He taught physics," Dave Medley explains.

"I always heard what Vic Ponzer was saying, but he never once said anything to me personally," Larry Miller recalls. "So I don't know if I had a problem or not because he never said anything. Greg's dad was a talker. Heck, he ran a bar and restaurant, he needed to talk to be a good host. He never came to me and complained. I liked Vic. Dixon's dad was the nicest man you would ever want to meet. Troy's dad was fine. Medley's dad was fine. I never could get Alan's dad to say anything. On the other hand, Billy Meier's dad went off on me one night."

"We were playing Dixie at home. Billy visited Dayton College in Ohio for a football scholarship and he missed a day of school. We played a game that night. Billy could've gone anytime. Could've gone on Saturday. Instead, he waited until Tuesday to make the trip and I was ticked. I told Billy, 'You didn't make practice so you're not going to start tonight's game.' Billy was fine and we beat the team handily without him. If we played Covington Catholic, I probably would've started him. I thought I would make a point. We're playing the game and all of a sudden Mr. Meier is at the other end of the floor hollering at me."

"I look over at Dave Schadler on the bench and I said, 'Dave, you've got 'em.' He said, 'What do you mean, I got 'em?' I said, 'I'm going to talk to Mr. Meier. I don't know what he wants.' So I stood up in the middle of the game and walked over to Norman. By the time I reached him, he's backed out into the hallway out of the gym. There's nobody in the hallway because the game's going on. I don't know what he was doing. He said, 'What are you doing? You're not going to play him.' Norman could probably kill me because he's such a big strong man, but at the time I was too dumb to know he wouldn't, so I just walked on back to the game. He never said anything else. That was it," Miller recalls of the confrontation.

Billy Meier recollects the incident from the Meier family perspective. "I had a football visit to Dayton. I planned to go and I was going to miss school, but I would have been back in time for practice. The morning I left, it snowed and we were off school. I still traveled to Dayton. I thought I'd still be back in time for basketball practice. Since it snowed, Coach Miller called practice at 11:00 a.m. Well, at 11:00 a.m., I was in Dayton. I couldn't be found. I was up there with my dad. I didn't know anything about practice. I returned to attend practice. I drove up to school and nobody was there. I called Coach Miller and he said, 'No, we had practice at 11:00 a.m.' He asked why I didn't tell him I was going to Dayton. I didn't because I planned to be back in time for practice. I missed a day of school. Well, Coach planned on sitting me out a quarter of the Dixie game. When the second quarter rolled around, he was getting ready to put me in, but here comes my dad out of his seat at the top, boom, boom, boom walking down and taps Coach Miller on the shoulder behind the bench. Dad said, 'You had your quarter, now I want mine.' So, Coach told me to sit down. I ended up sitting out the whole first half. It was more of principle for Coach. I never blew off practice, but he took it the wrong way. My dad's reaction cost me another quarter," explains Billy of his benching.

Norman Meier, Billy Meier's father, is an enormous man. He's also a good man. He even makes his son Billy look small. Norman worked his entire life at Eaton Asphalt and always supported Billy's athletic endeavors. That one time, Norman allowed his support to fall a little off course. Coach Miller and Norman Meier didn't put the incident behind them until twenty years later at the 20th year reunion of the team.

CHAPTER 27
Players' Varsity Years Before 1981

*"Observe due measure, for right timing is in all
things the most important factor."*
~ Hesiod

McKinley, Meier, Dixon, Ponzer, Mullins, Dougherty and Medley each received varsity experience before their senior years, but in varying degrees. Troy McKinley actually played varsity as a freshman. Troy started varsity as a sophomore and averaged fifteen points a game. Billy Meier started several games as a sophomore. Dave Dixon started as a junior. Greg Ponzer, David Medley, Sean Dougherty and Alan Mullins received more limited playing time. When Ponzer, Medley and Dougherty were juniors and Mullins a sophomore, Simon Kenton's roster included four solid senior players: Tim Bene; Alan's older brother, Danny, who also started at quarterback in football; Greg Allender, a solid all around player; and Mike Medley, Dave's older brother, a great shooter and valedictorian of his class. Danny Mullins lacked Alan's quickness, but competed with an unmatched ferocity. Danny hated to lose. In the 1979-1980 season, the Simon Kenton varsity played their way to the District finals, and despite losing, earned their first Regional berth in twelve years.

During midseason of the 1979-1980 year, the Pioneers won fourteen games and lost only two, both in overtime and on last second shots. The team opened the season by winning the Boone County Tipoff Tournament, the Pioneer's first tournament victory in eleven years. They also won a Christmas tournament in Breckinridge County, Larry's old coaching position. Larry Miller recalls why he scheduled Breckinridge County. He attended a basketball clinic held by Gale Catlett, then the University of Cincinnati head basketball coach. John Wooden attended as the featured guest. After speaking,

John Wooden agreed to take questions. Larry Miller laughs when telling the story how after Wooden announced his willingness to speak one on one with any coach, all the coaches left Gale Catlett to go over to talk to John Wooden. Larry in true carpe diem, seized the moment. Larry told Coach Wooden that he coached a team lacking confidence. Coach Wooden offered a practical and simple solution: "Win a few more games and your players will build more confidence." Larry took the advice and scheduled a few more teams Simon Kenton could handle to build their confidence.

During the season, as a junior, Troy McKinley set a team scoring record for a game with forty-one points. The 1979-1980 team compiled the highest victory total for the school since 1951 with twenty-one. The local media ranked them number two in the 9th Region behind the Holmes Bulldogs led by Dickie Beal, who played college basketball the next year at the University of Kentucky. Many, including this author, believe Dickie Beal to be the best guard to ever play Northern Kentucky high school basketball. Dickie dominated a game with his phenomenal quickness on both ends of the floor. The opposing team would dribble the ball up the court. Beal would steal it, drive, and score. This would be repeated for 32 minutes. No one stopped him.

Troy McKinley, as a junior, led the team in average, 19.7 points; rebounds, 10.1; and free throw percentage, 85.1. David Dixon led in field goal percentage with 62.3%, a new school record. Dixon would also surpass the single game scoring record of Troy McKinley set earlier in the year, by scoring 45 in a game. Dixon and McKinley reached these levels six years before the implementation of the three point shot. Greg Allender set a school record with 142 assists in a year. The team set a school record by making 53.4% of their field goals for the season.

The 1979-1980 year reflected harmony between the senior players and the younger players on the team. Mike Medley and Danny Mullins, being Dave Medley and Alan Mullins' older brothers, helped in the team relationships. The year before 1978 - 1979 was not so peaceful or successful.

Todd Penick, during the 1978-1979 year, was a senior basketball player. Todd saw nothing beneficial about sharing time with the super sophomores, Troy McKinley, Dave Dixon and Billy Meier. Possessing a bad attitude, Todd Penick attempted to intimidate everyone.

The threat to Todd Penick's playing time led Coach Miller to be threatened with his coaching position by School Board Member, Chlorine "Jake" Menefee. Jake informed Larry Miller through Dave Schadler, play Todd Penick or else. Larry Miller ignored the demand and resented the intrusion into his coaching decisions. Larry also refused to back down. His response would be to not play Todd Penick at all.

Dave Schadler recalls Jake "going after" him, too. "Well, it didn't end with Penick. I drove a school bus in the mornings and Jake drove behind my school bus. I swear to goodness he followed me on my bus route. I don't know what he was doing, other than trying to catch me doing something wrong. He abused his authority as a board member. To understand him you needed to know Jake may have decent intentions, but lacked an education or personal ability to deal with situations properly," Schadler explains of Jake's intrusions.

Greg Ponzer, Sean Dougherty and Dave Medley played and started junior varsity their freshman year. Their sophomore and junior years they played junior varsity and varsity. Having their three "big and tall" players (Billy, Troy and Dave Dixon) focused on varsity gave Sean, Greg, and Dave little opportunity to win the junior varsity championship. This disappointed the group since their team at Twenhofel had won the 7th, 8th and 9th grade championships.

Greg Allender and Mike Medley started at guard the 1979-1980 year. Danny Mullins and Troy McKinley started at forward. Billy Meier started at center, but couldn't stay healthy, so Dave Dixon replaced him at center. Billy Meier, after suffering an injury, failed to finish the year. Billy's absence from the lineup hurt the Pioneers. In the regional game, the Pioneers lost to Highlands. "Billy didn't play and Highlands barely beat us. We would have won and maybe made it to state," Coach Miller remembers. Miller wanted a second crack at the invincible Dickie Beal and the Holmes Bulldogs.

The 1979-1980 team suffered a disappointing ending. The Pioneers lost to the Highlands Bluebirds in the first round of the regional, 77-72. The Pioneers would have what every team has after losing their final game of the year - next year. However, they were returning a lot of talent and size.

CHAPTER 28
The Development of the Team

"Being busy does not always mean real work. The object of all work is production or accomplishment and to either of these ends there must be forethought, system, planning, intelligence, and honest purpose, as well as, perspiration. Seeming to do is not doing."
~ Edison

A whole different attitude in Simon Kenton basketball came to town with Larry Miller," Sean Dougherty said. "He implemented a drill oriented program. You got in shape, you played hard and you didn't stop playing hard. If you stopped, you ran."

Coach Miller and his staff focused on the incremental improvement of their basketball program and team. This included Coach Schadler and Coach Miller playing against the front court in practice and cutting them little slack in the process.

"When I was in high school at Simon Kenton, our team could have been better. I wanted to provide our kids the type of coaching and training we never received," Dave Schadler explained of his desire to make a positive difference. "I looked at my weaknesses. I didn't want them to have any weaknesses. We stressed weight training. We stressed a physical toughness other high school kids never obtained. I wasn't trying to hurt them, but we refused to allow anyone to be tougher or more physical than our boys. We taught them a physically tough practice wasn't to be feared. In fact, I believe they accepted the challenge willingly. Larry and I always played against them. We were men still in shape. Hell, they never beat us. We'd go up and down the floor and bang the hell out of them," Dave Schadler explained of his playing in practice.

Dave Schadler realized his charge of toughening up the front court in creative fashion. "I used football pads. I don't even remember what I called the drill. I think ping-pong. I'd have someone throw the ball up and everyone had to go for the rebound. Whoever grabbed the rebound was required to put the ball right back up. When they tipped it back, I'd give them a body shot like they'd receive in a game against good teams. If they came down with it, when they'd go back up, I'd whack them a good one. The managers helped me too. We stuck them pretty good. I don't know how many of the old-fashioned three-point goals in games we made, but in games our big guys would go up, get fouled and stick the ball right back in the hole because they were used to it. We also used a drill we called the meat grinder at the end of practice. We'd place the whole daggone team in the lane and allow them to grab a position. They'd be hot and sweaty and have to rub their bodies against each other. We'd throw the ball up and the first guy who made two baskets would be able to leave the drill. The drill became a fierce competition. We saw bloody noses. Greg Ponzer would win the drill more times than not because he loved the fight. I'll never forget Troy McKinley finally won it once. We always wanted more aggression out of Troy."

The summer before Troy McKinley's senior year, Larry Miller accepted a summer job painting the inside of Simon Kenton. This gave Larry the ability to keep the gym open. Coach Miller wasn't allowed to coach, but Troy McKinley was allowed to shoot.

"Coach Miller wasn't allowed in there, but I'd ride my bike up to school every day. I placed an old pitchback for baseball, the square netted stands underneath the basket. I shot at least a hundred free throws. If I didn't make 92, I would shoot a hundred more. I also worked on my moves and shooting. I would shoot for hours," Troy McKinley recalls of his summer routine.

Bones McKinley also remembers Troy practicing all summer. Bones spoke to Larry Miller first and Coach Miller assured him Troy would receive a basketball scholarship. Bones preferred Troy focus on basketball during the summer rather than work a summer job. Troy would earn money at home detailing cars. Coach Miller, at Bones' request, ordered the same brand and size of basketball used during high school games.

Bones next asked Bob Abel if Troy could come to the school on summer mornings and shoot baskets. Bob Abel explained the gym couldn't be opened and someone would have to chaperone Troy.

"I said, 'Bob, you're talking about Troy. You know he wouldn't throw a paper wad on the floor, much less tear something up.' You draw up a contract stating if Troy tears up anything in the gym, I'll pay for it. I'll sign it," Bones explained in frustration.

"Bob Abel explained the Board would still not allow it. I explained to him that Covington Catholic, Holy Cross and Holmes practice twelve hours a day in summer programs, and all I wanted was Troy to be allowed to shoot by himself."

"Coach Miller told me about his painting job and I could send Troy up to school. Coach would unlock the gym and while he painted, Troy could shoot all he wanted."

"So Troy woke up early and arrived at school by eight. He'd be in the gym four hours. He picked ten spots around the top of the key. He'd shoot ten from each spot and then move. He shot a minimum of a thousand every day. I'd stop by at noon sometimes. His senior year, he would pull up to shoot with the confidence he would make it. Troy practiced constantly," Bones boasts proudly.

Dave Dixon also focused on basketball during the summer before his senior year. "Between my junior and senior year, we held practice at the gym during the summer. I would run down from home, three or four miles away. Dave Schadler played with us. I drove toward the basket. I faked to the left, faked to the right and went up and shot right in his face. He said, 'Daggone. I'm done.' He walked over and sat down on the bench. After practice, Larry and Dave asked me to the office for a talk. They told me, 'Just about everybody in Northern Kentucky thinks Troy McKinley is a better player than you are.' I was included in that list, by the way. They said, 'We're not so sure of that.' They said, 'You're going to be hard to hold under 25 points a game next year.' They were obviously attempting to build my confidence since they knew I lacked confidence," David Dixon recalled.

Dave Medley remembers Coach Miller making it clear to him his supporting role on the team. Medley also agrees with Billy Meier's recollection that Coach Miller encouraged and fostered physical play.

"Coach Miller never told me to stop fouling. He conducted physical practices. He used drills where no fouls could be called. The whole point to the drill was to take the ball strong to the basket even if you have three guys hanging on you. They used a drill where they threw the ball into the center of the court and you had to dive for it. We had a drill where everybody's in the paint. It's a free-for-all. No dribbling. Everybody's in the paint pounding. Coach Schadler beat the hell out of us with pads during the drill. He enjoyed it. I still have a scar on my eye thanks to Dave Dixon," Dave Medley recalls.

Dave Medley recalls another unique drill. " I still have matching gashes on my legs from the box drill. Coach Miller built these plywood boxes. He learned the drill from a Soviet basketball coach to increase vertical jump. We would stack the boxes, two foot and one foot boxes. You'd put a foot box on top of two foot to make a three-foot box. There might have been four-foot boxes. Standing still, you jumped to reach the top of the box. We would do that over and over and over. Take a break and move to a taller box. I missed the boxes once and then twice. I can't believe no one ever broke an ankle," Dave laughs.

Coach Miller recalls he borrowed the box idea from a Purdue University clinic he and Dave Schadler attended. The coach at the clinic obtained the concept from Russian coaches. Coach Miller kept the boxes in his garage and the players came over to use them whenever they chose. Coach Miller later covered the boxes in carpet to avoid the gashes Dave Medley received.

Ron Coleman, Booster President at the time, recalls the players working out on a contraption used to develop jumping. He also recalls watching Coach Miller at practice always watching the clock and score in scrimmages to practice game situations. He also will never forget one play where Coach Miller showed Billy Meier how to soft hook the ball off the glass over a tall defender. Ron recalls Coach Miller explaining, "We'll need that play down the road," as if he saw the future.

"If you twisted an ankle, Coach Miller's therapy involved submerging your ankle into a bucket of ice. You didn't just leave it there for a few minutes. You left it there for a half hour to an hour until you were close to frostbite. You preferred to go back on the court because playing on a bad ankle was infinitely better than leaving your foot in a bucket of ice for an hour. Also, we practiced at 7:00 a.m. on Thanksgiving Day and Christmas Day. Coach Miller held college-level practices. Football practiced twice a day before the season. We practiced basketball twice a day during the season. After the explosion, we practiced in the morning. Then we practiced again at night," Dave Medley remembers.

Greg Ponzer recalls the team consisting of a collective group of fighters. "Billy Meier was a great athlete with physical size and determination. We all had a little bit of a screw loose. We weren't your constant nice guys. We all came from a little different backgrounds, but we all lived in the same community and we were all tough in our own little world. We were fighters. Billy Meier wouldn't back down from anybody. Alan Mullins and Sean Dougherty were football players. They were small, but tough. Dave Dixon in his freshman year probably couldn't chew gum and walk at the same time.

By our senior year, Dave Dixon didn't take smack off anyone!" Greg Ponzer explains with pride in his teammates.

Coach Bill Pelfrey, Jr. summarized the team's talents. "We had size, we had strength, we had jumping ability, we had shooting ability, we had three kids six-six or better. We had a six-six kid who could take it outside. We had a six-six kid who could hit a three-point play before the three-pointers. We had a ball handling guard who was quicker than lightning who was unselfish and who was willing to dish the ball off. We had a senior second guard who could also play tough enough to move inside to the three position to allow Troy to go outside. They were truly a team. Not only were they unselfish, they actually liked each other. They did not care who received the credit," Bill explains.

Greg Ponzer developed as the enforcer of the team. "I didn't plan it that way," he said. "I believe my football mentality spilled over on the basketball floor. I was a football player first. You must be aggressive in football. I couldn't shoot very well. I was a two guard that couldn't shoot. From twenty feet, I was out there shooting bank shots. I couldn't shoot it any better to make a swish. I fired it up there and hoped it hit the backboard and went in. I was an average ball handler. But I could move and guard. Typically, Larry placed me on the other team's best offensive player. I could shut them down. I took pride in doing so and liked the challenge. But being the enforcer, I don't know? You know how it is, if you act tough sometimes, people shy away from you." In a dramatic game later in the 1980-1981 season, Greg Ponzer proved how effective he could bank in shots in Scottie Pippen fashion.

"You have to realize, Greg used to get the hell beat out of him by his older brothers all the time," Sean Dougherty said. "Their fights were scary. Greg wasn't intimidated by anyone. He was a hitter. Greg was my best friend, but I can remember practice becoming tense at times."

Billy Meier remembers all the drills. "It was a free for all. You could push. You could chew. You could kick. You could claw. You could gouge. No fouls," explains Billy Meier, as if he misses the drills.

"Greg and I had an unspoken bond. I instinctively knew what Greg was doing on the court and he knew what I was thinking," Billy Meier recalls. Drinking buddies sometimes simply know each other best. The Yankees had Martin and Mantle. The Pioneers had Meier and Ponzer.

"I was called for a lot of fouls I didn't really commit. The coaches told me it was because of my stature. If I bumped somebody a little, I thought it's a bump, but the referee thought it a wallop. I fouled out a lot of games and had four fouls on me in many and I don't believe Coach Miller ever, ever,

ever said a single word to me about fouling too much. I don't believe I can ever remember him talking to me about watching my fouls. Remarkable," recalls Billy Meier of Coach Miller's acceptance of fouls. "Not one, 'Billy will you stop fouling'." For the 1980 - 1981 season, Billy actually only fouled out one game, the last one the Pioneers would play that year. In twelve games, Billy had four fouls.

Today, filming your team and your competition is quite common from middle school to professional sports. In 1980-1981, a few coaches at the high school level studied film. However, fewer still watched basketball film with their players and made it a party. "Coach Miller always had us over to watch game film. We'd have pizza. His wife and young son, Bart, would be there. We'd watch film and have a good time. It was all part of his plan to bring us all together. I wonder how many other teams in 1981 in our region did the same," Greg Ponzer recalls of film study. "They came over every Sunday," Joyce Miller recalled of the film sessions. "We had something to eat and they watched game films. It was a lot of fun having those kids around all the time." Since the Millers had no family in the area, the players and coaches became the Miller's extended family. "They were kids you liked to have in your house," Joyce Miller explained. "I had a young son. Bart was three at the time. He enjoyed the players and they enjoyed being around him. Larry loved his players too," Joyce says wistfully.

Coach Miller's love usually came in the form of tough love. "My favorite tactic was to call a timeout, choose one player and rip him," Larry Miller says with a grin. "I remember overhearing Bob Medley asking Bones McKinley, 'Well, who's he going to get this time?' I always liked to rip on Troy. Troy could take it and when the other kids saw you rip your best player, they could take it when you ripped them," Miller explained of his psychological ploy.

Larry Miller's offense involved passing the ball to Troy McKinley, and if Troy didn't have a shot, he passed down under to Dixon or Meier. "I was our first option. I would basically come off a screen or go to the free throw line. If I had the shot, I was to take it. If not, we had David and Billy. We had two six-six guys to pass off to. Then if they weren't open, we took a shot on the wings," Troy McKinley recalls.

Coach Miller developed his own version of a match up zone. "Teams struggled with our zone. You'd hear their coaches scream 'man to man'. And we're not really in a man. Then they'd scream, 'they're in a zone'. So teams never solved our defense," Billy Meier explained.

"Coach Miller was a math and physics teacher. He's very analytical. He told the team we're going to call our zone the pentahedron. We're like, what, pentahedron? What the heck's that? By the time our senior year came around, we had it down pretty good," recalls Troy McKinley.

"Pentahedron defense was half man-to-man and half zone. You set up like you were in a zone, but if someone came in your area in the zone, you played man. I'm sure there's a lot of teams and college teams that do this now, but for a high school team then, nobody ever did it. We never faced it. If a man came into your area, you went man-to-man on him. If he passed the ball away, you were back in zone. We did do man-to-man too. We rarely followed one man around specifically. Whoever was the closest to us, we'd pick them up," Billy Meier describes. Webster's dictionary defines pentahedron as "a solid figure having five faces." The definition fit the Pioneer defense, five players forming a solid barrier.

As their senior year arrived, the coaches chose their cast for the team. Four seniors and a junior would start: Billy Meier and Troy McKinley at forward, Dave Dixon at center, Alan Mullins at point guard and Greg Ponzer at the other guard. Two seniors would back up the starters, Dave Medley for the big men and Sean Dougherty for the guards. These seven knew each other, liked each other and knew how to win. It all began in grade school. Now, it would be their one last chance to capture basketball glory in high school.

During their entire time playing together, while they fought on playgrounds and practices, there is not one single story or incident anyone can recall where during a game, they yelled at each other in anger or an unencouraging manner. Their expectations as a team, their own and others for them, was high as the season arrived. They began their school year with their school blowing up, a classmate dying, one of their fathers nearly dying, a case of mononucleosis and another of meningitis, practice at other schools, school at night, disrupted routines and the taste of a disappointing football season all in their rear view mirror.

CHAPTER 29
Expectations

"There is a tide in the affairs of men which taken at
the flood leads to fortune.
Omitted, all the voyages of our lives are bound in
shallows and misery.
We are at that tide and we must take it as it serves
or we shall lose our venture."
    ~ Shakespeare

The *Kentucky Post* serves as the Northern Kentucky daily evening newspaper. The *Post* named Simon Kenton High School as the preseason number one for the Ninth Region for the 1980-1981 season. However, the preseason ranking was not an issue which consumed the players thoughts. When asked if the expectations stressed him, Sean replied, "No, it was fun." Dave Schadler saw the potential for the team. "We believed we coached several players who could play college basketball," Dave Schadler explains.

"As a group of players, we never sat around and said 'we're going to go to state' or 'we got to win the regional.' We never really made it an issue. As a group, we played one game at a time. We never, during practice, in the locker room or away from basketball, spoke about goals. We were just playing ball," Alan Mullins recalls of the team's attitude.

Dave Medley thought the team could win their regional. "I felt we had a shot to go to state. Going to state is a dream for any high school basketball player in Kentucky. Especially if you've watched for years from the stands and tasted the atmosphere. You wonder what it's like to play on the hallowed floor of Rupp Arena," Dave Medley explains of the dream.

"We didn't really sit down and talk or think about it," Greg Ponzer explains. "We played ball. We would go to practice. We would play the games. We'd play them one at a time. I know that's a cliche. The big question mark entering the year was whether we guards could handle pressure. We had the star. Troy McKinley was one of the top players in the region, if not the <u>top</u> player. The *Post* preseason picture in the paper was in the new gym with Billy Meier, Troy McKinley and Dave Dixon on the front page with Larry Miller. And it's titled: No. 1 in the Region. They wrote we would go as far as our guards would take us. The guards only played junior varsity ball really. But Alan, Sean and I didn't really think about experience. We just wanted to play."

Greg Kroth began life as a miracle baby. In today's medical world, prenatal care is able to address premature birth issues with medical technology and knowledge not available over forty years ago when Greg Kroth came into the world in 1963 at two pounds six ounces. The doctors gave his parents the heartbreaking news: "He won't survive." Ignoring this prediction of mortality and the host of issues facing him, including his ability to breathe and his heart to pump being in jeopardy, Greg also faced life with a dislocated right knee and hip and two club feet. Greg grew up in hospitals. His primary place of residence would be Shriners Hospital in Lexington, Kentucky. This hospital generously treats children without any financial payment. Greg lived through nineteen surgeries in twenty-one years. He calculates that he spent an entire seven years of his life in the hospital. One of his surgeries lengthened a leg three inches.

When Greg Kroth attended Twenhofel Middle School, basketball coach Bill Pelfrey, Sr. taught physical education. Pelfrey, Sr. allowed Greg to volunteer as his "gym assistant." "Gym assistant" soon became manager for the basketball team. This role involved helping the coaching staff with the many mundane but necessary tasks such as picking up basketballs and cleaning up the locker room. Despite his noticeable and permanent limp, Greg performed his responsibilities with pride. He viewed his role cheerfully as one in which he could participate and be part of something special.

When Greg Kroth attended Simon Kenton his sophomore year, Coach Pelfrey, Sr. recommended him to the football coach Bill Gaines. Greg attended training at Kent State the summer between his sophomore and junior year and training at Eastern Kentucky University between his junior and senior year to become a formal trainer. A trainer helped wrap legs, treat minor injuries, ice sprains and triage injuries. In Greg's senior year, 1980-1981, he became the basketball trainer for the varsity boys basketball team.

Greg Kroth recalls Coach Miller's Bill Parcells-like disdain for injured players. He confirms Dave Medley's recollection of ice buckets for sprains. He also remembers Billy Meier always being injured including a groin pull his entire senior year. During games, Greg Kroth also filmed the play-by-play for the coaching staff for film review.

Greg Kroth's long days at school earned him the Most School Spirit Award from his classmates his 1981 senior year.

Bill Pelfrey, Jr.'s son, Doug won a job as the basketball team's ball boy. Bill Pelfrey, Jr. remembers Doug's journey all the way to the NFL. "As a ten-year-old, his goal was to go to Simon Kenton where he was the ball boy the 1980-1981 season. However, his friends went to Scott High School and he followed them to Scott. At Scott High School, he starred as a place kicker. Despite having a full collegiate scholarship in baseball offered, he walked on to the University of Kentucky football team. When he arrived, they had ten place kickers on the squad. Of the ten, only one had a scholarship. Doug rode the bench for two years. After a coaching change where Bill Curry replaced Jerry Clayborne, the school brought in Jan Stenerud, the famed Kansas City Chiefs kicker, as a consultant. After working with the kickers, Jan Stenerud told Bill Curry, 'This kid may be scholarship, but this one over here (Doug Pelfrey) is your best kicker.' Doug received his first opportunity in a game against Central Michigan. It was a 50-yarder. Doug split the uprights and stuck as the kicker," his father explained with pride. The Cincinnati Bengals would later draft Doug Pelfrey and he became one of the most accurate field goal kickers of all time. It all started as a ball boy for Simon Kenton. Sean Dougherty jokes that the Simon Kenton basketball team was so good in 1980-1981, they needed a professional football player as a ball boy.

"I'd like to live up to our number one preseason ranking by the coaches," said Larry Miller at the time. "I feel we could very well be the team to beat in Northern Kentucky. But we're not the only good team around."

The *Louisville Courier Journal* ranked the Pioneers 19th in the *Courier's* preseason state poll. A team called Louisville Moore ranked No. 1. The *Courier* selected Troy McKinley one of the top 20 players in the state.

The following was the official roster for the Pioneer team as they began their 1980 - 1981 season:

Player.	Pos.	Ht.	Yr.
Dave Dixon	C	6-6	Sr.
Sean Dougherty	G	5-7	Sr.
Troy McKinley	F	6-5 1/2	Sr.
Dave Medley	F	6-1 1/2	Sr.
Billy Meier	F	6-5 1/2	Sr.

Player.	Pos.	Ht.	Yr.
Greg Ponzer	G	5-11	Sr.
Larry Callahan	C	6-3	Jr.
Alan Mullins	G	5-11	Jr.
Jeff Williams	F	6-1 1/2	Jr.
Tony Brosky	G	5-11	Soph.
Joey Bruckner	C	6-0	Soph.
Tim Downs	F	6-1	Soph.
David Gray	G	5-8	Soph.
Robbie Heeger	F	5-11	Soph.
Jeff Hester	G	5-7	Soph.
Rob Jennings	G	6-1	Soph.
John Meier	C	6-2	Soph.
Doug Norton	F	5-11	Soph.

CHAPTER 30
The Cheerleaders

"Commitment to the team - there is no such thing
as in-between, you are either in or out."
~ Pat Riley

The eight varsity cheerleaders, four seniors and four juniors, were every bit as special as the basketball players. From a jury, civic organization, group of friends, a team, and even cheerleaders, someone always emerges as the natural leader of the group. Tami Elliott became the captain of the cheerleaders because the other girls looked to her as their leader. Her captain position is a credit to Tami since she cheered in elementary school and seventh grade, but not again until the eleventh grade. Tami failed to make the eighth grade team at Twenhofel. Captains for Simon Kenton's cheerleaders were also chosen in part by scores from tryouts. Scores included teacher and performance assessments of the cheerleader. A cheerleader also needed a clean slate on behavior and discipline.

The Simon Kenton Class of 1981 may have had, to the great delight to their male classmates, the prettiest group of girls to ever be in one class in the school's long history. The class enjoyed more attractive girls than simply the cheerleaders. Tami Elliott was certainly one of the beautiful young ladies. Tami had brown hair, brown eyes, a cute face and the typical curvy, toned physique of an athletic cheerleader. When she smiled, she warmed hearts. Along with all these positive attributes, Tami was always polite, friendly and possessed country wholesomeness and kindness. "Tami was their leader. She was willing to call to arrange events, to organize and to help me with uniforms. She was just a very, very sweet girl," remembers Linda Whittenburg, the 1980 - 1981 cheerleading coach. Her senior year, the student body voted Tami the football Homecoming Queen. Dave Dixon, her cousin, had the honor of serving as her escort. Tami also played tennis and received the senior superlative, Most Attractive. She also won the Principal's Award.

Mary Zimmerer and Tami Elliott were close and dear friends. While Mary's 'best friend' was Jill Brueckner, Mary and Tami shared the traits of 'All-American' girl next door. Mary had big blue eyes and the face of an angel. Sweet, smart, athletic and nice to a fault, Mary had few to no enemies, plenty of friends and boys who adored her. Mary also became a top art student. She chose to attend vocational art school to advance her objective of a career in graphic design. All the boys from Simon Kenton who rode the bus with Mary from Simon Kenton to vocational school enjoyed having a pretty cheerleader in their midst. Mary won the Vocational Student award. "Mary was so much like me, a perfectionist," Linda Whittenberg recalls. "She wanted it done right and she worked everybody to death to get it. She was like the team cheerleaders' cheerleader." Mary and Jill Brueckner were the only cheerleaders to make both football and basketball Homecoming Court their senior year as voted by the student body. Mary also served as the Art Director for the 1981 yearbook including designing the cover. Her design won the vote by the yearbook staff as they considered more than one. Connie Beach, yearbook faculty representative, still believes it is a "really big deal" to have the cover designed by a student. Connie had advised on twenty-five yearbooks and the 1981 yearbook remains her favorite.

Mary Zimmerer and Jill Brueckner grew up on Pelly Road in Independence living as next door neighbors with their families. They grew up best of friends. Tall and athletic, Jill was a pretty blonde. "Jill was so sweet and respectful, and she also had a lot of talent," Linda Whittenburg said of Jill's years as a cheerleader. Her senior year, Jill won basketball Homecoming Queen and also won the senior superlative, Best Personality. Jill also was elected to the football Homecoming Court which Tami Elliott won.

In an almost bizarre coincidence, Jill and Mary would both give birth to twins later in their lives. Neither had a family history of twins. Adding to this strange event, Mary's only sister Martha and Jill's only sister Kim also had twins! Mary jokes it had to have been the creek water which they all drank as little girls. At Kenton Elementary, Mary and Jill performed a cheerleading routine to "True to Your School," by the Beach Boys and "Saturday Night" by the Bay City Rollers at the school's annual variety show. During their years at Simon Kenton prior to receiving their drivers licenses, Jill and Mary rode their Schwinn ten speeds up to the school for summer practices. Later, each had Volkswagon bugs. Jill's car was light blue and Mary's red. Mary claims she once stuffed the entire cheerleading team into her car. Self sufficient, Mary even changed the oil in her own car. Mary alternated weeks with her sister Martha cleaning their house for the $10.00 a week allowance.

Mary's father, Jerry, claims he wanted his daughters to be able to stand on their own and not be dependent on a man. Mary's mother and father both worked. Jerry Zimmerer worked as a salesman for Double Envelope. Mary's mother, Becky, worked as a surgical nurse at St. Elizabeth Medical Center. Once, when the hospital security guard failed to lift the gate because Becky forgot her card, Becky drove through the gate to timely make an emergency surgery she had been called to. Mary also recalls her mother always brought her dinner to school while Mary practiced cheerleading. Nice girls, but no saints, at age fourteen, Jill and Mary once drove Mary's brother Dave's jeep to one of their boyfriend's house. Neither could drive a stick, so Mary worked the brake and clutch and Jill worked the gas and gears. Mary feels fortunate they didn't die in a crash.

The fourth senior on the team, Krista Isler, stood taller than even Jill Brueckner. An outstanding gymnast, Krista was quiet, yet full of fun. Her dark hair and brown eyes made her a statuesque brunette. "Krista was a wonderful gymnast. With talent, it was probably a tossup between her and Tonda as far as who was the most talented gymnast," Linda Whittenburg said. "Krista had a grace about her. When she walked, she flowed." Krista later earned a spot on the Cincinnati Ben-gals who cheer for the NFL's Cincinnati Bengals.

The smallest of the girls, Tonda Hignite became what the cheerleading world calls a 'flyer.' This means if the girls needed to throw someone in the air or place one of themselves at the top of a 'build', Tonda received the nod. A talented dancer, Tonda developed into the team choreographer. Bouncy, full of smiles and a bundle of energy, the strawberry blonde cheerleader spelled cheerleader. "Tonda was the girl who put together our routines and dances. Very talented. She was the one on top of our builds," Linda Whittenburg recalls.

Charlotte Woods was the classic high school girl who looked like a college girl. Possessing sultry good looks, Charlotte accentuated her dark eyes and hair by frequently wearing black out of uniform. Athletic like the other cheerleaders, Charlotte also had a fire and rebel inside her. "Charlotte was a very hard worker. She worked hard and did what she was supposed to do. She was also very emotional," Whittenburg remembers.

Thin as a rail, Pam Meenach had the look of a runway model. With Krista and Charlotte, Pam completed the trio of pretty brunettes who cheered on the team. A very talented gymnast, Pam could flip and jump with the best. In a remarkable achievement, Pam taught herself gymnastics. "Pam was my sweetheart and always well-behaved. Really good team player," recalls Linda Whittenburg. Pam failed to make the 5th or 6th grade cheerleading teams at Whites Tower. Persisting, she made the 7th grade team at Twenhofel. In her senior year in 1982, Pam won Captain of the varsity cheerleading squad.

Deneen Reimer was a great gymnast who, like Tonda Hignite, Charlotte Woods, and Pam Meenach formed a junior quartet on the squad. This group of four would have continued future success as seniors. "Deneen was quiet and never a problem. She had quality skills and was a team player," recalls Linda Whittenburg.

Linda Whittenburg admired her girls. "They were all nonstoppable, if that's a term. They were like little EverReady bunnies. They went to practice all the time. They wore me out. They were always willing to practice. 'Can we have practice tomorrow?', they always asked. They were really hard workers. They had definite ideas about what they wanted to do, and I just trusted in their instincts and in their talents. I usually just let them do it. I occasionally offered some input or an opinion, but they were just so talented. They were all equally good."

As the 1980-1981 school year began, and before Linda Whittenburg joined them, the varsity cheerleaders had no coach or sponsor. Tami Elliott recalls it being difficult without a sponsor. On their own, the cheerleaders chose to practice in the gym when it was available or in the hallway of the school.

"We just basically pretty much kept on the same schedule and same regimen on our own," Tami Elliott explained. The girls simply followed what Rhonda Reeves, their prior coach, had taught them.

"She was the one who built the program, and we went by her standards. She was our prior sponsor. Before she left, she conducted the last tryouts. She built certain standards, district and regional. We usually won district and regions. She developed the rules, the practice schedules, the goals and the demands. Mrs. Reeves built a good program. We had a sound background," Tami explained.

Ms. Reeves was the former, Rhonda LaFollette, 1971 Simon Kenton graduate. Her brother, Dexter, a Piner firefighter, was injured in the explosion at the school. Ms. Reeves' philosophy for the girls involved school first, team second and competition last. This concept is lost in modern cheerleading where competition commands all the attention. Ms. Reeves also demanded good character in cheerleaders. She expected cheerleaders to raise school spirit. The girls chose themes for each basketball or baseball game. They decorated locker rooms, buses and road ways. They made signs for every player on the team and ribbons for every student. The girls made the ribbons themselves. Themes included "Fork the Devils" for the Dayton Green Devils or "Lick Lloyd" included giving out suckers to students. For "Crunch Connor" they gave out Nestle Crunch bars.

Although Mike Tolliver's wife helped for a while, no one wanted the job as cheerleading coach as the 1980 - 1981 school year approached. In a revelation of self initiative, the cheerleaders practiced on their own without a coach. Then one day, Mike Tolliver, the Assistant Principal, stopped in Linda Whittenburg's class to speak to her about the cheerleading coach position.

"I was low woman on the totem pole. I had to. Mike Tolliver, the assistant principal came to me. I did not have my tenure, and you had to have four years to have tenure back then. After four years, if you receive tenure, then you have a permanent lifetime teaching certificate. Now they have to have continuing education units to keep their certificates. It's not just across the board. So I was not tenured and it was my third year. He said, 'We need you to do this.' So I did it or else," Linda Whittenburg laughs of her recruitment. Linda never cared for sports. She also didn't care for cheerleaders. Now she was assigned to coach cheerleaders!

Linda Whittenburg would contribute. She jokes she would inform the girls when they made a build or formation which arm or leg was out of alignment. "Oh, gosh, they were so good. Going in, I had very little work to do. I just showed up and filled out forms and ordered uniforms. I did the paperwork and the organizing. I had to sponsor and to chaperone. It was time consuming. Talent-wise, it was a given with that group. They were also very nice girls," Linda remembers.

The results of the cheerleaders' hard work catapulted them to the 33rd District Championship, 9th Region Championship and third place finish at State in 1981.

The cheerleaders took cheering seriously. "The girls were cheerleaders first. Entertainers second. It wasn't about a show. They cared about the teams. They cried over losses and laughed and enjoyed the victories. They exuded school spirit," Linda Whittenburg remembers proudly. They cheered at all the home and away football and basketball games. Occasionally, they even cheered at a baseball game. The squad always needed money. For one set of uniforms, a relative of Tami Elliott made terry cloth outfits. A picture with the team wearing them shows eight young pretty girls posing in a sitting chorus line. Mary Zimmerer's mother, Becky, made sweats for the entire team.

Simon Kenton also offered a Pep Band, a Pep Club and Rifleers. The Pep Band played at basketball games to play their part in firing up the crowd. The Pep Club also focused on helping school spirit before and during games. The Rifleers had uniforms and performed routines with wooden rifles at football games. Sharon Nie, a senior in the class of 1981, wore a coonskin cap and buckskin as the school's mascot. A large group of school fans who filled the bleachers called themselves the Rowdies.

The Pioneer fight song always helped fire up the crowd. Called "Here Come the Pioneers," Robert Roden, the Simon Kenton band director in the 1970's wrote the song. Tragically, Robert Roden died in the Beverly Hills Supper Club fire. The Beverly Hills Supper Club in Southgate, Kentucky was the showplace of the Midwest when it burned from faulty aluminum electric wiring May 28, 1977 resulting in 165 deaths of guests and staff. Beverly Hills was the biggest supper club between Las Vegas and the East Coast, with national acts of the time such as Joey Heatherton, Phyllis Diller and Frankie Vallie and the Four Seasons, performing there regularly.

The following is the text of the Pioneer fight song:

Here come the Pioneers
Back them with our cheers
Our team will win tonight
'Cause they're all right
Fight Fight Fight
Fight boys, for SK
Beat them the fair way
We're proud to say that we're from S - K - S

P - I - O - N - E - E - R - S

Here come the Pioneers . . . (repeat song)

The faculty at Simon Kenton High School for 1980-1981 grew close in and out of school. They also became huge sports fans. "A bunch of teachers that were hired at Simon Kenton in the early '70s. We were all boomers, and there was a big turnover for some reason at Simon Kenton. There were retirements for teachers who had been there since the school opened in 1937. They were retiring and leaving. I know in my wife's group, they called themselves the Dirty Dozen because twelve of them were hired that year. All twelve of them were still there in '81. We were a bunch of recent graduates conscious of social service and all of us went into teaching," explains Dwight Searcy of the relationships. "We founded the Bleacher Teachers. Shawna Cartwright started it. We even attended the away games in 1980-1981. We arrived early so no one could keep us from filling up the seats behind the Simon Kenton bench. Teams at other schools arranged their students' cheering section behind the opposing team to hassle them. We provided a buffer between our team and the opposing hostile cheering sections. We made sweatshirts and T-shirts which we wore to the games," Dwight Searcy explains.

"Many times after basketball games, faculty who attended the games gathered at someone's house to rehash the game and just socialize," recalls math teacher Mike Collins. Mike Collins also remembers Larry and Joyce Miller were extremely popular with the faculty. "Larry had to put up with a lot from the 'old timers'. When he first came to Simon Kenton, he met resistance from many of the long-time supporters of the program which had frankly been a long-time losing program. We even made up songs about what a 'horrible' coach he was and how he didn't know anything and sing them to him," Mike Collins laughs of the ribbing Larry Miller.

CHAPTER 31
Mutual Respect

"It's not the critic that counts, not the one who points out how the strong man stumbled or how the doer of deeds might have done them better. The credit belongs to the man who is actually in the arena, whose face is marred with sweat and dust and blood; who strives valiantly; who errs and comes up short again and again; who knows the great enthusiasms, the great devotions, and spends himself in a worthy cause; who if he wins, knows the triumph of high achievement; and who, if he fails, at least fails while daring greatly, so that his place shall never be with those cold and timid souls who know neither victory or defeat."
   ~ Theodore Roosevelt

Coach Miller knew he coached a special group of cohesive young men who also had a winning attitude. He provides the following description.

"Alan Mullins was the only junior we really played in 1980-1981. Alan was a great athlete. Not real big. Quick. Fast. Real smart. Probably one of the smartest kids I ever coached. Never questioned."

"Sean Dougherty was little. If he hadn't been so small, he could have been a great player. He was a good player, but he could have really been great if taller. He was quick as a cat. He could bring the ball down the floor and he could really defend."

"Greg Ponzer was one of the toughest kids I ever coached. We listed him at 5-10 and that's probably stretching him. He was off and on shooting, but he could score. He was a great defender too. He and Billy were our enforcers. Those two would fight each other in practice. They just liked to get after each other. If you want kids to win, they must be competitive. I don't know how else you'd describe it."

"Dave Dixon was the fastest kid on the team at six foot six. He out ran everybody in sprints. Dave is a tremendous athlete. He could jump out of the gym. He wasn't very strong. We listed him at 185 pounds and that's probably stretching it. He could flat jump and score. Also, I recall Dave Dixon never came to school on his birthday because his Mom said he didn't have to. Funny."

"Billy Meier was big and strong. We listed him at 200. He was a phenomenal athlete. We were playing at Bishop Brossert when he was a junior and we were thumping them. We were playing 1-3-1 zone and Billy was playing baseline. He was running from the corner and this guy was wearing him out. They'd run him to one side and Billy would run over there and their guy would make another basket. I'd holler at him, 'Get over there quicker."

"So the kid would line up on the other side.. Billy would run and the kid would shoot and score from that side. The kid made about three or four buckets in a row. So we called a timeout. Billy said, 'Coach, you want me to take him out? He's wearing me out. Let me put him in the bleachers.' I said, 'Billy we're up 30, we don't need to be putting anybody in the bleachers,' because he'd done that at Lloyd."

"Dave Medley was a strong kid, real brainy, real smart kid, could do anything you asked him to do. He didn't have the size of the other guys. If Dave had played on any other team, he'd have been a star. He could be a good player, but we had three 6'6" guys and there wasn't any place for Dave but in the back up role."

"In Troy McKinley, I have not seen a better shooter. I was a head coach for eighteen years. I never had anybody that could shoot like him and I had some really good shooters. He had unbelievable eye-hand coordination. He's also a good ball handler. He was a good passer. Troy could do it all with a basketball. He wasn't a great athlete. And in four years, I don't think Troy said six words to me."

In speaking about his players, Coach Miller held a special affinity for each of them for different reasons, but he especially loved Greg Ponzer's toughness.

"I really liked Greg. We're closer now probably and I don't see him hardly. But he was a hard kid to get close to then. But you had to like him. I mean, God almighty, when he came out on the court, he was ready to play. You know, he didn't care who got in front of him. He's going to go get the ball for you. He had that football safety mentality," remembers Coach Miller of his second guard.

There is an expression: respect is mutual. It is always difficult to find someone expressing respect for someone who fails to reciprocate respect. Professional athletes after a critical game can always be heard expressing accolades on the competition. The same principle applies in everyday life. The Simon Kenton players respected Coach Miller and he respected them.

"I thought he was great. I never had any ill feelings toward him. He hollered, but he hollered at everybody. But it wasn't cussing. When he would get mad, he would get mad. But I never took it personally. I never had and never will have anything bad to say about him," Troy McKinley explains.

Alan Mullins also respected Coach Miller. "I did, for the most part, did everything he asked me. I understood what I was supposed to be doing. I never really veered away from that except the Lloyd game," Alan Mullins recalls.

Dave Medley had a good relationship with Coach Miller, but there were moments. "There were times when you didn't want to get on Coach Miller's bad side. I remember after a Highlands game, middle of the season senior year, I twisted an ankle going up for a lay up and charged a guy. Made the lay up, but came down and twisted the heck out of my ankle. Coach didn't want me to sit on it. He didn't want me to let it get stiff. He wanted me to get back in. I tried, but I was just hobbling around. Eventually, I went to the emergency room that night," Dave Medley explains regarding his injury.

"My relationship with Larry was a good relationship. Larry Miller coached us as a coach and not as a friend. He was a disciplinarian for us. He practiced tough love. There was times where he walked out of practice on us," remembers Greg Ponzer. "He would say if you guys don't want to do it, don't want to be here, then fine. We won't practice today. But he was a fair coach. Demonstrated by the meeting he held at the beginning of the year about starting guards. I believe he knew more of what we had than we knew what we had and he really pulled the most out of each of us. That's a great coaching trait," explains Greg Ponzer of his opinion of Larry Miller as a coach.

"The kids never ruled this team. Never. We started practice. We practiced hard. We left practice. We knew who the coach was. I think we became extensions of him. There was never loss of respect for Larry Miller. He was also an excellent bench coach," adds Greg Ponzer.

"We lost five games that year in 1980 - 1981, and I know at least three of the games that we lost, we were thinking, 'man, we're going to have a hell of a practice.' At least three times after those five losses, we walked into the gym out of the locker room and the volleyball net was set up in the gym. Coach Miller and Coach Schadler were standing there. They held volleyballs in their hand. We thought what's going on? They'd throw the volleyballs to us and told us to play volleyball for two hours," recalls Billy Meier of playing volleyball at practice.

"His practices were about competitiveness. Most of the enjoyment of practice was competing against somebody else. Physical, hard, pressing, offense and defense. We became the best physically conditioned team around," Sean explained.

"Dave Schadler filled a different role on the team. Dave was kind of the guy that would cuddle us and talk to us. He really liked Billy Meier and me. We kind of bonded with him a little bit because I think Dave, being 31, on Friday nights liked to get out a little bit just like we did. He would come in with his coffee and I'm sure he wasn't feeling too good those days," laughs Greg Ponzer.

Every basketball and football team includes players who play against the starters in practices. The backups role is to vigorously help the starters properly prepare and improve. Better subs adds up to better starters. Coaches rarely complain about having too much talent on their team.

Tim Downs played the support role to the best of his ability. Every day he endured the rigors of practice along side the starters. Yet, as a sophomore, he only rarely played in varsity games.

One practice Tim Downs and Larry Callahan failed to live up to the expectations of Coach Miller and Coach Miller summarily threw Tim and Larry out of practice and to the showers. After reaching the locker room, Tim required the use of the toilet, not the urinal. Callahan hit the showers. Tim dropped his shorts and sat down on the commode. In seconds, Coach Schadler burst into the locker room, yelling at the Tim's effort and performance. Tim recalls Coach Schadler didn't care about Tim's location on the toilet. With the door open to the booth where Tim sat, Coach Schadler continued his shouting and screaming for what seemed forever to Tim Downs. Tim can't remember if he was even able to finish his business. He remembers the yelling and the uncomfortable location he found himself in.

Tim also recalls how competitive Billy Meier practiced. In the "ball at center court, first one to get it" drill, Tim remembers beating Billy Meier to the ball once and heading towards the nearest basket. As Tim raced down the court in anticipation of an easy layup, Billy Meier followed in hot pursuit. Before Tim reached the basket, Billy grabbed Tim's jersey from behind at the top and as Billy pulled, Billy ripped the jersey and shorts all the way down. Tim stood in the middle of the court practically naked. It may have only been a drill, but Billy Meier had no intention of allowing Tim Downs to beat him. Not even once.

Coach Miller also dealt with having three starting guards and only two guard positions. "Sean, Greg and I were real good friends all through pee-wee football and growing up. When we arrived at high school, divisions occurred. Mostly about playing time. It really became an issue as a sophomore, I played a little varsity. When we played junior varsity ball together everything was fine. Coach Miller would bring us up and let us dress varsity," explains Alan Mullins. "A couple other games during the season when the varsity would win in a blow out, I received opportunities for playing time. Sean wondered why I'm playing a little more than he was. Actually, it all worked out. We settled it that year. As I've looked back, I wasn't old enough to understand it at the time, but I admire how Coach Miller thought ahead. He saw me as someone with speed, quickness and the ability to handle the ball. He recognized it and groomed me even as a sophomore by giving me opportunities and placing me out there in situations," adds Alan Mullins.

Billy Meier remembers there would be moments mild mannered Dave Dixon would leap out of his cage. "There were practices on Saturday. I always thought it was funny how Dave Schadler would stumble in. He'd tell Greg and me, 'Smells like you guys had a good time'. We were sweating beer. He'd strut away with a grin on his face. I actually believe Coach Miller and Coach Schadler were always afraid they were going to make one of us mad and we would quit. I saw Dave Dixon in a practice jump up in Larry Miller's face. They were nose to nose going at it. Dixon was mad about something. I can't remember what it was, but we were all standing back thinking 'Wow. Is this Dave Dixon in his face?' They were jawing hard. I thought how the hell is he getting away with that? Coach never made him run. Never made him do anything. I'm thinking is it because he knows if he makes him mad and he quits, he doesn't have quite the team that he had before?" Billy Meier wondered about the incident. In reality, the Coaches loved to see fire in their players bellies, particularly someone like Dave Dixon, the introvert.

"I didn't have mental toughness that probably Troy, Greg, Sean, Alan and Dave Medley had. I had the athletic skills, but I was weaker mentally. I always felt I was trying to prove something after not playing for so many years," Dixon recalls of his insecurity.

Dave Schadler remembers most of the Northern Kentucky coaches got along, but Larry Miller was always competitive. "It was a fraternity. I'm talking about the basketball community. Several of the former coaches were principals. They'd meet informally at places like the Greyhound Grill. They were having a conference drawing to play in this conference preview Larry Miller's first year. I wasn't in the meeting, but Simon Kenton drew Holmes to play in that tournament. Coach Reynolds at Holmes had one of the top teams in the state. Simon Kenton was not a very strong team at that point and had a first-year coach. Reynolds said, for all the right reasons I'm positive, 'Well, let's not play Simon Kenton. Let's let Simon play someone else.' I'm sure it was for all the right reasons: new program, new coach, first-year head coach. Larry had never been a head coach before. 'Let's allow you guys play someone where you're going to be a little bit more competitive'. I've been told that Larry responded with, 'The hell with that. We'll play Holmes'."

CHAPTER 32
The Season

"If I always appear prepared, it is because before entering an undertaking, I have meditated long and have foreseen what might occur.
It is not genius which reveals to me suddenly and secretly what I should do in circumstances unexpected by others; it is thought and preparation."
~ Napoleon

To assist in the healing process of the Simon Kenton community, the contractor accelerated the construction of the new gym ahead of the remaining reconstruction so the gym was available to host the opening home game of the season, November 28, 1980.

"With the new gym, the school bought us brand-new uniforms and brand-new warmups. Everything was brand-new," remembers Sean Dougherty of the beginning of the season.

"We went from a gym that held 350 to a gym that held 1,500. In the old gym, you ran into a concrete wall," Sean Dougherty recalls of the old court. Sean remembers hurting himself his junior year when hitting the wall attempting to save a pass. Mary Zimmerer recalls that in the old gym the cheerleaders had one foot to stand in between the wall and playing area. The new gym would provide plenty of room for the cheerleaders to perform their routines and cheers.

Before the beginning of the regular season, the Pioneers scrimmaged Loveland High School in Cincinnati, Ohio. Billy Meier suffered an injury in the game. Meier going down resulted in Dave Medley receiving an opportunity to start at forward to begin the season.

Coach Miller recalls the hoopla prior to the Pioneers' opening game tipoff at Simon Kenton. "The superintendent came and threw out the first ball. Television cameras were there because we were from the school which had exploded and now we're back playing in a new gym. All three Cincinnati television stations covered the game," Coach Miller recalls of the opening night.

"The St. Henry Crusaders had a pretty nice ball club and they played right with us for a long time. We pulled it out at the end. We ended up winning 79 to 61, but St. Henry played real well," Coach Miller recalls of the first game of the season.

Dave Medley recalls his season suffering an embarrassing beginning at the first home game. "I remember tripping coming out of the paper hoop the cheerleaders built when I jumped through the hoop. I think I might have gone through first that time. For whatever reason, I went through first. I don't know why. But I remember almost falling on my face," Dave Medley laughs.

Troy McKinley recollects a strange irony about the St. Henry's warm-up routine considering the school being a Catholic school. "Every time we played at St. Henry, they always warmed up to the song "Hells Bells" by AC/DC. I'm like, what is this? I just thought that was odd for them to warm up to that song," Troy chuckles.

Greg Ponzer scored the first point in the new gym on a free throw. "I probably wasn't the guy that was supposed to make the first basket in Simon Kenton's new gym. Troy probably would have taken the shot. So it probably didn't work out according to the script," Greg Ponzer laughs. No one believes Greg Ponzer didn't know exactly what he was doing.

"I think it was a lay-up going to the basket early in the game. It was just one of those things. I was a terrible free throw shooter. I think I probably had two free throws and made one of them. I grew up with the old gym. I used to love sitting in that old gym watching the guys play basketball. It was loud, too. You could have a hundred people in there and it was pretty darn loud. But moving to the new gym was a crowning of what we were hoping to accomplish. Sometimes when people get something new, it changes the attitude a little bit," Greg Ponzer explains.

The McKinleys good-naturedly agree with Greg Ponzer's assessment regarding the first points. Mary McKinley's uncle, John Coleman, scored the first points in the "old gym" and the McKinleys wanted to hold the family tradition.

Mike Tolliver, assistant principal at the time, recalls the season would be the first time in school history the school worried about sellouts. "I can remember we had to worry about sellouts for the first time and the fire marshal controlling how many attended games. The ironic part is that when we played other schools at their gym, they had sellouts there as well. I remember having to warn teachers that if you want to attend the game, arrive early. Almost all of the games were sold out," Mike Tolliver recalls of the attendance records.

The Pioneers' traveled to Dayton, Kentucky on the Ohio River for their second game. The Dayton Green Devils never threatened to win a district or regional. The legendary John Wooden of ten U.C.L.A. championships fame coached Dayton in 1932 as his first coaching job out of college. He coached basketball and football at the school. He also taught. Dayton gave Simon Kenton an unexpected close game before losing, 66 to 61.

"Billy Meier wouldn't play until late December. He didn't play the first six or seven games. Every other year, he injured himself at the end of the year and didn't finish it. This year he decided to get hurt at the beginning of the year and didn't start it. It hurt us in the early games. So we had Billy out. Dave Medley started for him. We had Sean, Greg and Alan coming out of football and they weren't really ready for basketball," Coach Miller recalls of the team's slow start.

"We didn't leave the gate very well even though we did win the first two games. Then we traveled to Frankfort to play in the Capital City Classic. We played Shelby County. They had a nice team and even went to the state tournament that year. They won the 8th Region. They beat us 58 to 51," Coach Miller recalls. The loss by seven points would be the largest margin of defeat for the Pioneers for the year.

"The game was a stepping stone for us because they manhandled us pretty good," Greg Ponzer recalls. "I remember Coach Miller storming into the locker room after the game. It was the most emotion I ever saw from him. He slung his clipboard. His anger was aimed at the big guys over rebounding. He knew it was a game for us to show what we could do in the State of Kentucky. We were confident in Northern Kentucky. Shelby County was a chance for us to make a name for ourselves down state and we just didn't take advantage of the opportunity."

"Those guys at Shelby were a short, stocky, physical ball team. I felt like I couldn't do anything in that game," Dave Dixon recalls of the defeat. Dave Medley only remembers how mad his Dad was at the Pioneers after losing to Shelby County.

"I remember losing to Shelby County because it was the first team we played which was not from Northern Kentucky," Sean Dougherty recalls.

"Shelby was a powerhouse we watched perennially down state. They beat Holmes in the championship when Charles Hurt, who later played for the University of Kentucky, put his arm up through the net and rim to knock Doug Schloemer's shot out."

Sean Dougherty recollects a very quiet ride back on the bus after the Shelby County loss. The players knew the coaches were disappointed and the players feared the coaches call for practice for the next morning. When the players showed up to the morning practice, the coaches placed volleyball nets in the gym, instructed the team to play volleyball for two hours, and left.

"We'd do things other than regular practice. We'd scrimmage and do odd things. The kids were under a lot of pressure. They had been through the explosion. Heck, it was harder on them than even me because of their local roots," explains Coach Miller of utilizing diversion techniques.

"We had all the expectations. They wrote articles 'Number 1, Simon Kenton the first time ever'. Simon Kenton never won the 9th Region and now here we were ranked Number 1. Can they do it? Can they actually pull it off? That was a lot of pressure on the kids. I was too young to realize it," Coach Miller adds of the pressure.

"I was barely thirty. I wasn't at home. Those kids were at home. Their friends were reading this. My folks were down in Hardin County. They didn't know where Simon Kenton was on the map. You put pressure on yourself as a individual, but these kids were trying to live up to all their buddies, their parents and everybody saying they're a good team. 'How come you don't win them all by thirty?' Everybody thinks you're supposed to win by thirty when you've got the best team," Coach Miller explains of the expectations.

After losing to Shelby County, the Pioneers played the Newport Wildcats at the Simon Kenton home floor. Simon Kenton formally dedicated their new gym the same night, December 12, 1980. The school brought back players, coaches and the athletic director from the 1938 basketball team, the school's first. Newport also enjoyed a solid team in 1980 - 1981, but at the time of this game, injuries plagued them. Troy McKinley recalls Newport was "always our nemesis in middle school." The Pioneers won the dedication game 63 to 56 over Newport. Next up for Simon Kenton would be another other Kenton County public high school, the Dixie Heights Colonels. One of Dixie's players that year, Mark Pike, would later play over a decade as a special teams specialist for the NFL Buffalo Bills and play in four Super Bowls.

"We went to Dixie Heights, a big rival at the time and our kids played pretty well. We beat them by twenty, 80-60. It was our best game to that point of the season. Troy had a big game, thirty-six points and thirteen rebounds. Dixie Heights had a pretty nice team and Troy still had thirty-six. Dave Dixon had fifteen points and eleven rebounds. Greg Ponzer scored eighteen points. Then we played Lloyd. Lloyd used a slow-down offense. Their coach always wanted to slow the play down. We still beat them 67 to 49," recalls Coach Miller of the Dixie and Lloyd games.

"We then played our top competition for the Region that year, Covington Catholic, in the first round of the Newport Catholic Invitational. Billy was back for the game, but he wasn't very good. We enjoyed a three point lead with about a minute and a half to go and ended up losing. We suffered a couple of turnovers at the end of the game. Troy fouled out with a minute and a half to go too. They made a shot at the buzzer to beat us by two, 64 to 62. Don Turney grabbed a pass and hit a bank shot at the horn for Covington Catholic. The Colonel fans mobbed the floor. Our team was down after that game," Coach Miller recalls of the second loss of the season.

Next up on the Pioneers schedule was the Campbell County Camels.

"We went to Campbell County and beat them handily, 83-68. They had a good player and one big kid, but we had three," Larry Miller recalls. "Then we went to Connor and Connor beat us by one, 67-66 in their Invitational. We played Connor twice that year. They had a nice team with all juniors but one. We never beat them. They were all about 6-1, 6-2 and pretty strong kids," Coach Miller explains of the Connor obstacle.

Dave Dixon hated losing to Connor because Dave's father worked with one of the Conner player's fathers, Bill Blasingame. "You can imagine the crap my dad took at work after they beat us twice. That's why to this day I'd like to play that game again," Dave Dixon stresses of his disappointment.

"We next went to Highlands. The Highlands Bluebirds were the class of the region at the time. They were at home, but we still beat them by sixteen, 85-69," Coach Miller recalls.

Troy McKinley suffered a funny "equipment" problem at Highlands the year before. "I forgot my tennis shoes. I only had my gold Converse and I had to wear them. They were low cut. I always wore high tops. None of my teammates on the bench wore size fourteen. So I was stuck. I looked silly in those gold shoes. I don't remember how many points I had that game, but I banked in like a forty-footer at the buzzer. Everyone on our team wanted me to start wearing those shoes all the time. I said, there ain't no way," Troy

McKinley laughs of his 'golden slippers'. Dave Medley would hurt his ankle during the 1980 - 1981 Highlands game and miss three games.

"We went to Boone next and Boone had a really nice team. We won only by three at Boone, 70-67, but they had two great players," Coach Miller recalls. Dave Dixon scored twenty points. Troy's twelve rebounds and twenty-five points led the team. The rematch with Campbell County which followed the Boone County game was closer, but still a 67 to 62 Pioneer victory.

The rematch at Simon Kenton against Covington Catholic followed at the Pioneers home gym. In obtaining their revenge, the Pioneers won the game by thirteen, 77-64. Billy Meier began improving and had fourteen points. The Pioneers followed this victory by pounding Walton-Verona, 76-66. Next would be Scott High School where Troy McKinley scored twenty-one points and fifteen rebounds in crushing the Eagles, 73-52.

On January 28-31, 1981, the Lloyd Invitational matched two teams each from the Ninth Region and Tenth Region. Simon Kenton played the state ranked Mason County from the Tenth Region. Simon Kenton received no state recognition at the time. As far as the state rankings, the Pioneers were off the radar, off the map and off the screen. Simon Kenton was ranked as high as seventeenth in the state pre-season poll. After the season began, the Pioneers were never ranked. The Pioneers made a shot at the buzzer to defeat Mason County and won 71 to 69. Dave Dixon recalls giving the Mason County players a hard time and smack talk flying back and forth. Dixon backed his talk up with twenty-six points and nine rebounds. Troy McKinley poured in twenty-two points and grabbed an amazing twenty rebounds. Dave Dixon missed a shot on a pass from Greg Ponzer, but followed it and made the winning basket.

The Pioneers still lost in the Tournament semi-finals. "Lloyd beat us. Lloyd had a nice team and they played that slow-down game. Everybody hated it. We didn't shoot it very well, and Troy was six for fourteen. That's not Troy. He always shot over sixty percent. They ended up beating us by one, 45-44. It was controversial. We had a couple of bad calls from the referees," Coach Miller said of the team's fourth loss.

Simon Kenton traveled to the Newport Wildcats' home court for the next game. Despite Newport regaining their health, Simon Kenton won 69-62. Greg Ponzer recalls during the Newport game he came down with an elbow and struck a player named David Simpson. "He was probably one of the biggest guys in the region and definitely the toughest. I caught him right underneath the throat, and boy, he chased me the rest of the darn game.

Calling me everything he could call me," Greg Ponzer laughs. "I didn't blame him."

Dave Medley doesn't recall how the Newport game concluded, but remembers a tough practice after the game. The rematch against Scott followed the Newport game. Troy McKinley would shoot seventeen out of twenty-two from the field and nine out of ten from the line and score forty-three points. Larry Miller remembers the game well. "He didn't make his first seventeen field goals, but his first seventeen shots including free throws. He had probably thirty and this woman came down out of the stands at Scott. She didn't know if I or Dave was head coach. She just chewed Dave out. She got in his ear cussing him and hollering at him to take 'that McKinley out.' Dave's standing there shaking his head. He said, 'Ma'am, I'm not the head coach. Cuss him out and pointed at me'," Coach Miller laughs recalling the angry Scott lady.

"I was not going to take him out until he missed a shot. He finally missed one and we took him out. I was hoping he would take the record that night. So I took him out for good at forty-three. The record was forty-five. Dave Dixon had set it the year before," Larry Miller recalls of his decision.

"I took Troy out and our scorer, Joey Freimuth, sent a guy over and said 'McKinley's got forty-three, that's two away from the school record' and suggested I should put him back in. Here we are up thirty-five on Scott. They're our sister school. They allowed us to use their building. I called Troy over. 'Troy, you got forty-three, you want to go back in and break the record, forty-five?' He said, 'Nah, Coach, I'll get it some other time'. I said, 'Okay'. I didn't want to argue with him," Coach Miller grins proudly of Troy's unselfish decision.

Dave Medley scored nine points at Scott. "Everybody was wanting me to shoot too because I never broke double digits the entire darn season," Dave laughs.

After the Scott game, an incident occurred at school between Larry Miller and Mike Tolliver, the assistant principal. "The next day, I'm sitting at lunch and everybody always wanted to take their shots at us. One of the highlights of our day was when Larry and I had lunch with the faculty at Simon Kenton. They were ate up with the basketball team. They had their opinions too. We're sitting there, and Mike Tolliver walked up and said some sarcastic remark about 'you should not beat schools by that margin. If you had any class, you would have taken out your starters earlier'. So Larry stood up, and he and Mike got into it. At lunch. All the school kids there. I mean, it was amazing. I'd like to hear what the kids remember about the argument. We weren't adults all the time. Imagine the students watching the head coach and assistant principal going at it," Dave Schadler laughs regarding the confrontation.

After easily vanquishing the overpowered Scott Eagles, 98-62, Simon Kenton defeated the Lloyd Juggernauts to avenge their prior tournament loss, 61-55. The Pioneers then played the Holmes Bulldogs, finally without Dickie Beal whom Holmes lost to graduation. After thumping Holmes 95-71, the Pioneers played Dixie Heights again and smoked them again, 89-57.

"We were at practice one day, and I said to Troy, 'alley-oop one, I'll jump up and see if I can dunk it.' So we did it a couple of times. We weren't supposed to do it in games. Then we played Dixie. I'm standing on the block. Troy's got an open shot from the free throw line, but he alley-oops it to me and I dunk it. The next time or two down the court, I drove the baseline and dunked it again. Then Troy, on the next possession, alley-oops it to me, and I dunk it again. They were absolutely perfect passes, just tremendous passes. I couldn't believe Coach Miller let us," Dave Dixon laughs of the dunkathon. Coach Miller then emptied his bench.

During the season, at the time, the KHSAA prohibited dunking during pregame warmups. The Pioneers often times had Assistant Coach Bill Pelfrey, Jr. watch out for the referees to come out of their locker room so the players could dunk during pregame to fire up the crowd. When Billy Meier was recovering from his ankle injury earlier in the season, the coaches allowed him to shoot around in practice. Greg Ponzer failed in his 'duty' assigned to him by Billy to look out for the coaches and they caught Billy dunking on his busted ankle.

The good feelings from the Dixie game would not last. The Pioneers traveled to Hebron, Kentucky to play the Connor Cougars in a rematch.

"We had to play Connor again over at Connor. Even though we played better, the score didn't indicate it. They ended up beating us by five, 75-70, and our team was really down. We had been on a run. We'd won four or five games there easily and then Connor beat us. Kids were down and I was too," Coach Miller recalls of the team loss.

The Pioneers played one final regular season game.

"We had one more game before the season was over. We went to Boone County and we really hyped it. We wanted to play well against Boone County. First quarter of the game, Billy gets thrown out. They claim he threw a flagrant elbow, which he probably did, knowing Billy. I never argued it. We brought in Dave Medley, and he played a great game. We beat Boone by twenty-seven on their floor, 87-60, and their court is where the District

Tournament was going to be the next week," Larry Miller remembers of the trip to Boone County. Later in this story, someone else besides Billy Meier would be tossed from a critical game for an elbow thrown at Billy Meier.

"I distinctly recall we didn't do anything special in preparation for that Boone game, but when we stepped on the floor that night over at Boone, it was a different mind set. I don't know what spurred it or where it came from, but we picked our intensity up," Alan Mullins recalls. The night of the Boone County game, Troy McKinley grieved the death of his uncle, Dick McKinley, Bones brother. "We wanted to go into the District on a good note. My brother, Dick, had died and was laid out that night. We went to the funeral home, then went on to the game," Bones McKinley explains. Kentucky high school basketball. Nothing like it.

"We get over there and the score is Boone County ten and Billy Meier ten. Billy made the first ten points," Bones said. "Billy and a Boone player mix it up underneath. They're going down the sidelines and the ref's back-pedaling. Billy just, bam, nailed the player right in the teeth. 'You're outta here,' yelled the referee. Everybody liked to have our side. What are we going to do now, Billy's got all the points. But Dave Medley came in and played a great game. Troy caught fire too, and we beat them by thirty," Bones remembers. Dave Dixon boasted a double/double with twenty-one and thirteen. Sean Dougherty broke double digits with ten points. Troy had twenty-five points and eleven rebounds. Alan Mullins had nine assists.

As the season ended, heading into District, the Pioneers amassed a solid nineteen and five record. However, as Connor, Lloyd, Covington Catholic and Shelby County proved, the Pioneers were far from invincible. Simon Kenton also weren't ranked in the state. In the 9th Region, the Pioneers were neck and neck at the top of the local polling with the Covington Catholic Colonels whose motto was "with a spirit which will never die.". The District battles would begin the determination of who would represent the 9th Region in the state tournament..

As the 1981 regular season closed, Troy McKinley pulled off a remarkable feat. He led the 9th Region in field goal percentage, .623; points a game average, 25.3; and free throw percentage, .821. Nobody is able to recall a basketball player to achieve this triple objective on any level. Players who win scoring titles like Michael Jordan and Alan Iverson generally do not win field goal percentage or free throw titles. Wilt Chamberlain probably led in points and percentage from the field, but not the free throw line too. Troy was also fifth in rebounds at 10.6 per game. He broke the career scoring record at Simon Kenton previously held by Gene Coppage who played from 1949-1953.

However, the Pioneers were not a one man show. For the year, Dave Dixon averaged 15.8 points, Billy Meier 10.3 and Greg Ponzer 10.1. The team averaged 30.9 rebounds a game. Their guards averaged nearly five assists a game. Larry Miller kept statistics on everything. The team averaged .524 field goal percentage. They averaged .639 free throw percentage. Dave Dixon blocked 45 shots. Troy McKinley blocked 38. Alan Mullins averaged only three turnovers per game, a remarkable achievement for a point guard. The team averaged 71.8 points and allowed only 61.6 points a game. The team grabbed eight steals a game. Coach Miller knew how many lane violations, bad passes and even charges each player took. Players other than the seven main players scored only 38 total points in the season.

Prior to the season, the Pioneers planned on playing in as many tournaments as possible. Principal Bob Abel recalls he and Larry Miller discussing the benefits prior to the season of playing in tournaments. Despite playing in four tournaments, Simon Kenton lost every one. However, the Pioneers gained valuable experience.

The Pioneers in their five season losses were never were blown out. Their worst loss was by seven points to Shelby County.

A controversy behind the scenes almost hijacked the season. A prickly issue came from an anonymous sour grapes complaint. The complaint involved whether or not the Simon Kenton players had lost their eligibility. Bert Bennett, Kenton County superintendent, received an anonymous complaint that Simon Kenton had played in a game at the end of the season the year before which resulted in their eligibility being jeopardized. Bob Abel recalls the concern both he and Bert Bennett expressed with the issue. However, after an investigation, the game in issue occurred before the end of the state tournament and the KHSAA determined the end of the state tournament as the end of the season. Therefore, the eligibility for the players was not lost. It was a technical close call which nearly hijacked the drama to come. The eligibility question never became public knowledge.

CHAPTER 33
The Walton Game

"The hen is the wisest of all animals
because she never cackles until after the egg is laid."
~ Lincoln

The 33rd District Tournament would be the fifth tournament of the year for the Simon Kenton Pioneers. Unlike the other tournaments, losing before the finals of the District would end their season. The 33rd District included five of the top ten teams in Northern Kentucky. "It's too bad we have so many good teams in this district," said Walton Coach Bob Eads prior to the tournament. The lower bracket of the tournament included the following teams: Simon Kenton (19-5), St. Henry (17-15), Walton-Verona (26-6) and Boone County (16-9). The upper bracket included Connor (17-7), Lloyd (18-8) and Dixie Heights (7-17). The Pioneers played the St. Henry Crusaders for their first 33rd District tournament game held at Boone County High School.

"We always had a competitive relationship with St. Henry. We respected each other. Respect means something. Many kids don't really respect each other. The 33rd District was the toughest district in the Region that year and probably still is today in the Ninth Region," Greg Ponzer recalls.

The scoreboard read 17-17 after the first quarter of the St. Henry game. At the half, the Pioneers led by one, 29-28. Simon Kenton increased their lead by the conclusion of the third quarter, 48-43. Either team had a chance to win until the final five minutes when St. Henry ran out of steam and the Pioneers took over the game. Seniors filled the rosters of both teams. Knowing it could be their last high school game, both teams laid it on the line. Simon Kenton won the fourth quarter 26-11 to win the game 74-54. Troy McKinley tossed in twenty-four points for the game. Billy Meier added seventeen points. Greg Ponzer dealt out eight assists and scored eleven points. Dave Dixon sat out much of the game after picking up three fouls in the first quarter. "They hung together when the pressure was on and came through. That's what it takes to win a championship," Larry Miller commented after the game relative to his team's poise. After the game, Larry Miller wrote "Teamwork" on the locker room blackboard to emphasize what won the game for the Pioneers. Simon Kenton would need teamwork and persistence against their next opponent, the Bearcats of Walton-Verona who defeated Boone County on the Rebels home floor, 65-56.

The next basketball game between the Pioneers and Bearcats would go down in history as one of the greatest high school basketball games ever played, anywhere at anytime. It was played March 6, 1981, a Friday night. Sean Dougherty remembers so many fans packed into the 2500 capacity gym at Boone County High School "the building was sweating." Actually, the gym 'perspired' so much, it created dangerous slippery floor conditions.

The referees for the classic game, Dan Sullivan, forty-six at the time, and Tom Hummel, thirty-six, recall parking blocks from the high school and witnessing over a thousand fans being turned away. Both long time officials, neither referee ever beheld a larger crowd at Boone County High School.

WHKK sports radio called the game. Dale MacMillan handled play by play and Hardy Tribble provided the color commentary. Hardy Tribble interviewed Larry Miller prior to the game and commented to the Coach about the substantial crowd gathered in the arena. "I like that kind of game," remarked Coach Miller. "All our players are up emotionally and all are healthy. We really have seven starters. The team is quiet because they feel the tension and pressure. I want the enthusiasm to come spontaneously, not because of what I say to them. It's a great atmosphere for a basketball game."

Hardy Tribble also spoke to Walton head basketball coach Bob Eads. A graduate from Boone County, Bob Eads claimed he also never observed such an extensive crowd of supporters for two schools at Boone County. "We have a mountain to climb tonight. We're ready to play. I see it in their eyes. Good things happen to good people," Bob Eads stated with cautious optimism.

Led by the towering 6'10" Andy Burns and their mercurial 5'11" point guard John Anderson, the Bearcats always hustled and played team basketball. Curtis Carpenter, 5'11", and Les McCubbin, 6'0", started at the forwards. Junior guard Kevin Martin at 6'0" completed the starting five. Mirroring Simon Kenton, Walton started four seniors and a junior. The Pioneers owned an easy height advantage over the Bearcats and the two regular season games between the two teams resulted in easy Pioneer victories. Therefore, the Pioneers possessed plenty of confidence playing the Bearcats for a third time. However, this District game would be played on a neutral floor. Yet, regardless of venue, other than Andy Burns, the Bearcats of Walton couldn't match up with the front line of Simon Kenton. "Curtis Carpenter and Les McCubbin were both good shooters. They were tough. They compensated for their height disadvantage with scrappiness," Andy Burns assessed of his teammates in a retrospective interview. Off the bench, the Bearcats turned to 6'2" senior Danny Mockbee, their version of Dave Medley. Walton played more games than Simon Kenton during the year and made it to the finals of the Class A early state season tournament before losing.

Despite the Pioneers being favored, a cliché is a cliché because it's true. The cliché that's why they play the game it's always true in sports. Upsets unexpectedly happen in every sport.

Dave Schadler said he felt butterflies in his stomach prior to the game. "We had a good relationship with Bob Eads. For some reason, before the game we didn't want to talk to him while Eads wanted to be real friendly. I believe we pissed him off that night. It was cut and run time for us. We needed to reach the regional tournament. I thought our guards outplayed their guards that night, but we could not cover their forwards. Meier and Dixon were really a nonfactor because they couldn't defend their smaller matchups. Their forwards were draining 15-foot jumpers, and we couldn't get out there to guard them. It seemed like if there was a big rebound, Andy Burns grabbed it. If there was a big shot, their forwards made it," Dave Schadler stressed with held over frustration. "I remember standing up the whole game. We couldn't sit down. Everybody in the gym stood. I remember yelling stuff at our players. Calling them this and that. The Bearcats were just playing their butts off. We were done. We were done for," Schadler recalls of game's outlook.

"The gymnasium was packed. You couldn't even take the ball out of bounds because they allowed the people to stand on the sidelines. It was like playing in a pit of people. It was the most amazing game. It was one of those, wow, this is it," Andy Burns remembers.

Both schools sported blue and white colors, so the Pioneers came out in their royal blue uniforms while Walton wore white. Dave Dixon and Andy Burns jumped at center court and Dixon, despite Burns four inch height advantage, controlled the tip to begin the game. The Bearcats immediately played man to man defense and Greg Ponzer put the Pioneers in the book first by uncharacteristically draining a shot from the top of the key. After

Curtis Carpenter tied the score with 7:21 to play in the first quarter, Walton pressed full court. The Pioneer guards broke the press and Billy Meier put back a tap on a Dave Dixon miss. Next, Simon Kenton's man to man defense forced a walk on Curtis Carpenter. At 5:06, Walton called their first time out. Dale McMillan from WHKK radio reported condensation was forming on the floor. After a foul by McKinley and an Andy Burns miss of a free throw, Greg Ponzer made a 18 foot bank shot for a 10-4 Pioneer lead. This would be the first of many long bank shots on the night by Greg Ponzer. He had it working off the glass.

Les McCubbin made an 8 footer to close the lead to 10-6. After another Walton turnover, McKinley scored again for a 12-6 Pioneer lead. After Alan Mullins fouled him, Kevin Martin made two free throws to close the gap to 12-8 with 3:13 remaining in the first quarter. Next, Andy Burns fouled Billy Meier, but Meier missed both free throws. Dave Dixon and Andy Burns traded baskets to create a 14-8 Pioneer lead with 2:40 left. After a McKinley miss, Kevin Martin made a scoop shot (14-12), followed by a 8 foot bank shot by Greg Ponzer (16-12). On a save out of bounds from Andy Burns, Les McCubbin made a 18 footer at 1:24 (16-14). Next, Billy Meier fouled Danny Mockbee on a rebound on a McKinley miss. Earlier in the year Mockbee had suffered an emergency appendectomy. Fully recovered, he came to play on this night. Dave Medley entered the game for Billy Meier and the Pioneers. Andy Burns tied the game at 16-16 with 40 seconds left in the quarter. After Anderson scored for Walton, the Bearcats took their first lead 18-16 at the end of the first quarter. Walton-Verona shot a blazing 66% from the field, 8 for 12, in the quarter. Simon Kenton shot only 8 of 19, but led in rebounds 8 to 3. The strategy of Walton clearly manifested itself from the first quarter. The smaller Walton players intended on driving to the basket despite the Simon Kenton 6'6" front line.

Dixon won the tap over Burns again to begin the second quarter. Walton showed a 2-3 zone and Dave Dixon scored to tie the game. Dale McMillan from his microphone commented Simon Kenton played like "Santa Anna at the Alamo. Give no quarter." Andy Burns made one free throw of two for Walton to regain the lead 19-18. Sean Dougherty fouled John Anderson who made both free throws for a 21-18 Walton lead at 6:04. Ponzer "had Anderson covered like a blanket but Anderson still got it in" was the radio call as Walton went up 25-23. A Mockbee foul sent McKinley to the line who made both free throws to tie the game again. Dale McMillen commented from his radio table, "McKinley at the free throw line is like the gold at Ft. Knox. You know it's there." McKinley fouled Anderson who finally missed a free throw, but he made the second, 26-25 Walton. Greg Ponzer banked another 17 footer off the glass for the Pioneers to regain the lead 27-26. Mullins replaced Ponzer after Ponzer fouled Mockbee who calmly hit both free throws, 28-27 Walton. Next, Anderson hit a jump shot, 30-27 Walton. Mullins then fouled Anderson who again made both free throws, 32-27 Walton. Coach Miller called a timeout. Afterwards, Anderson fouled Mullins who missed the one and one, but Dixon scored from the top of the key to close the Walton lead to 32-29 with 1:21 left. As McKinley grabbed a rebound, Dale McMillen commented "Simon Kenton is really getting after people defensively."

Dixon fouled Mockbee with 43 seconds left and Mockbee made one free throw, 33-29 Walton. Burns picked up his second foul on Sean Dougherty. Sean Dougherty made both free throws, 33-31 Walton. Kevin Martin made a last second scoop shot for a 35-31 Walton halftime lead.

At the half, as both coaches spoke to their teams regarding adjustments, the Bearcat fans believed they had an upset in the making. The Pioneer fans, still confident, experienced a tinge of doubt.

To begin the third quarter, Dixon won his third tip with the taller Burns and Ponzer made a 19 foot bank shot to close the gap 35-33. Meier goaltended a Burns shot to make the score, 37-33 Walton. The intensity in the game grew and grew. Every possession the entire game counted and every player treated each possession like it counted. Next, Dixon made a shot on a stick back, 37-35 Walton. Dixon fouled Burns at 6:08 and the basket counted, but Burns missed the free throw, 39-35 Walton. As Walton remained in a 2-3 zone, McKinley made a jump shot over it to bring the Pioneers within two, 39-37. The teams traded fouls with Ponzer and Burns both picking up their thirds. Sean Dougherty came in for Ponzer and made a sixteen foot shot to tie the score 39-39 at 4:13, the eighth tie in the game. Burns and Dougherty traded baskets for another tie 43-43 with 1:53 left. Martin scored for a 45-43 Walton lead to end the third quarter of the close contest.

Burns won the fourth quarter tip and the teams continued to battle each other by trading baskets and fouling each other. At 3:01, Ponzer picked up his fourth foul. Out of a Simon Kenton time out, Carpenter made both free throws for a 61-53 lead. Walton had made 25 of 29 free throws for the game and now enjoyed an eight point lead with only three minutes remaining. The lead was Walton's largest. The dream of the Pioneers began to fade. Sean Dougherty came in for Ponzer due to the foul situation. Dave Dixon scored and was also fouled on the shot. But, Dixon missed the free throw and the Pioneers trailed 61-55 with 2:49 left. Then, Sean Dougherty picked up his fourth foul. Now desperate, Coach Miller unleashed the "bumble bees"upon the Bearcats. Dale McMillen reported from the radio: "Aggressive Simon Kenton is all over the basketball." Simon Kenton stole the ball and Kevin Martin fouled Mullins, but Mullins missed the free throws with 2:16 remaining. Simon Kenton's Troy McKinley grabbed the rebound and was immediately fouled by McCubbin. McKinley made one of two free throws to make the score 61-56 with 2:07 left. At 1:45, Sean Dougherty picked a pocket of a Bearcat. Over a 2-3 zone, McKinley drained a 10 footer to pull the Pioneers within three, 61-58. Alan Mullins followed with a steal of his own and Ponzer missed a shot, but Kevin Martin fouled out with his fifth foul. Freddy Poore replaced Martin for the Bearcats.

Ponzer missed the free throw and Burns made 2 free throws after being fouled to increase Walton's lead, 63-58. With 58 seconds left, Troy McKinley scored to keep the deficit at three. "Everybody is standing," reported an excited Dale McMillen on the radio. With 37 seconds left, Sean Dougherty fouled out. Billy Meier came in the game for Dougherty. Meier previously left the game limping. John Anderson missed the free throw and Dixon and Burns tied up, but Walton controlled the jump ball. Carpenter then slipped on the floor to turn it over. Next, Anderson fouled Ponzer who only made one free throw, 63-61 Walton. Burns grabbed the rebound on the Ponzer miss. However, the ball went out of bounds with 18 seconds left in the game. Simon Kenton called their final timeout. Ponzer missed a shot and McKinley fouled Burns with :07 seconds left to play in the game. Dale McMillen then announced over the radio that when he earlier told Coach Eads of Walton "Bobby you got a pretty rough draw," Eads replied, "Boone County and Simon Kenton got the tough one."

"Both Sullivan and Hummel, the referees, sucked the whistle in. They sent the bees after us, Ponzer, Mullins and Dougherty. They started slapping and stealing the ball," Andy Burns laments about the Pioneers coming back from the 8 point deficit. Dave Medley was forced to play lots of minutes in the fourth quarter due to foul trouble on the starters. Andy Burns was sent to the free throw line for a one and one bonus.

If Burns made the free throw, game over. In 1981, there were no three point plays. There was only seven seconds left. Preparing to lose, Tim Downs and the varsity reserves decided they would not shake hands with the Walton players and run straight to the locker room at the final buzzer. In despair, they planned their exit before the final seven seconds ticked off.

Simon Kenton, out of timeouts, couldn't ice Burns at the free throw line. Andy Burns deliberately walked to the charity stripe. " I wasn't too nervous. I saw the scoreboard. We were up two points. The chance of them, even if I did miss it, to come down and score would be slim," recalls Burns of the game situation. As Burns stepped to the free throw line, Billy Meier walked behind him and remarked, "Andy, you guys played a great game. You deserve to win." As Billy passed Burns, Andy looked at Billy and thought to himself, "Is he messing with me?" or "Is he really congratulating us?" It didn't matter. Andy Burns was thinking. "Billy was always a sarcastic SOB and he and Ponzer were always jawing. I looked at him, but didn't say anything," recalls Andy Burns of the Meier remark.

Troy McKinley remembers standing at his spot under the basket behind the lane line waiting for Andy Burns to shoot and saying to himself, "I can't believe this is over. We've lost."

Greg Ponzer lined up in the lane filled with the same defeatist thoughts as Troy McKinley. "We probably had more than twenty team fouls at that point. Today, you receive two shots. You didn't have that back then, just a bonus situation. Andy was a heck of a ballplayer. All he needs to do is make the free throw and we're done. I'm thinking we were going to lose. We're done. We're out of here. The hype is over," Greg Ponzer thought from the lane.

Mary McKinley sat in the stands crying. The Pioneer cheering section sat in stunned silence. The cheerleaders stood in despair as they clutched their sweaty hands in nerve racking anticipation.

Andy Burns remembers he wasn't a great free throw shooter, but thought "I can end this game." As Andy Burns began to shoot, the Walton Verona fans belted out "Nah, Nah, Nah, Nah, Hey, Hey, Hey, Hey, Goodbye" to mock the Pioneers and their fans. No one ever told the Walton fans about Lincoln's hen observation.

As tired sweat rolled down Andy Burns arms and forehead, he dribbled the ball a few times. The free throw he was ready to shoot would seal a great upset. He raised his long arms and lifted the ball in his huge hands. He released the ball toward the basket. As it sailed toward the goal, the Simon Kenton crowd held its collective breath. Then hope sprung forth from their chests. Burns ironed it. Troy McKinley, blocking his man out, grabbed the rebound and immediately threw an outlet pass to Alan Mullins. At half court, Alan saw Greg Ponzer streaking down the right side in front of him. Mullins riffled it to Ponzer who banked in a driving layup at the last second as the horn sounded. Overtime. Pandemonium struck as the floor flooded with crazed Pioneer fans, relieved cheerleaders and a drained, but exhilarated team and coaching staff. The Walton-Verona players, coaches and fans watched in disbelief and shock.

Dale McMillen screamed from the radio, "We're going to overtime. This place has busted lose!"

"We went over to the bench and the team was just in a frenzy because the place was in a frenzy. I mean, it was just everywhere. Larry Miller was trying to coach us and nobody was listening. That's when I told the guys we needed to shut the F up and listen. 'Shut up and listen', I yelled." remembers Greg Ponzer. This poise came from the player who had just tied the game.

The outburst earned Greg Ponzer the title of Captain of the team from that moment forward. "Larry put me in that position after that moment. After that point in time, before every game, I would be the one to go out to mid-court and receive the instructions from the officials. Prior to that, we didn't have a designated captain," Greg Ponzer recalls of his new captain status.

Under the rules of qualification, only the winners of the semifinals in the District would advance to region. "It wouldn't have been a disgrace to lose to them, but we had beaten'em and I thought we were playing real well, especially after the Boone County game, the last game of the season. I thought we were at the top of our game," Larry Miller recalls. Dale McMillen reported on the radio, "We've seen some kind of basketball tonight." However, there was more basketball to play.

As overtime began for Simon Kenton, Dougherty was gone with five fouls. McKinley, Dixon, Meier, Ponzer and Mullins each had 4 fouls. Therefore, as the overtime commenced, all five of the players the Pioneers sent out to play found themselves strapped with four fouls. For Walton, Martin was gone. Anderson and Burns each had four fouls and McCubbin and Mockbee had three each. The referees claim they called the game straight up. The teams simply banged the tar out of each other with punishing defense.

In the three minute overtime, the Bearcats double teamed Troy McKinley in hopes of slowing Troy down. However, John Anderson, the Bearcats' leader and top scorer, fouled out on a charging foul early in the overtime. But, Andy Burns scored for a 65-63 Walton lead at 2:05 left in the overtime. Dixon responded with a basket to tie the score 65-65 with 1:39 left. This was the twelfth tie for the game. The teams next traded steals. At 1:10 Simon Kenton called a timeout. Out of the timeout, Curtis Carpenter, considering all the other players' foul situations, remarkably committed only his first foul on Billy Meier with 1:05 left , but Billy missed the first free throw. Walton called a timeout, but Billy Meier still made his second shot and the Pioneers led, 66-65. Alan Mullins then picked up his fifth foul to foul out with 1:02 left in overtime. It was the first and only time Alan Mullins fouled out in a game for the year. This forced Greg Ponzer to move to the point guard. "Boy, it was ugly watching that," Alan Mullins laughs of Greg Ponzer playing point. "It was awkward on my end since I wasn't used to not handling the ball. It was the only game I fouled out all year. We were still pressing and pushing the issue. I wasn't playing tentative with four fouls. None of us would. We would just play the game like we knew we should be playing. I just happened to pick up a foul being aggressive. It was awkward being on the sideline watching. I was supposed to be out there. Greg wasn't supposed to be handling the ball, bringing it up court, but he could. But there was never a sense of doom or 'we're dead now' or anything." "Ponzer is the only thing left as a guard," Dale McMillen remarked on the air. Freddy Poore missed the free throw and McKinley grabbed the rebound. With thirty-one seconds left, Carpenter fouled Ponzer and Ponzer made both free throws for a three point Simon Kenton lead 68-65. Freddy Poore threw a pass out of bounds, but Medley threw the in bounds pass to Carpenter who scored and Medley fouled him. To this day, Medley agonizes over his double error. Carpenter made the free throw and the game was tied 68-68, the thirteenth tie. Simon Kenton had the ball and twenty seconds to use. McCubbin fouled McKinley with five seconds left in the overtime and Walton called a timeout. However, there was no icing McKinley. Troy made both free throws for a 70-68 Pioneer lead with only five seconds to go. However, the Bearcats would not go easy into the night. Carpenter on a full court pass from Poore made a remarkable fifteen footer at the buzzer to send the game into double overtime. Now, it was the Bearcat fans turn to storm the floor while the Pioneer fans felt the win escape them.

Dale McMillen yelled into his radio microphone, "I don't know how much pressure you are supposed to take!" Dale McMillen also reported on the air that referee Dan Sullivan joked the basket was no good as the clock expired. Simon Kenton won the tip in double overtime, but missed their first shot. Then, Walton decided to hold the ball the entire overtime for one final shot. Simon Kenton also switched to a 1-3-1 zone. "They held the ball because they were getting tired," recalls Sean Dougherty of the Bearcat strategy. The plan fell apart when Poore, playing for Anderson, threw the ball out of bounds on a cut to the basket by a teammate. The Pioneers took the ball down court and held the ball themselves. Simon Kenton called a timeout with fourteen seconds. Out of the time out, Dale McMillen reported Ponzer was two inches from an over and back violation before Ponzer found Troy McKinley who passed to Dave Dixon who drained a short shot. The Bearcats collapsed on Troy McKinley expecting him to shoot, but Troy saw an open Dixon for an easy basket. It was the only two points scored in the second overtime. One second remained on the clock. McCubbin threw away a desperation in-bounds pass and Simon Kenton escaped with a 72-70 victory. The Pioneer cheerleaders and players leaped with relieved joy. Their fans stormed the court again. This time, the game was over.

"We grew up with the Walton kids. We played ball with them from grade school through high school. We were on teams together. There was a great deal of mutual respect. But that game is a pit in their stomach that they'll never get over," Greg Ponzer reflected on the victory twenty-five years later.

Andy Burns will never forget the crushing defeat. "When the game was over, of course, I was demoralized. The crowd was just like a sea of people. I remember I was trying to get to the locker room. Back then, there was respect, but Walton and Simon Kenton weren't gentlemen rivals. My girlfriend, who ironically went to Simon Kenton, said she was trying to stop me, and I ignored her. But I didn't even see her. I was just trying to get to the locker room. Once I got in the locker room, we were just emotionally crushed. I was mad at myself for the free throw. People will never forget that for whatever reason. It wasn't where I lost the game, but I could have clinched it. I could have sealed it and I didn't seal it," Andy Burns explains of the miss. "I don't think we were meant to win that game. We would have never won the region. It still puzzles me everyone remembers my missed free throw rather than Freddy Poore's turnover."

While Andy Burns dated a Simon Kenton girl, Dave Dixon was faced with consoling his girlfriend, a Walton student, after the game. Dave is glad he consoled her rather than having to have her console him. "I'll tell you, in Walton, those people still hold grudges over that game. It's amazing." Billy Meier recalls of the narrow victory.

Ron Coleman, the Simon Kenton Booster President, knew many of the Walton parents. After the game, he walked across the floor and met up with some of them. When he expressed what a great game it was to the Walton faithful, they ignored him in anger and frustration. He regrets ever extending the olive branch because the pain was too fresh and intense for his Walton friends.

The Chairman of the Kenton County School Board, Jake Menefee became so excited at the Walton-Verona game, the referees threw him out. "Well, the next night at the District finals game against Lloyd, Jake showed up and handcuffed himself to the bleachers so that he wouldn't be able to be tossed out," Bill Pelfrey, Jr. laughs.

"I don't remember if he threw something on the floor, but I know for sure that he was sitting down across from the bench. He's sitting across from the bench and I remember him getting up and walking over to the referees and saying something to them," recalls David Schadler of the incident.

"I remember one of the referees was Tom Hummel. Jake got on the floor and said something to him. Hummel had the police come toss him out. Jake was still on the school board. Of course, by that time, he's real supportive and all that of the team. Boy, if we'd lost, he'd have jumped on us. But they threw him out. I watched it and I just loved it. I said to Larry, 'They kicked Menifee's ass out of that game.' And Larry said, 'Well, I hope they kicked him out for the whole tournament.' But they didn't. They let him back in the next game," Dave Schadler laughs of Larry Miller's reaction.

For the game, Simon Kenton's scoring included the following: McKinley 27, Ponzer 17, Dixon 14, Meier 8 and Dougherty 6. For Walton, Burns and Anderson both had 19 points, Carpenter 11, Martin 10, McCubbin 8, Mockbee 3 and Poore 2.

"I think it is one of the best basketball games I've ever seen. Tremendous tension," Larry Miller recalls. The 'bumblebees' forced Walton-Verona to turn the ball over seven times in the last three minutes of regulation. Larry Miller gave a post game interview to WHKK. "Mathematically it's impossible to press. With two on the ball, someone must be open. Pressure from the crowd and game helps even things out. It's a shame they had to lose the game. They may be the second best team in the Region. Those forwards can beat you. Bobby does a great job. McKinley wants to play in Lexington. It's going to take a good ball club to keep us from going with him in the lineup. The crowd brought us back. Our kids don't quit. I think that will be the difference."

Tom Hummel, currently the Gray Middle School principal in the Boone County school system, coached football at Campbell County at the time. In 1979, he refereed his first game at the state tournament at Rupp Arena. Hummel recalls the Simon Kenton/Walton game as the classic little vs. big. He refers to the game as "the single most intense game" he ever officiated. Hummel tossed Jake Menefee for running out on the floor and taping him on the shoulder at the end of regulation. Hummel had no idea who Menefee was or doing out on the floor. Hummel requested the deputy from the Boone County Sheriff escort him out of the gymnasium. His officiating partner, Dan Sullivan joked with Hummel all the senior citizens would hate him. Bob Abel remembers Jake ran out on the floor because he thought Hummel waved off the Ponzer shot. The referees remarkably called no technicals in the game.

After the District game between Simon Kenton and Walton-Verona and in later years, whenever Hummel refereed at Walton, an older gentlemen sat behind the scorers table and shook his head at him the whole game and yelled "Don't you have anything better to do?"

In 2004, Dan Sullivan retired from two stints as Superintendent at Newport Schools in Campbell County. Sullivan officiated games for 22 years before retiring in 1987. Sullivan recalls Boone County's gym opening in 1956 and the ventilation not being sufficient to handle large crowds. In a twist of fate, Sullivan's son, Dan, would later marry the Bearcat star, John Anderson's sister, Julie, a cheerleader for the 1981 Bearcat team. His son Dan is now the principal at Walton-Verona High School. Sullivan was not supposed to referee the game until he was called. Hummel and Sullivan received $25.00 for the game. When Sullivan returned to Walton the next year to referee a game, the Poore family would yell at Sullivan - "You son of a bitch. You cost us a state title." John Salyers, from WHKK radio, believes the loss nearly killed the Walton coach, Bob Eads.

Simon Kenton played the Lloyd Juggernauts in the District Final on Saturday, March 7. Lloyd had previously beaten Connor, the Pioneers old nemesis, in the other 33rd District Semifinal. "I didn't think we could beat Connor," Coach Miller said. "I'm going to be honest with you. I'm not sure we could have beaten them if we had to play them again."

Simon Kenton beat Lloyd by only two to win the District.

Alan Mullins remembers the Lloyd game being anticlimactic. "It was almost a sense of why are we even playing this stupid game. It's for a district championship, but at the same time, both teams qualify for the regionals. We thought we beat Walton in an incredible game, so why are we playing this game? The advantage it's suppose to give you is a district winner plays a district loser from one of the other districts in the region, but because of upsets that isn't always an advantage," Alan Mullins explained.

Greg Ponzer remembers the awards ceremony after the District tournament. "Billy Meier and I didn't make the All-District team. Larry Miller came down the bench after the tournament where Billy and I were sitting and he got us together and said, 'You boys were cheated. You boys should have been on the All-Tournament team for the district.' Billy and I didn't think about it or care. Who gave a darn, we didn't really care. We were going to the Region," Greg Ponzer explained of his lack of concern for personal accolades.

The next step for Simon Kenton would be the Regional and the Regional winner earned the right to play at Rupp Arena, the venue the Pioneer boys began experiencing from grade school.

CHAPTER 34
Andy Burns

"The longest road in the world is the road to redemption."
~ Unknown

Unfairly, Andy Burns will forever live the remainder of his life as the Bill Buckner of Walton. Bill Buckner, for non-baseball fans, was the Boston Red Sox first baseman who allowed a routine ground ball to pass through his legs during a World Series game. If he had fielded the ball, the Red Sox would have won the World Series. The Red Sox lost the game on the error and lost the next game to lose the World Series. Buckner had to move from Boston to avoid fan abuse. The label applied as much to Freddy Poore as Andy Burns for throwing away a pass, but it's Andy Burns who carries the cross for the Bearcat loss in the 1981 District semifinal.

Andy grew up in Walton on South Main. His father, Claude C. Burns, drove a bus for the Kenton County School District and taught school at of all places, Twenhofel. Claude actually drove the bus to and from school from his designated bus route which included Green Road where the bus picked me, Eric Deters, and my brothers up every morning. In 1971, Claude Burns taught social studies and history at Twenhofel. This same year which found Andy Burns turning seven, Claude Burns tragically committed suicide. I'll never forget the day. I waited for the bus with my brothers at the end of the driveway. The bus never came. We found out later why. Claude pulled his bus off to the side of the road and shot himself. The news shocked, horrified and scared me, and Claude was my bus driver. I can't imagine how the unfortunate event harmed Andy. I never met Andy until I interviewed him for this book. We were the same age at the time of his father's death. As with any death of a parent, but even more so a suicide, the tragedy would follow

Andy and his family in the form of not only the loss, but the burden which resulted. Andy shares the tragedy with Dave Dixon whose father later also took his own life. When Andy Burns learned of Dave's loss, Andy recalls calling Dave to offer his support. Andy Burns recollects how his young years changed course after his father's death which cheated Andy's fate.

"When I was in high school, my mom explained the plan they had for me included attending Twenhofel and Simon Kenton. My father's suicide changed the course of my life," Andy Burns reflects.

Andy Burns would become known as a 'late bloomer.' "God always puts you in positions to best suit you. I think being at Walton gave me an opportunity to develop. I didn't start until my sophomore year," recalls Andy Burns of his basketball career.

During his senior season, Andy dated a girl from Simon Kenton High School. His surreal connection or disconnection to Simon Kenton High School is Shakespearian. At his ten year class reunion from Walton-Verona, Andy heard the jokes from his classmates about how they could have been state champs "if Burns could have made a couple of free throws." Andy attended and graduated from Northern Kentucky University after his Walton-Verona years. Andy played basketball at NKU. Andy obtained an educational social studies comprehensive with a math and history minor and actually student taught history at Simon Kenton with Tim Moore, the Pioneers public address announcer. Today, Troy McKinley is Andy's son Drew's Sunday School teacher at First Church in Burlington, Kentucky.

Andy Burns maintains a good natured and positive disposition. "I owe it to my mom. I've been spiritually grounded all my life. I've always depended on my faith, and I always believe things happen for a reason. I attended Northern and had great years there, but I also faced challenges. I wasn't treated fairly. You can never change those events. I always kept a positive outlook. I can only change what I can change. The coach, Mike Beitzel, was a Bobby Knight wannabe. He played the head games. Beitzel created a totally different world in basketball than my high school coach, Bob Eads. My mom never involved herself in athletics. I lacked guidance. I probably could have played at a Division I school being six ten and played for a better coach. I lacked foresight. I received letters from countless schools. The University of Cincinnati came and watched me a couple of times, but I never responded to them. Northern locked their horns into me from the beginning of the season. They offered me a full ride. I thought, my mom's a widow, I'll stay local. I didn't think through my other options," Andy Burns explains of his failure to properly explore his options.

Andy Burns's mother worked for an attorney as a legal secretary for years. Even at 72, she still works full time at a law office.

"I ran into Coach Beitzel a few years ago and he hasn't changed," Andy said. "He walked up to me and said, 'Man Burns, man, you're heavy.' He doesn't think before speaking. He doesn't realize the impact of what he says to kids. I actually made a comment to him, ' I'm doing all right, Coach, after the psychotherapy I needed for a couple of years after school.' But anyway, he came up to me and said, 'Yeah, I saw Troy McKinley the other day.' I said, 'Oh, really.' He said. 'I was recruiting him. Man, if you had hit those two free throws, I'd have had Troy McKinley.' That's what he said to me. At first I thought to say I would've prayed Troy never played for you at Northern," Andy Burns muses of the 'butterfly effect' of his missing the free throw.

After a time in Indiana and Louisville, Andy moved back to Walton with his family. He drove around town revisiting his old stomping grounds. "It was Lloyd Clements. He was on the corner there at Alta Vista and Depot Street. I saw him sitting on his porch. I drove down the street and happened to see Lloyd sitting on the porch. I said to myself, there's Lloyd Clements. He worked as the janitor. We bonded with the janitors because they were always around the gym with us. They became part of the team. I walked up to Lloyd and he looked at me and I asked; 'Hey, do you know who I am?' He couldn't remember my name. I said I'm Andy Burns. He said 'Andy Burns, man that game at Simon Kenton, if you'd have hit those free throws'. I just stood there thinking. How long have I been gone now and this guy still recalls the missed free throw."

To complete the Andy Burns' contribution to the story, a history and genealogy buff, Andy Burns traced his roots directly to Simon Kenton himself. Maybe the ghost of Simon Kenton, and not Billy Meier, distracted Andy Burns the night he missed the free throw.

CHAPTER 35
Region

"Destiny is not a matter of chance. It is a matter of choice."
~ William Jennings Bryan

In 1981, the Ninth Region tournament was held at Holmes High School in Covington, Kentucky. The Holmes gym included substantial seating capacity which is why, along with Connor High School, the school was usually chosen as the site for the Ninth Region tournament. The floor of the Holmes court is in a pit below the stands and the lighting is insufficient. Players played in a yellow fog. The two highest seeds, Covington Catholic and Simon Kenton, found themselves at opposite ends of the bracket. Simon Kenton drew the Newport Wildcats in the first round on Thursday, March 12, 1981. The Pioneers had defeated the Wildcats twice in the regular season.

"There weren't a lot of African-American kids playing varsity basketball in Northern Kentucky at that time. Newport and Holmes had African-American players. Lloyd or another school would have one or two occasionally. When you played against Newport, you played a different game. They didn't have much size, but they were quick and tough," Coach Miller reflects of the challenge Newport presented.

"It got rough during our game with Newport and we had a little fight. Greg Ponzer took control of the game. I don't know what he said, but when he came out of a pile of players there was blood all over his elbow and it wasn't his. I came over and said, 'You all right, Greg?' He said, 'I'm fine, Coach, wipe that blood off'," Coach Miller recalls of the incident.

"Whatever happened in that pile, after the incident, we blew them out. It wasn't close after the pile up which happened in the third quarter. We were ahead by six at the half, nine after three, and then fourteen for the game, which is a good win in the Regional Tournament because everybody in the Regional Tournament can play," Larry Miller explains of the margin of victory.

Dave Schadler remembers the game well, too. "They were playing hard. Meier or Dixon were into it with Mayes, a big six-five guy. Someone got fouled. I don't really remember who got fouled. Whether it was them or us. It was after a pile up. Both teams are lined up. Our guys were disciplined. Their guys are squawking. Meier and Dixon had the look in their eye and they're ready to play. Ponzer said something to Mayes. I looked at Greg and wondered what he was doing. No telling what he's doing. After that, Newport quit, and we handled them easy. I asked Ponzer after the game, 'What did you say to him?' He said, 'I just told him to shut his ass up and play and get it over with.' Years later, I learned my wife's cousin played on the same Newport team we played in 1981. He was a sophomore at the time; Sean Turner was his name. I asked Sean, 'Do you ever recollect that incident?' 'Yeah,' he laughed, 'Greg Ponzer scared the hell out of our guys. Our guys were scared to death of Ponzer'. I said, 'What are you talking about?' He said, 'Ponzer told him we'll meet you on the street and we'll kick your ass just like we'll do in this game.' They were done," Dave Schadler grins of the intimidation the Pioneers laid on the Wildcats. The Pioneers won the game 65-51. One reason why the Pioneers pulled away is Newport's star and the player Greg Ponzer spoke smack to, Mitch Mayes, fouled out in the third quarter.

Simon Kenton played the Campbell County Camels the following night in the semi-finals on March 13, 1981. A Friday the 13th game. Pioneer fans showed up three hours before game time. Before the game, the Simon Kenton band and cheerleaders joined together to perform a "Rocky" dance routine. The Pioneers played that night as tough as "Rocky" punched. Like Newport, the Pioneers defeated the Camels twice during the season. Like Newport, the Pioneers beat them three times. The Pioneers won 66-53. Troy McKinley led the way with twenty-eight points. Sean Dougherty had a career high eleven points and five assists for the game.

On Saturday, March 14, 1981, the regional finals involved the rubber match with the Covington Catholic Colonels. "I've been preaching for Simon Kenton to forget tradition ever since I've been there," Coach Miller said at the time. "These kids are winners. It's going to take a good club to beat us. But that's what Covington Catholic has. They're playing good. They've won eighteen straight. But who beat them last? We did. It should be a dandy." Fans from both teams packed the Holmes gymnasium before the game. Pioneer fans sat and stood on one side and Colonel fans on the other side. Intensity and anxiety filled the gym's atmosphere. Charged up fans taunted each other. Alan Mullins' older brother, Danny, became involved in a fight in the stands before the game started and was kicked out," Greg Ponzer recalls of the excitement. Depending on whose side you are on, Covington Catholic's student cheering section is great or obnoxious. In 2006, the Colonels cheering section received a special recognition at the state tournament for their antics cheering on their team who lost in the first round. The student cheering section practiced a routine, new at the time, but not now (they may have created it) where the students held up newspapers over their faces as the Pioneers were introduced before the game. "No respect," remarks Sean Dougherty of the antic. "We jumped out pretty good. We were up 34-26 at the half and then I don't know what happened. It was like you turned us off and Covington Catholic turned it on. They outscored us in the third. Nothing stopped them," Larry Miller remembers.

"I called two timeouts and we changed defenses. We tried different schemes, but nothing would stop their run. The horn sounded at the end of the third quarter and the Colonel players ran off the floor to their bench and celebrated. They grabbed the lead 43-42. Our kids grabbed a little resolve and came out the fourth quarter and made a statement. Troy scored sixteen in the last quarter. Troy McKinley decided, 'I'm going to State Tournament and I'm going to take my team with me,' Larry Miller recalls proudly of his team's resiliency. The Pioineers won 77 to 66.

"I don't ever remember the game being in doubt," Dave Schadler stated with confidence. "They couldn't match up with us."

Steve Berling of Covington Catholic was always a basketball star. In the regional finals, Steve played according to his own account the worst basketball game he ever played on any level. Greg Ponzer shut him down and Steve scored only three points. On the defensive side, Steve guarded Troy McKinley who scored over thirty on him. Steve has the good humor to laugh about the game today.

Alan Mullins recalls Greg Ponzer busting a Covington Catholic player in the mouth. "All of a sudden, out of the middle of this pile of players, emerges Greg walking out with this serious look on his face, as if he's ready to kill somebody. He's looking down at his arm and blood is running down his elbow. I look back behind him and Tommy Blank from Covington Catholic is on the baseline holding his face in his hands. Sure enough, Greg popped him an elbow and bloodied Tommy's mouth," Alan Mullins remembers of the scene. Sean Dougherty remembers another Ponzer play. "The player was the other guard, not Tommy Blank. This guard cut across the baseline against our zone and the next thing I knew, he was laying flat on his back. Greg stood there looking at him. Greg just went bam and took him out. They lost that guard. Covington Catholic games were always very physical, very confrontational," explains Sean of the rivalry. "They weren't dirty. It was simply physical."

Greg Ponzer played baseball against Tommy Blank since childhood and recalls they always went after each other. "We were running down the floor on a fast break and Tommy inadvertently mixed up my feet and kicked me. We tangled up. At the same time, I took my elbow and caught him right in the mouth. He was madder than hell. No fouls, no nothing. Nobody saw it. That's what happened. We had those altercations all the time. Just competitiveness," Greg explains of the combativeness. "We respected each other."

Dave Medley explains the scene in the locker room after the game. "We sat in the locker room after we won the Ninth Region discussing what to place on the back of our jackets for winning. We spoke about our options and Coach Miller overheard the entire conversation and said, "Why don't you put on the back - State Champs,'" Dave Medley remembers of Coach Miller's challenge.

"Many people, though they practice positive thinking, don't fulfill their goals. Miller was focused. He was the right coach for our team. He had the right kind and amount of passion. People talk about passion in life, but to have focus and passion is special. We were winners. All through our lives, playing basketball and other sports, we won. Coach Miller wanted to win too. The coaches who coached at Simon Kenton before our team weren't the coaches for us. We needed and wanted a coach who never accepted losing," Dave explains Coach Miller's attitude.

The victory over Covington Catholic would be the first Ninth Region title for Simon Kenton since the Pioneers played basketball beginning in 1938. It took the Pioneers 41 years to win the Region. The team and coaches ceremoniously cut down the nets at Holmes in triumph. The win fell on Larry Miller's 31st birthday.

"It was a dream come true," Randall Wagner said of the title. "Those young men climbed the mountain out of the valley. I cried with joy."

CHAPTER 36
Going to State

"Nothing happens unless first a dream."
~ Carl Sandburg

After their Ninth Regional win, the significance of their accomplishment and the task before them seeped into the Pioneer player's and coaches's consciousness. "I don't remember having a party after we won the Region," Sean Dougherty recalls. "I remember being mobbed and it felt like we were at Holmes forever. We didn't care. We received the awards and cut down the nets. It was exhausting. We just played three games in three days. We normally played two games a week." Troy McKinley posed for photographs and even signed autographs at the request of rabid Pioneer fans.

"Time froze. All of a sudden it dawned on us and we collectively paused," recalls Alan Mullins. "The crowd reaction made us aware we accomplished something really special. But the very next day at practice, it was back to our focused mind set. We will play Knott County Central so we needed to get back to work."

Dave Dixon recalls the joy of giving radio interviews after the Ninth Region victory and his commenting about all the hard work the team put in their season being worth it. Dave Medley enjoyed the radio interviews too and his father's sentiment regarding the win. "I think it meant more to Dad we were playing at state than it ever meant to me and it means a lot to me," Dave Medley explains of his father's joy.

"The coaches just looked at each other. The parents, families, friends and fans were more excited than the players and the players were more excited than us," Dave Schadler recalls the celebration on the floor.

After the team finally left Holmes High School, a vehicular caravan followed the team bus to a party back at the Simon Kenton gym. Billy Meier recalls the exuberance. "We came through Independence and people packed the streets. The crowd caused the bus to slow down as it passed Ponzers. Greg and I sat in the same seat. We leaned out the window and people handed in beers. We collected a six pack of beer before we arrived back to school," Billy Meier laughs. A firetruck and police cruiser met the team bus near Pioneer Park on Madison Pike outside Covington. "I couldn't believe it. People came out in their night gowns, hanging out of windows, lining the streets. It was great," Assistant Fire Chief Rick Messingschlager observed.

Vic Ponzer drove his car behind the bus bringing the team home. He recalls three hundred people practically blocking the street at his tavern. "I think the boys played out of dedication. We've had so much tragedy this year, its great to have this. I'll tell you. They're a helluva bunch of kids," Vic Ponzer commented at the time. "It amazes you what kids can do," remarked principal Bob Abel as he walked through the confetti covered floor of the Holmes gym. "Everyone suffered, the faculty, students and parents. Basketball's been a release for the problems."

Ron Coleman, president of the Simon Kenton Athletic Boosters, sipped on Pepto-Bismol as he watched the Covington Catholic/Simon Kenton game. Part of the nerves Ron Coleman suffered involved his hiding under his seat two hundred blue T-shirts with Simon Kenton Pioneers Ninth Region Champs silkscreened on the front. "I was confident, but scared to death having the T-shirts made may be a bad omen," Ron Coleman worried at the time.

According to Ron Coleman, Lloyd Brueckner, cheerleader Jill Brueckner's father, failed to gain entry to the Holmes gym and listened to the entire regional finals game on the radio outside in his car.

The students and parents referenced the explosion when speaking of the Regional Championship. "The mood is that we're all champions now," said senior Eric Hummeldorf at the time. "We've overcome a lot this year." "They shot us all down. Everybody in the school," said senior Gene Kavanaugh at the time. "We needed something to kick us in the butt and make us stop feeling sorry for ourselves. It feels good to finally be a winner."

"Everybody rallied around the basketball team," Dave Medley's father, Bob explained. "They were winning and we needed some winners. They were dedicated. You can't really say that it was because of the things that happened this year, but they worked extra hard."

"The boosters organization at Simon Kenton was unbelievable. I remember coming home from school the night before games and found my bedroom completely decorated all through the regional tournament. Pillowcases dreaming of state. The cheerleaders and boosters decorated rooms, halls, lockers, vehicles, everything," Sean Dougherty recalls appreciatively.

Sean also recalls a bizarre showing of support from a local company. "F&C Athletics, the largest area athletic store for uniforms, came over to school and presented us with stuff for our state trip. They actually gave us jocks with our names embroidered on them, with State Tourney '81. Crazy. But we wore them and I still have mine," Sean Dougherty laughs of his embroidered jock.

The accomplishment of winning the Ninth Region and heading to the State Tournament was euphoric to everyone, including Coach Larry Miller. "That's why you coach high school in Kentucky. To go to the State Tournament. I didn't believe we could do it at Simon Kenton at first. I'll be honest with you. You usually have to coach at a place with a winning history if you're aiming to win a Region," Larry Miller explains of the victory. "And, it was all talent within a few miles from the school. We never recruited anyone."

Larry Miller may have been the only person in Independence who believed Simon Kenton had a chance to win the State Tournament. Bones and Mary McKinley believed it an impossible dream.

"When the team left for Lexington from Simon Kenton, the students picked up a chant," Bones said. "Down state, down state, down state.' It was 'Down state, down state, down state.' We drove up to the school when they loaded the bus and headed out. They allowed all the kids out of Simon Kenton for the sendoff. The kids changed their chant, from not 'down state', to 'win state, win state, win state, win state.' I told Mary, 'How naive'. Mary and I both thought out loud, 'We feel so sorry for our boys.' We didn't think we'd win a game," Bones McKinley recalls of his pessimism.

Greg Ponzer, naive or not, exuded confidence and shared his Coach's optimism. "Back then, and even today, the Ninth Region winner would go down to play one game. You'd lose and you'd come home. I remember telling everyone we weren't going down just to play one. We were going down to play four," Greg recalls of his plans. "Coach Miller always marked each game off as we won through the District and Region and he always put four games on the blackboard for the games in the State Tournament," Greg Ponzer remembers. "Coach Miller protected us from the distractions of any pomp and circumstance. He kept us in our routine. We also wore the same socks, the same jocks and the same jerseys for every game," Sean Dougherty laughs of their superstitions.

The flu struck Greg Ponzer before the State Tournament. "I caught the flu on the Tuesday the week of the State Tournament. Dave Schadler drove me over to Dr. Huey in Walton, renowned for giving you two shots for whatever ailed you. At first, I refused to go in, but Schadler made me. Sure enough, Dr. Huey gave me two shots. I made it through the worst part by Thursday, but remained sick the entire state tournament," Greg Ponzer recalls of his untimely sickness.

Knott County Central was the Pioneers first round opponent. Knott County Central, a short team, shot the lights out of it and played tough defense like all the Kentucky Mountain teams.

"I remember Coach Miller exhorting the junior varsity we played against at practice to play hard. Rob Jennings bloodied Dave Dixon's nose in our final practice before we left for state. Dave had a fit. We had to pull Dixon and Jennings apart. Miller's point was this isn't Northern Kentucky ball. We're going down state. No blood, no foul. It's going to be physical," Sean Dougherty recalls regarding the last practice.

Larry Miller passed out an agenda to his players before the State Tournament. He confidently instructed on the top of the paper to pack for four days. The following is an exact replica of the agenda Coach Miller prepared and distributed to his players and Linda Whittenburg gave to her cheerleaders:

PACK FOR 4 DAYS
THURSDAY

8:30	Leave
10:30	Arrive Holiday Inn North, Lexington
	Check in to assigned rooms
11:15	Leave Hotel to eat
12:15	Leave for Rupp Arena for first session
3:30	Leave Rupp Arena by end of third quarter in second game
4:30	Pre-game meal
7:00	Leave for Rupp Arena
9:00	DEFEAT Knott County Central
11:00	Eat in Hotel Rooms
11:30	Lights outs-Get a good nights sleep

FRIDAY

10:30	Wake up–Stay in bed until this time
10:30-11:30	Breakfast at Holiday Inn Restaurant
12:15	Leave for Rupp Arena for first session
3:30	Leave Rupp Arena by end of third quarter of second game

4:30	Pre-game meal
7:00	Leave for Rupp Arena
9:00	DEFEAT (Virgie v/s Clay Co. winner)
11:00	Eat in Hotel Rooms
11:30	Lights out–Get a good nights sleep

SATURDAY

9:00	Wake up
9:00-9:30	Breakfast-Do not eat too much we play at 11:30
10:00	Leave for Rupp Arena
11:30	WIN GAME
Eat after game	
4:00	Very light pregame meal
6:45	Leave for Rupp Arena
8:00	WIN State Championship!!!!!

SUNDAY

| 11:00 | Check out at Hotel |

RULES

1) No one in your room that is not a member of the team.
2) No telephone calls after lights out.
3) Get as much rest as possible, you can party after we win the Championship.
4) Plus all other common sense rules.

The physics teacher who coached practice to the minute, planned his team's State Tournament to the minute.

"I refused to allow the boys to have a great time and lose an opportunity to win. Most teams receive few, if any chances. The state doesn't seed. It's a blind draw. We happened to receive a decent draw for the first game," Coach Miller explains his objectives.

"I remember leaving school in the morning. We left around 8:30, after school began. It was a big shebang. The entire school watched us leave. We arrived in Lexington and dropped our luggage off at the hotel. Coach wanted to take us over to the afternoon sessions because we didn't play until the last game Thursday night with a scheduled tip of 9:00 or 9:30," Alan Mullins recalls of the trip to Lexington. "We walked in the arena down underneath the floor where only players and not fans enter. Then we walked up to the top deck. We had a moment of awareness, holy smoke, we're in Rupp Arena. We're going to be playing here in a couple hours," Alan Mullins recalls of the aura.

Greg Ponzer remembers watching one of the earlier games and reminding his teammates they were not there to play one game, but four. Greg also recalls Larry Miller keeping Billy, Sean and him in separate rooms to avoid shenanigans. Regardless, Greg planned to celebrate. "I kept a nice bottle of Jack Daniels underneath my bed ready for the party. I kept it there waiting for me," Greg Ponzer laughs of his stash.

History served as a sobering reminder that Coach Miller's optimism may be misplaced. Teams from the Ninth Region survived to play in the finals in 1924, 1935, 1944, 1954, 1965, 1967 and 1978. In seven opportunities, the 9th Region lost every chance to win a State Tournament. In 1978, Holmes lost to Shelby County in overtime, 68 to 66. In 1967, Covington Catholic lost by a point on a controversial shot at the buzzer. The Ninth Region appeared to have a curse. Coaches and others from the Ninth Region believed the region jinxed. Curses and jinxes can be tough to break. History, many times, repeats itself.

CHAPTER 37
Ticket Scandal

"I've got the tickets in my pocket, now baby, we're gonna disappear, We've waited so long, waited so long."
 ~ Eddie Money's "Two Tickets to Paradise."

For the first time in its history, Simon Kenton dealt with a byproduct of their success - the pleasant problem of ticket distribution for the State Tournament.

The KHSAA gave each school in the tournament six hundred tickets. Half of the tickets were for seats behind the goal. The other half, for seats higher up in the arena. Nobody knew the location of the seats provided to Simon Kenton because the school had never played in the State Tournament. "All Simon Kenton knew was that white tickets cost $7 and the blue tickets cost $5," Larry Miller recalls.

Teacher Dwight Searcy is able to recount every detail of the "ticket scandal" which rocked Simon Kenton. "When the tickets came in, Joe Stark, the athletic director, controlled our allotment. Central office notified Joe they needed tickets for central office personnel. There were two-hundred-fifty white tickets which were supposed to be the better seats. The central office took a whole bunch of the white tickets. Well, that word got out. Then the rumor spread that Mr. Abell, the principal, had the rest of the white tickets and he was negotiating a deal with a travel agency who would sell them, and no white tickets would be available for teachers and students. We were going to be stuck with all of these bad blue tickets. The story about central office was true, but not the travel agency rumor," Dwight Searcy explains. Bob Abel explains that junior varsity player Larry Callahan's father, Bob Callahan, worked at Greyhound bus line. Bob Abel contacted Mr. Callahan only to discuss bus transportation for fans. Bob Abel actually gave his two tickets to Reuvan Hinsdale and his wife. Hinsdale has a Kenton County school named after him. A former superintendent for the district and huge basketball fan, Reuvan hired Bob Abel as Assistant Principal at Simon Kenton under Bob Barnes. Bob Abel would sit under one of the goals at the State Tournament.

"It turned out Mike Tolliver drafted a "privileged" teachers list and many teachers didn't have a chance to buy a ticket. Mike thought those who saw all the games ought to have a chance at a better seat. Mike Collins attended all the games too, but his name was left off the "privileged" list. Mike Collins signed up for blue tickets from Shawna Cartwright who also wrote up a list. Teachers became angry with each other. It was insane," Dwight Searcy laughs.

"They sold the tickets to the public in the lobby of the gymnasium from the concession stand," Dwight Searcy said. "The school limited the number of tickets parents and others coming in could buy. They sold out in one hour the Monday of the tournament. The rumor spread that tickets were available in the cafeteria. Parents descended like a mob on the cafeteria. As a lunchroom monitor in the cafeteria at the time, I witnessed the mob. You wouldn't believe the language. Two women walked out screaming at each other cussing up a storm. One spoke about Bob Abell. She yelled, 'I could scratch his eyes out.' You wouldn't believe it. People were screaming. Students running around."

With all the controversy, Searcy recognized an opportunity for his musical talent. "Mike Collins and I borrowed the tune of the Beatles 'Ticket to Ride' and changed it to 'Ticket to Hide' and wrote a song parody," Searcy chuckles.

Coach Miller shared his own humorous ticket scandal story. "People who had never attended a game craved to attend. The athletic director and the superintendent preferred the white tickets. My wife, Joyce, couldn't even land a white ticket," remembers Larry Miller. "Joyce and I drove to Rupp Arena the night before the tournament. We reached the Arena and I looked at the sections because I had never been to Rupp. It was only the third year of Rupp Arena. I looked at Joyce and I said, 'Joyce, remember the section on those white tickets? Those are the ones up at top. Your blue tickets are on the floor.' Joyce enjoyed calling all the teachers when we got back. The teachers upset that they had lost out on the best tickets now owned the best tickets," Larry Miller laughs of the incident. A classical "the first shall be last and the last shall be first" if there ever was one.

Simon Kenton actually received 1,043 tickets to the tournament. After Simon Kenton sold its initial allotment, school officials obtained 550 more tickets from Lexington late Monday before the tournament.

CHAPTER 38
Dwight Searcy's Songs

"None are so old as those who have outlived enthusiasm."
~ Thoreau

Simon Kenton High School in the late 1970's and early 1980's employed several husband and wife teacher teams. Dwight Searcy and his wife, Beverly, were one of many couples who taught at the school. In addition to teaching social studies, sociology and psychology, Dwight Searcy had possessed considerable musical talent. Mr. Searcy, as the students referred to him, developed into a huge Pioneer basketball fan. Dwight's wife, Beverly, taught Home Economics at the school. The two Searcys would teach together at Simon Kenton for twenty-seven years. Coach Miller's wife, Joyce, taught math and Coach Miller taught physics at Simon Kenton. The two couples, Searcys and Millers, became fast fans. At parties in the homes of teachers, Dwight Searcy pulled out his guitar and made up songs about Coach Miller and his team. "I've always been fairly talented at being able to do parodies," Dwight Searcy boasted. "I also wrote political commentary songs." Math teacher, Mike Collins, became a partner in crime, or music, with Dwight Searcy. They formed a talented tandem at pep rallies.

After Simon Kenton won the Ninth Region, Dwight Searcy and Mike Collins gave an Emmy performance at the school assembly pep rally. The parody created for the pep rally involved a work of spontaneous collaborative creativity as recalled by Dwight Searcy. "The morning of the pep rally, in second period sociology class, the students and I spoke about the big pep rally. I happened to have my guitar at school. I brought it to school every once in a while to play songs for my students. I'd sit on the desk and play. Well, we began talking about the pep rally and ideas formed in my mind, and I began making up words. The kids helped me with both' the rhyming and words. We used the tune from Hee-Haw, where the two guys stand next to each other with one facing the front and the other one has his back to the crowd," Dwight Searcy explained of the parody origination.

A popular television show in the 1970's, the country variety show "Hee Haw"starred the late Buck Owens and the great Roy Clark. The show also entertained with a host of comedians and young buxom women wearing short shorts and cleavage blouses. It was all corny good fun. Jokes and music filled the hour-long show televised on Saturday nights. Many skits became weekly staples with a variable topic. One weekly musical skit was "Where Oh Where Are You Tonight". The song began with two singers standing side by side with one facing the audience and the other facing away from the audience. The singer facing the audience would sing a verse and when the chorus arrived, the other singer would turn around to face the audience and chime in. Every refrain ended with a "fart" sound from the mouth from the singers followed by the words "you were gone." Mike Collins and Dwight Searcy performed this duet parody at the pep rally prior to the State Tournament to the hysterical delight of the entire student body. The following words written by Dwight Searcy and his students is now legendary:

WHERE OH WHERE ARE THEY TONIGHT
(Tune - HEE HAW; Where Oh Where)

They told us we'd lose in the 33rd district
That big Andy Burns was too much for us.
But the Pioneers came back; now the Bearcats are cryin'
And the whole town of Walton has learned how to cuss.

Where oh where are the Bearcats tonight?
We had to leave them home all alone.
All around the ninth region the Bearcats are known.
But they played the Pioneers and "phzzzzzzt" they was gone.

Then came the night at the regional finals.
Turney got rollin' and CovCath was hot.
But how 'bout this team? You know there's just no quittin'
Turney fouled out and "Hey look what we've got!!!"

Where oh where is CovCath tonight?

We had to leave them home all alone.
All around the ninth region the Colonels are known.
But they played the Pioneers and "phzzzzzzt" they was gone.

Now there's shootin' Big Mack and dunkin' Dave Dixon
And rebounding Billy make up the big three.
With Mullins, Medley, Dougherty and Ponzer.
We'll bring Knott County right down to its knees.

Where oh where is Knott County tonight?
They might as well pack up and go home.
Cause around Rupp Arena they just don't belong.
They'll play the Pioneers and "phzzzzzzt" they'll be gone.

"I caught a lot of heat from the Walton folks for my song. They re-mained heart-broken over their double overtime loss to us in the district tournament," Dwight Searcy recalls. A Walton-Verona alumni and former Walton basketball player himself. Walton saw Dwight Searcy as a regular Benedict Arnold.

CHAPTER 39
Pioneer Express

"Life is enthusiasm, zest."
~ Sir Lawrence Oliver

The Collins family grew up on Moffitt Road, one of the longest and windiest country roads through southern Kenton County south of Independence. Farms dot the landscape. The youngest of five sons, Richard Collins attended Simon Kenton like each of his older brothers. All of them received childhood nicknames which they hold to this day. The oldest, Lennie, would be called Skinner, followed by Rock, Fit, Boze and then Smell.

Richard Collins was Smell. Smell received his nickname, according to his recollection of family history, from when still in diapers, he preferred to escape the clutches of his parents and smell rather than have his diapers changed. The name stuck. Everyone called him Smell. One would think someone named Smell may be an undesirable. Nothing would be further from reality. A member of the Pioneer Class of 1981, his class voted Smell Mr. Simon Kenton. One of the farm boys or grease monkeys from the rural area outside the City of Independence, Smell also practiced his comedic talents. Tall, and as skinny as a narrow board, he knew everyone. After Simon Kenton won the Regional, Smell's school spirit sprung into action. The Collins brothers passed an old yellow school bus down from brother to brother. They each used it for their own group excursions. Being from a family full of mechanics, Smell took the old school bus and with his merry band of 'dirt farmers' including classmates Kevin Beighle, Kevin Friedman, Tommy Humphrey and Joe Schmiadie, Jed Deters, a 1978 Simon Kenton Graduate, the author of this book, and a host of others, painted the bus blue and white, named it the Pioneer Express, cleaned out all the seats for room for a keg and headed off to Rupp Arena filled with Pioneer fans. Before leaving, the gang drove the bus to Simon Kenton to join in the send off of the team. The 1981 Yearbook captured the completed product. On the way to Rupp Arena on Thursday, the tournament's first day, the Pioneer Express Bus crashed the Walton-Verona High School parking lot. Hooping and hollering from the bus, the Pioneer fans agitated Walton students who ran outside and unsuccessfully tried to block the bus in. Andy Burns watched in horror from a class window. His blood boiled at the mockery.

Equal in spirit to his little brother, Lennie Collins, or Skinner, owner of Nicholson Service Center, two miles south of Simon Kenton, felt compelled to paint the entire back of his gas station blue and white with a huge SK adorning the concrete blocks. It remains faded, but remains there twenty-five years later.

There are too many stories of creative spirit to recount here. Another which deserves mentioning is the SK Starlettes. A group of Simon Kenton male teachers and students dressed up as cheerleaders and called themselves the SK Starlettes. The group included Tim Moore, Gene Kavanaugh, Brian Wyatt, Bill Boyle, Dave Moore, Jody Cuzick and Carl Fitzer.

Proving you never know where spirit may lead you, Smell Collins be-came and remains the dynamic Pastor of Piner Baptist Church in Piner, Kentucky, a few miles south of Independence. His flock doesn't call him Smell. His old friends still do.

CHAPTER 40
Knott County Central

"Just Do It."
~ Nike Logo

The Kentucky High School Athletics Association (KHSAA) regulates high school athletics in Kentucky. Founded in 1917 with nineteen schools, the KHSAA has conducted the boys' state basketball tournament since 1918, first at Centre College in Danville and later at locations in either Lexington or Louisville. Held in March each year, and known as the Sweet Sixteen for featuring champions from sixteen state regions, this tournament is the premier high school sporting event in Kentucky.

Rupp Arena is located in the heart of downtown Lexington. Opened in 1976, it is named after University of Kentucky coaching legend, Adolph Rupp. It's seating capacity is listed as 23,500 for arena events. The University of Kentucky Wildcats play their home games at Rupp. In the lower seating area, chair-back seats fill the seating sections. There is also a student standing-room area behind one goal. The upper area is bleachers. Rupp has no luxury suites. Rupp Arena is known as an intimidating venue for opposing teams of University of Kentucky. Multi-purpose, Rupp also hosts big-named concerts and other sporting events. In 1981, Rupp Arena hosted the Kentucky High School State Tournament.

Knott County holds the distinction of being the third to last county formed in Kentucky out of the one hundred and twenty total counties. The town of Hindman is the county seat of Knott County. This county seat is the town where the county government, including the court system is found in each Kentucky county. Every county in Kentucky has a county seat which contains a town square with a courthouse as the centerpiece. Knott County is named after former Governor James Proctor Knott. It is the only Kentucky County without a river touching its borders. It's also a mining county. Coal mining is prevalent in the Eastern Kentucky mountains. On December 7, 1981, Pearl Harbor Day, the same year as their appearance in the state tournament against Simon Kenton, a mine exploded in the Knott County town of Topmost killing eight men. Knott County also boasts Alice Lloyd College, a four-year college, which provides post secondary education. Lucy Krippenstapel, my maternal grandmother, attended the college on the path to becoming a school teacher. Lucy attended the college while traveling from Harlan County, also a mining mountain county. In honor of my mountain roots, I named my son Parker Riley Harlan. In 1980, Knott County's population was 17,940. Kentucky's current Attorney General, Grady Stumbo hails from Knott County.

The KHSAA scheduled the State Tournament, the 64th in 1981 for March 18, 19, 20 and 21. The $1 program featured the team photographs and advertisers. Countless basketball camps advertised their benefits. Simon Kenton's team photograph is the only team photograph which included the players and cheerleaders, varsity and junior varsity for both.

In their first state tournament game ever, Simon Kenton didn't play very well. "I was scared to death and I didn't even get in that game," Dave Medley remembers. "I think as a team we were just nervous," Sean Dougherty agrees with Dave Medley. "When we came out on the floor for the first time, I led the team out. I can remember running onto the floor and looking up and going, holy smokes. The floor felt different. The atmosphere was different. The adrenaline was even greater than when we won the region at Holmes when we played before 5,000. This was a 23,000 - 24,000 seat stadium. The floor actually gave. The floors in high schools are wood on concrete. It was on a whole different level," Sean Dougherty explains.

Simon Kenton played the Knott County Central Patriots who finished 15-13 during the year. The Patriots upset a thirty-three and one Breathitt County team to win the Fourteenth Region. Knott County Central had lost to Breathitt three prior times during the season, then beat them in the Regional Final. Harold Combs coached the Patriots. No starter for Knott Central exceeded six foot two in height. The Patriots and the Pioneers were the only two teams in the State Tournament without an African-American player. A crowd of 14,000 gathered at Rupp Arena for the Pioneers first game.

"At the pre-game meal, I'm sitting with Dave Schadler and my wife. One of the managers said, 'You've got to come back here, Coach.' I said,

'Why?' He said, 'Dixon's eating peppers.' I said, 'What are you talking about?' I walk back to the players table and Dave Dixon is popping those hot peppers in his mouth, one after the other. I didn't know how many he had eaten, but there's a stack of stems. 'Dave, what are you doing?,' I asked. 'I love 'em, Coach. I love 'em,' he said. 'Dave, we're going to play basketball in four hours you shouldn't be doing that.' He kept saying, 'I love 'em, Coach.' We were at the Continental Inn in Lexington. It had a big buffet. I always fed them four hours before a game so it didn't make any difference what the kids ate, but he was chomping on those peppers. I knew he wasn't going to be very good for the game, and he wasn't," Larry Miller remembers.

Knott County utilized its quickness and cohesive team play to keep the much larger Pioneers off guard. The Patriots kept Simon Kenton off balance by using a head-fake and either cutting to the basket or dishing off to the open man inside. The crowd witnessed Knott County run out to a 16-10 first-quarter lead. Six of those points came on easy inside baskets against a confused Simon Kenton defense. In turn, Simon Kenton scored its 10 first quarter points on jump shots.

"We were better than Knott County, but played terrible. One of the keys to winning state though is beating somebody you can and receiving a draw where you beat a team the first game without playing very well. The reason is everybody is jittery," Coach Miller explained of the narrow victory.

"You don't get a chance to do all that stuff they showed in 'Hoosiers' where the coach showed the players the goals are still ten feet. It's so monitored. You step off the bus and walk in. They walk you to your locker room and they say, 'Coach, we'll be back to get you.' You don't leave. You don't do anything. They come and walk you to the floor. They meet you coming off the floor and walk you back to the locker room. They don't let you touch that floor before the game or after the game," explains Coach Miller of the controlled atmosphere.

"The referees let them beat the hell out of Alan Mullins, and Dave Dixon didn't show up," recalls Dave Schadler.

"They out-rebounded us. They out-hustled us. They were an old mountain team. We were in awe of the game. It didn't affect my shooting because I couldn't shoot to begin with, but no one shot well. I didn't play well. You hope you can get through that first game. It doesn't matter if you win by one or if you win by twenty. You just want to move on," Greg Ponzer explains.

After the game, Troy McKinley's legs began to tighten up and cramp. The pain worsened. Troy thought the flu was hitting him. "I sat in a bathtub for a long time and rubbed Ben-Gay all over my legs. I thought, I can't get sick now, but my legs were killing me. I don't know if I had a 24-hour virus or worse," Troy McKinley remembers.

Larry Miller refused to allow the players' parents to see their kids during the tournament. This included the sick Troy McKinley.

CHAPTER 41
Virgie

"How do you go from where you are to where you want to be?
"I think you have to have enthusiasm for life. You have to have a dream, a goal, and you have to be willing to work for it."
    ~ Jim Valvano

The Virgie Eagles finished 28-3 and won the Fifteenth Region. Coached by Bobby Osborne, he claimed his team was "the best tournament team I've had." Virgie won fourteen in a row and never lost a game against anyone in their Region that year. They were run and gun and scored 100 or more points in four games. All of this *before* the 3 point shot and during only eight minute quarters.

"Virgie had a kid named Todd May, who rated the second best player in the state behind Manual Forest of Louisville Moore. Only a junior, he stood 6'8" and 195 pounds. I remember Friday night would be the largest crowd to ever watch a high school basketball in Kentucky because everyone wanted to watch Todd May," Coach Miller remembers of the next game. However, before the Pioneers played on Friday night, Rupp Arena hosted another tournament game. "The other game was Owensboro against Louisville Moore. Moore had Manuel Forrest. They rated Manuel Forrest the second best player in the country behind Patrick Ewing. He even rated ahead of Michael Jordan, also a high school senior. Michael Jordan, Patrick Ewing and Manuel Forrest were three of the ten National Parade High School All-Americans," Larry Miller recalls. Dave Schadler described Todd May. "Only a junior, he played like an animal. Every college recruited him. He was an athlete. Could run, could jump, the whole package. However, your second game you feel more familiar with Rupp. I felt like we belonged. In the hotel that day, Larry and I strategized. We focused obviously on Todd May. We knew we couldn't stop him, but we could limit him. We knew that if we played our game, we could win. However, we were underdogs," recalls Dave Schadler. Todd May averaged a remarkable twenty-eight points and seventeen rebounds a game that year.

"They were claiming it to be the largest crowd to ever see a high school basketball game in Kentucky. They expected 18,000-19,000. It set a new record," remembers Dave Schadler of the crowd. The record lasted a day.

Louisville Moore, behind Manuel Forrest, thumped Owensboro in the first game. It was the Pioneers turn to receive, according to the prognosticators, their thumping. "It was a shoot-out. Troy McKinley got hot and Todd May was good. It was up and down the floor and fire it up. We'd get ahead and I'd think we'd be all right, but they had this little guy named Rodney Rowe who caught fire. He ended up with thirty. I expected Todd May to hit a bundle and he had thirty-one. But Rodney Rowe was just unbelievable. I tried Sean Dougherty on him. I tried Greg Ponzer on him. Didn't matter. Rowe went wild," Coach Miller recalls of Rowe's unexpected performance.

"I couldn't guard Rowe. I couldn't get close enough to elbow him and it wouldn't have helped anyway. They were tough," Greg Ponzer laughs.

When Dixon fouled out thirty-eight seconds into the fourth quarter, Simon Kenton played with a small lineup. They still couldn't contain Rowe who hit eight straight points early in the fourth quarter to tie the game at 69-69. The fourth quarter continued the shootout.

With seven seconds left in the game, McKinley hit a layup and a free throw for the Pioneers' final points and an 84-81 lead. Rowe's basket with a second remaining completed the 84 - 83 Pioneer victory.

Dave Schadler remembers he coached his big men the best he could. "We played man-to-man the whole time. Todd May didn't get any stickbacks against us. David Dixon was just a mental mess. I kept telling Dave and Billy all day long before the game, 'you're gong to have to stick your ass in that guy and you're going to have to box him off or he's going to eat us up on the offensive boards. When you catch the ball, don't shoot jump shots, jump hook it, because he'll knock it back in your face.' All day long I'm on them. Troy sat silently in the corner of the hotel room. I never said anything to Troy because if I said anything to Troy, I always figured I'd just mess him up. The other guys, I knew how to yank them. I knew that Billy would listen to me. Dixon normally did, but he was just screwed up. I kept telling Larry,

'He ain't right. He ain't right. Get him out of there.' Larry's still stuck with him," Dave Schadler recalls of his frustration.

"Late in the game, Virgie switched to man-to-man. They played zone most of the night. They came back out of a timeout and put Todd May on Troy. I adjusted and put Troy out on the top. Todd May wasn't their best defender, but he was their star. He was their 6-8 star, but he couldn't guard Troy. So Troy either took it to the basket or they'd double team and Troy would hit somebody for a lay-up or he'd get fouled. Troy kept scoring. It was a wild one," remembers Coach Miller of the Virgie shoot out.

Virgie Coach Bobby Osborne was equally impressed with McKinley. "We tried to keep a fresh man on him. He's an excellent player. We tried to cut him off in the first half, but we didn't play with the intensity we normally play with. I think we took them lightly. They didn't have a real good game last night when we saw them," Coach Osborne expressed in regret after the game.

"Our game against Virgie was one of the classic state tournament games. It was a great offensive show between Rowe and May on their side and Troy on ours. Troy saved us," Coach Miller states with appreciation.

Legend has it Joe B. Hall, head basketball coach of the University of Kentucky, turned to his recruiter, Joe Dean, during the Virgie game and said, "Why in the hell didn't you tell me about this kid," referring to Troy McKinley. Dwight Searcy would have been happy during the Virgie game to know Kenny Price from "Hee-Haw" was in the stands during the Virgie game rooting for the victorious Pioneers.

"As soon as we reached the locker room after the Virgie game, Dave Schadler gave us the stats. A bunch of reporters by then were after us. Everybody begged to talk to McKinley. Reporters gave me a hard time. I shoved Troy McKinley into the locker room away from the reporters. Reporter Gene McLean wrote me hard for that move. I walked out the door and he said 'I want to talk to McKinley.' I said, 'No, not tonight; tomorrow night.' 'He ain't going to be here tomorrow night, I want to talk to him,' he said. I said, 'No, we'll be here tomorrow night'," Coach Miller recalls of his confidence.

After the Virgie win, Coach Miller kept the team on his schedule. "It was early Saturday morning. We took them to the hotel, fed them Big Macs, cheeseburgers and french fries and went to bed," Coach Miller explained.

"While Dave Schadler ran out for the McDonalds, Joyce looked for a place to wash the teams uniforms because our next game was eleven o'clock the next morning," Coach Miller explains of the time problem.

"They always give out the cheerleading awards on Friday night. So if you play the last game on Friday, you're lucky to leave there by midnight. Joyce, Connie Beach and Shawna Cartright broke into an apartment complex to use a washer and dryer and wash the uniforms. It was unlocked, but it was private property," Larry Miller laughs of the uniform washing caper.

The three ladies began washing the players and cheerleaders uniforms at the team hotel. The hotel tried to help, but they only had a giant commercial washer for linens. The ladies soon smelled bleach and knew the uniforms would be ruined. The night manager stopped the machine and the ladies took the wet uniforms out and put them in a giant drink cooler. They put the cooler in Connie's Beech's car and drove off looking for a laundry mat. They never found one. The desperate ladies found an apartment complex unlocked and used the laundry room. They ran out of quarters though and couldn't dry the uniforms. After a policeman drove by to give them a scare, they drove the wet uniforms back to the hotel where they hung them up in the cheerleaders rooms. As they hung up the boys' uniforms, they found embroidered jocks. It was 3:00 am when the three ladies returned. They found Larry Miller was still awake working on a game plan. He couldn't believe the ladies were still out working on the uniform washing problem.

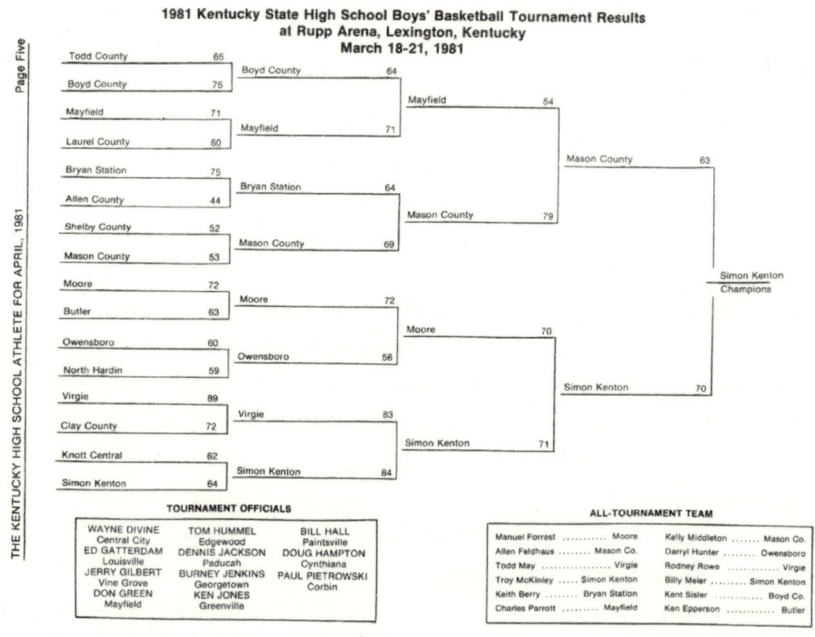

1981 Kentucky State High School Boys' Basketball Tournament Results
at Rupp Arena, Lexington, Kentucky
March 18-21, 1981

Todd County	65						
Boyd County	75	Boyd County	64				
				Mayfield	64		
Mayfield	71	Mayfield	71				
Laurel County	60					Mason County	63
Bryan Station	75	Bryan Station	64				
Allen County	44			Mason County	79		
Shelby County	52	Mason County	69				
Mason County	53						Simon Kenton Champions
Moore	72	Moore	72				
Butler	63			Moore	70		
Owensboro	60	Owensboro	56				
North Hardin	59					Simon Kenton	70
Virgie	89	Virgie	83				
Clay County	72			Simon Kenton	71		
Knott Central	62	Simon Kenton	84				
Simon Kenton	64						

TOURNAMENT OFFICIALS

WAYNE DIVINE
Central City
ED GATTERDAM
Louisville
JERRY GILBERT
Vine Grove
DON GREEN
Mayfield

TOM HUMMEL
Edgewood
DENNIS JACKSON
Paducah
BURNEY JENKINS
Georgetown
KEN JONES
Greenville

BILL HALL
Paintsville
DOUG HAMPTON
Cynthiana
PAUL PIETROWSKI
Corbin

ALL-TOURNAMENT TEAM

Manuel Forrest .... Moore
Allen Feldhaus .... Mason Co.
Troy McKinley ..... Simon Kenton
Keith Berry .... Bryan Station
Charles Parrott .... Mayfield

Kelly Middleton .... Mason Co.
Darryl Hunter .... Owensboro
Rodney Rowe .... Virgie
Billy Meier .... Simon Kenton
Kent Sisler .... Boyd Co.
Ken Epperson .... Butler

CHAPTER 42
Louisville Moore

"Always think of passing the ball before shooting it."
~ John Wooden

The Louisville Moore Mustangs won the Seventh Region. Their star, Manuel Forrest averaged 33 points a game while leading his team to a 28-5 record. Through their District and 7th Region, they never even played a close game. Coach Tom Finnegan boastfully called Forrest "the greatest player in the history of the State of Kentucky." Considering basketball's storied history in Kentucky, this was quite an anointment by his coach.

Meanwhile, Coach Miller could feel his team clicking. "Dixon still hadn't given us a real good game, but Meier was playing the best he's ever played in his life. Greg was playing well. Alan was phenomenal. He didn't give the ball up," Coach Miller reflects of his team's play.

Greg Ponzer recalls knowing Louisville Moore was good, but had no idea Manuel Forrest was a Parade High School All-American with Patrick Ewing and Michael Jordan. "I walked out before the games to meet with the referees. Manuel Forrest came out for their team. The referees introduced themselves to him. They joked around with him 'Now, what did you say your name was, Darrell Griffin.' They spoke to Manuel Forrest with admiration. I'm standing out there being ignored, while they're comparing this guy to Darrell Griffin who played at Louisville and earned the name "Dr. Dunkenstein". I'm thinking, damn what are we getting ourselves into. I'm this little white guy and he's this big 6'7" two hundred pound black guy. Forrest also really didn't think too much of us. You could tell. He clearly wasn't thinking this was going to be much of a game," Greg Ponzer recalls of the pregame meeting. Yet, the game would match the dramatic excitement of the Walton-Verona game.

John Salyers, now field representative for Kentucky U.S. Senator and Hall of Famer Jim Bunning, provided the man on the floor commentary for WHKK broadcast team. Prior to their radio broadcast of the semifinals game, John interviewed Happy Chandler. A Kentucky icon, Happy served as Kentucky's Governor, U.S. Senator and Major League Baseball Commissioner. Happy's political career spanned decades. In 1981, Happy Chandler enjoyed his retired celebrity status. He also led the University of Kentucky fans at Rupp Arena after a basketball game in the singing of "My Old Kentucky Home." In a word, Happy Chandler was simply a gem. His grandson, Ben Chandler, who was sworn in as an attorney the same day I was sworn in, became Kentucky's Attorney General and now serves in the United States Congress from Lexington.

At the end of the interview, Happy spoke about Simon Kenton High School having a chance against the navy and white, Louisville Moore. An underdog many times in his political career, Happy may have seen a little of himself in the Pioneers.

As the semi-finals game began before 16,000 fans, the Pioneers unexpectedly took control despite McKinley picking up two fouls in the first 1:07 of the first quarter. In a remarkable display of faith in Troy, Coach Miller kept McKinley in the game with two fouls. In succession, Dixon made a layup, Meier made a stick back and a hook shot over Manuel Forrest, and McKinley drained a 17 foot jumper. Down 8-0, Louisville Moore called a time out. Out of the time out, Ponzer blocked a shot, but Manuel Forrest made Moore's first two points. McKinley answered with two more. After several misses and steals, Troy McKinley made two free throws after being fouled. After a Ponzer rebound in front of the 6'7" Phelps, McKinley made a 18 footer resulting in a 14-2 lead for the Pioneers. Moore finally scored again, but Dixon answered. After Forrest scored at 1:09 left in the first quarter after only shooting 3 of 9, the Pioneers held a shocking 16-8 advantage.

After a few steals and slam dunks by Manuel Forrest, the Mustangs closed the gap further. Louisville Moore used a box and one on McKinley. By the end of the quarter, the Mustangs nearly came all the way back and only trailed 17-15 at the end of the first quarter.

Forrest would begin the second quarter just as hot and despite McKinley being double teamed, the Pioneers continued to force the ball to him. Louisville Moore pressed and after earlier tying the game, took the lead 23-21 with 5:51 remaining. After a foul on Meier, the Simon Kenton bench received a technical foul and the Mustangs pulled away a little at 27-21. Meier made two back to back baskets including the second on goaltending by Forrest and the Pioneers trailed only 27-25. After a basket by Ponzer tied the score at 27, Forrest dumped in four more points. At 4:19 in the game, Moore led 31-27 and then the referee called a jump ball between the 5'10" Greg Ponzer and 6'7" Manuel Forrest at Moore's end of the floor.

"Ponzer took it as a personal honor to get Manuel Forest. He went after Manuel," remembers Coach Miller. Greg Ponzer would provide the most memorable moment of the tournament.

"On a rebound, after every held ball, they'd go to the jump ball. I don't know if it was an offensive or a defense rebound, but we both went to the ball. We had a contraption in high school called the leaper, we used to work on the machine, and I worked on my jumping. I liked doing that. I was 5'10", but I could dunk the ball," recalls Greg Ponzer. "Manuel Forrest and I were tied up. So we had to go to the circle right by one of the goals. I remember it was closest to our goal. We just had the jump ball. I had a knack of bringing my left arm up to jump. I'd sit there and jump with my left arm. And I just stole the tip from him. I didn't out jump him. I stole the tip. Just stole the tip. Dale McMillen announced on the radio broadcast that Manuel Forrest 'became a hot dog and he got burned.' Everyone made such a big deal about me out jumping Manuel Forest and it became legendary fun, but I didn't out jump him."

After the jump ball, McKinley scored. Following a McKinley rebound, Moore player Kenny Brown according to WHKK "really put a shot on Billy Meier." With 2:38 left, the referees called a flagrant foul on Kenny Brown and ejected him from the game.

"Billy and a boy named Brown had gotten into it before the half. I don't know what happened. I never did ask Billy. I didn't want to know," Coach Miller remembers. "They threw Brown out of the game. Evidently he made a flagrant foul attempt or hit Billy."

Billy Meier recalls what happened and professes his innocence. "Every time Troy or anybody would shoot from the outside, I would work to get inside position on Brown. I had worked around him and got inside position. Well, the ball went through the net. I turned around real quick and he was right there and we ran into each other head-on. He got ticked off and pushed me. Well, running down the court, I never said a word to him. He just got up next to me and took the swing, and it happened to be right in front of the referee. I mean it was a pretty good pop when I ran into him. I don't know if he thought I did it on purpose, but we started to run down the court, and he took a swing at me. He averaged seventeen a game. It's a gutsy call by the referee," Billy Meier comments on the ejection.

As Manuel Forrest continued to put on a show, Dale McMillen mentioned Forrest was "in a league by himself." At the 1:35 mark, Dale called "Manuel Forrest 37 - Simon Kenton 30." After a Dixon basket, Forrest scored yet again as McMillen yelled: "You have to see it to believe it." As the clock ran out on the first half, Louisville Moore led 41-36. Thanks to the quick start, the Pioneers held close. Manuel Forrest had 32 of the 41 points of Louisville Moore. The state tournament record of King Kelly Coleman of 68 was not out of reach. Despite the Forrest scoring, his team shot only 40%. The Pioneers shot 63%.

At the half, the WHKK broadcast team interviewed Arthur Hawkins, a former member of the KHSAA Board of Control, who pointed out he knew no Ninth Region team ever won the tournament. They also interviewed Marion Schadler, the Mayor of Independence. The Mayor explained the Pioneers had "a great bunch of kids and coaches." He spoke of the school explosion and the pulling together of the community.

Forrest won the second half tip and his teammate, Thompson scored. After a McKinley miss, Dave Dixon, picked up his third foul. After another Mustang score, Coach Miller called a timeout. After the timeout, the teams traded baskets, and Coach Miller still called yet another time out. The Mustangs led by their largest margin, 49-38. Coach Miller then stuck Sean Dougherty in the game. Dougherty provided a spark. Sean fed McKinley and Dixon on three jump shots and the Pioneers clawed back to 49-44.

McMillen remarked over the radio: "Billy Meier rebounds. He is as rugged as anything Louisville Moore's got." Seeing their lead shrink, Moore called a timeout. The crowd screamed with enthusiasm for the underdog Pioneers. After Dixon made two free throws, Manuel Forrest scored on a slam dunk to McMillen's radio call that Forrest was a "glider pilot." McKinley and Forrest began a tick for tack shoot out. McKinley continued to drain jumpers despite "having everything but bricks hit him" according to McMillen. As the third quarter closed, the Simon Kenton Pioneers trailed only 57-55. The crowd erupted in jubilant pandemonium for the underdogs. The radio broadcasted the background noise.

As the fourth and final quarter began with Forrest winning another tap over Dixon, Dixon picked up his fourth foul. Coach Miller left him in the game. Dixon made a hook shot, but fouled out at 7:00 minutes remaining on a blocking foul which McMillen called "a bad call." After a Dougherty 12 footer, followed by a Dougherty steal and layup by Ponzer, the Pioneers recaptured the lead for the first time at 4:09 remaining in the game. The crowd grew even louder and muffled the radio broadcast.

The drama grew as the game closed out. After McKinley made a couple free throws, the Pioneers led 67-64. At 2:50, the Pioneers played four corners offense. After a Mustang basket, Billy Meier lost the ball and the referees called a blocking foul on Dougherty. After Jim Hubbs made two free throws, Louisville Moore retook the lead 68-67 with 2:15 left. After successive misses by McKinley and Meier, Greg Ponzer was fouled. Ponzer missed the front end of a one and one and Forrest grabbed the rebound at 1:50. Sean Dougherty tied him up, but Forrest easily won the tap. Forrest missed a shot and Meier grabbed the rebound at 1:28. The Pioneers called a timeout. As Louisville Moore played a 2-3 zone, Ponzer, Mullins and Dougherty passed the ball around. With 56 seconds left, Ponzer hit Meier on a backdoor and the Pioneers seized the lead 69-68. McKinley fouled Forrest on a lob pass with 38 seconds left. After a "big deep breath" as described by McMillen, Forrest drained both free throws for the Mustangs to recapture the lead 70-69.

The Pioneers took the clock down to seven seconds before Coach Miller called a timeout. McMillen announced: "It's cardiac time." John Salyers predicted: "Look for Billy Meier under the basket when Troy McKinley gets the ball." He reminded the listeners of the McKinley to Dixon play against Walton-Verona in the District semifinal. Ponzer inbounded the ball to Mullins. Mullins passed to McKinley near the key. As McKinley elevated to shoot, he passed to Meier behind Forrest and Meier laid it in off the glass with a gentle soft hook with one second left. The crowd shook Rupp Arena as Simon Kenton took the 71-70 lead. After Ponzer knocked away the length of the court inbounds pass to Forrest, Dale McMillen screamed on the radio: "64 years of frustration could be over!"

"When the horn went off, Greg and I were on the opposite sideline from the benches where the local radio broadcast team was. It just so happened the last play occurred in front of WHKK's radio team, Dale McMillen and Hardy Tribble. At that instant, we felt something magical going on and they happened to be the closest people to us. They're local folks and we knew them. I just remember the look in their eyes was just unforgettable," Alan recalls of the WHKK team.

"Greg and I were hugging them and just jumping up and down, going crazy. It was unbelievable. You're in this sea of people and all of our fans were down on the court. But those guys were right there and they've been with us through the ride, through the district and through the regional tournaments," Alan Mullins explains.

Troy McKinley claims he planned on taking the shot and he wanted to take the shot, but saw Billy wide open under the basket. He followed Coach Wooden's tenet and looked to pass first.

"One game, I made a steal. We were playing a team who we were killing. I made a steal. I'm dribbling with my head down and Ponzer was up ahead of me. There was nobody else around. I went up and dunked the ball. At the last second, I saw Greg, but I went ahead and dunked it. Coach Miller ripped me. I felt horrible," recalls Troy McKinley of the isolated selfish shot. "That was always in the back of my mind when making the shot or pass decision."

"They gave Manuel Forrest Mr. Kentucky Basketball at the end of the season. Then for some reason, maybe because he didn't play in the Kentucky/Indiana All-Star game, they took it away from him. I think they gave it to Phil Cox who would later play at Vanderbilt. I thought that was kind of interesting. He was definitely the best player in the state, but they took it away from him," Troy McKinley remembers of the Forrest's title strip.

At the end of the game, Manuel Forrest refused to shake Greg Ponzer's hand. Greg also remembers the announcers telling Coach Miller how many points Manuel Forrest threw in. Larry Miller responded: "He may have had 47, but he didn't have 49, and that's what it took to beat us." Wise and true words.

Coach Finnegan was furious in the post-game press conference about Brown getting thrown out and believes no player had ever been thrown out of the state tournament. An attempt to check this fact at the KHSAA, confirms no one remembers anyone else being thrown out of a state tournament game. Regardless, the ejection dearly cost Louisville Moore.

Coach Finnegan refused to allow Brown to speak to the press after the game. Finnegan also issued a statement: "Kenny Brown is one of the finest gentlemen I know. He is president of the Moore junior class. I don't want his reputation hurt. His ejection was an unprecedented act in the state tournament." Coach Finnegan also claimed Forrest played with a pulled groin the prior three weeks. Finnegan waived his Friday imposed rule relating to player interviews. All the players refused interviews and Forrest left immediately after the game.

Coach Miller called the moment after the Moore game, "the greatest Saturday morning ever." On the WHKK post game interview, Coach Miller explained he called the same play as the team called against Walton-Verona. He proudly boasted, "Those kids can handle anything." He pointed out he hesitated to put Dougherty in because of Moore's size, but that the did a super job. As WHKK completed their broadcast, John Salyers called the Pioneers a "Team of Destiny". He remarked the pioneers "came out of the grave" against Walton-Verona and it appeared destiny had called them."

CHAPTER 43
The State Final - Mason County

"Trickling water, if not stopped, will become a mighty river."
~ Chinese Proverb

The eighth county formed in Kentucky, Mason County's history predated Knott County. It is named for George Mason of Virginia, one of our country's founding fathers. It is believed George Mason possessed not only great knowledge, but a great fortune. Nineteen Kentucky counties formed from the original Mason County established by the Virginia legislature in 1788. Kentucky would be formed out of Virginia in the same manner North Carolina gave birth to Tennessee. Simon Kenton himself, along with Thomas Williams, receive credit for being the first permanent settlers of Mason County. Because of the many Indian raids, Simon Kenton built a station for the protection of the many families coming to the county. Maysville would become the largest town in the county. The bridge built in 1931 across the Ohio River between Maysville, Kentucky and Aberdeen, Ohio is named after Simon Kenton. In 1980, the population of Mason County was 17,765. The championship game of 1981 would match a school from the county which Simon Kenton founded, against the school which bore his name from the county which also bore his name. It may have been coincidental geography, but worthy of note nevertheless. It would be an all "Simon Kenton" final.

Ron Dennis would only make it to one boys' varsity Simon Kenton basketball game during the 1980-1981 season, the state final against the Mason County Royals. His lack of attendance resulted not in lack of interest, but simple life obligations. Ron worked nights at Cincinnati Milacron. As the first firefighter on the scene of the explosion, he suffered temporary blindness and nearly died.

"I was working with my brother-in-law the Saturday morning of the finals over in Edgewood. He was doing some plumbing work on his house and listening to the radio. Simon Kenton won that morning. Beat Louisville Moore. I called my wife and said, 'You want to go to that basketball game tonight?'

'Well, I don't know,' she replied. "I said, 'Let's go'."

"We lucked out and got two tickets. We were plum all the way up in the top as high as you could go, and we got there right before half," Ron remembers.

Another firefighter who attended every Simon Kenton game of the state tournament from a wheelchair was Steve Sierveld. Ron Coleman and Bob Abel sat under one of the goals. Ron Coleman secured a press pass and had a great view of the action. On Ron's and Bob Medley's drive to the tournament, a car with an Ohio license plate passed them. On the plate was 'SK 1'. Ron Coleman and Bob Medley knew it was a good omen. All the excitement over the Pioneers resulted in the boosters selling $22,000 worth of t-shirts for the year. Ron Coleman, a great basketball enthusiast, has a tape of the actual 1954 Milan team beating the Muncie Central team which is the 'Hoosiers' story. Ron claims the game is boring and doesn't compare to the Simon Kenton games against Walton or Louisville Moore.

The Mason County Royals made it to the finals with a 25-4 record. Former University of Kentucky All-American Jack Givens said: "This makes it a lot of fun. I know no one expected Simon Kenton and Mason County to be in the finals, and I think it will be good for fan interest." Neither team had ever made it to the tournament or the finals.

Randall Wagner didn't have tickets to the finals game. "You couldn't buy tickets outside. Bobby Cornelius came up and said, 'Somebody wants you to have these two tickets.' And that's the way I got in. Bobby would never tell me whose they were. He also wouldn't let me pay for them," Randall remembers of his tickets.

"I remember riding over to the game feeling real confident. I remember walking into the game and Jack Givens is actually trying to go in. The lady at the gate at Rupp Arena is asking him who he is while she's waving us on in. I'm thinking, wow, what a turn of events," Dave Schadler laughs.

"I remember being so excited and thinking this is the dream game. Mason is coached by Alan Feldhaus. His sons played for him. Feldhaus played for the University of Kentucky. We grew up watching University of Kentucky," remembers Sean Dougherty. "But now we're playing on UK's floor. Our uniforms looked like UK's uniforms. We were blue and white down to our converse leather tennis shoes. This is what we played for our entire life. We watched these games as little boys. Win or lose, we were there. It was time to go after it. I can also remember being tired. My, Alan's and Greg's role was up and down the court. We spent energy out on the floor," Sean Dougherty explains.

Superstition entered the picture during the state tournament. Dave Dixon asked for the trainer to tape his left ankle the same before every game. Alan Mullins and Billy Meier listened to "Back in Black" from AC/DC each game. Troy McKinley put his uniform on the same way every game. Pictures prove Coach Miller wore the same suit he wore during the District and Region for every State Tournament game. Mason County's trek through the State Tournament began like Simon Kenton's. They won by a point over Shelby 53-52. They followed this squeaker with an upset over Bryan Station 69-64, one of the favorites to win the tournament. Jack Givens of the University of Kentucky played for Lexington Bryan Station years before. Then, in the semi-finals, Mason beat Mayfield in a blow out 79-54. Allen Feldhaus, Jr. a 6'4" guard was Mason's tallest player. Terry Jackson started at the other guard. Dave Orme started at center. Kelly Middleton and Charles Jackson completed the starting five at the forward positions.

Kelly Middleton's road to the state tournament involved overcoming adversity. The previous fall, Middleton lost control of his car on a road in Mason County and struck an immovable tree. Middleton suffered two broken jaws and a crushed cheek. After extensive plastic surgery, the doctors wired his mouth together. He lost thirty pounds and missed the first two games of the season.

Prior to the game, Dale McMillen from WHKK interviewed Mason County Coach Alan Feldhaus. Feldhaus worried about his players being tired and matching up with the Pioneers big men. Mason boasted a fifteen game winning streak entering the finals. Hardy Tribble interviewed Larry Miller. Coach Miller reflected on the rough beginning to the season from the explosion. He also commented on the size of the crowd developing. Dale McMillen claimed he called 1,800 games, and the game about to be played excited him more than any.

As Simon Kenton and Mason County warmed up for the game, the song "Fame" blasted through the Rupp Arena sound system. The Pioneers ran their layup and rebound lines. McKinley #40, Dixon #32, Dougherty #11, Medley #35, Meier #41, Ponzer #5 and Mullins #12 listened to the music as they warmed up in their white warmups. They knew an opportunity they would never have again was before them. As the National Anthem concluded the "home of the Pioneers" is heard shouted by Pioneers fans through the radio broadcast. After a long season, the time to seize yet another moment arrived.

Mason County controlled the opening tip, but received a block by the Pioneers on their first shot as their reward. However, Mason County grabbed a 4-0 lead on two baskets by Feldhaus. McKinley drained a 19 footer to put the Pioneers on the board. At 6:15, McKinley made two free throws. After a Billy Meier basket at 5:03, followed by a Mason county score, Mason County led 12-6 at 4:36. Simon Kenton adjusted into a 2-3 zone. After Alan Mullins missed a free throw, Dave Dixon blocked a Mason County shot. Later, Simon Kenton shifted back to man to man, but trailed 16-6 with 1:40 left in the first quarter when the Pioneers called a timeout. With :33 seconds left in the quarter, Kelly Middleton converted two free throws for the Royals to take a 20-9 lead. Mason County was the best free throw shooting team in the tournament and they proved it. Simon Kenton wasted a timeout when they failed to score as time ran out in the quarter. The Pioneers faced a 20-9 deficit at the end of the quarter.

As the second quarter began with Dixon controlling the tip, McKinley began bringing his team back. He hit two shots before Mason County answered with baskets by Middleton and Orme. Dale McMillen commented the Pioneers were not hitting the offensive boards and appeared tired. Sean Dougherty came in to pick up the tempo. After two Dixon free throws brought the Pioneers within six, the Royals completed a 3 point play and led 27-18. At 4:00, Kelly Middleton of the Royals picked up his third foul. Coach Feldhaus removed Middleton from the line up. Billy Meier made both free throws. As Simon Kenton trailed at 2:20, 33-25, McMillen again commented: "Simon looks tired." The Royals scored again and after the Pioneers failed to score in the remaining nine seconds, Simon Kenton trailed by ten at the half, 35 - 25.

The final game would be all adrenaline. "Troy McKinley had the first thirteen points in the final game. Nobody's playing but Troy," recalls Coach Miller of the first half.

"At halftime I told them, 'You know, we've come a long way. You seniors are never going to get another opportunity. I'm probably never going to get another opportunity to do this,'" recalls Coach Miller of his halftime talk.

Greg Ponzer stood up and reminded the team about Robert Williams. "After the blast, we were pretty messed up. We didn't have a regular place to practice. We had to keep late hours. We had no idea where we'd play our games. We were really disappointed. One day, Robert Williams' father came and spoke to us. He made us think that good could come out of anything. It really picked me up. That meant something coming from him. I reminded the team at halftime about Robert and I think it picked us up," stated Greg Ponzer at the time.

Alan Mullins credits Coach Miller with the right perspective. "To Coach's credit, they looked at the situation at halftime and they didn't panic. They didn't raise their voices. They just said, 'hey, we've got to get back in this – here's what we've got to do'. First, we've got to relax. We've got to get back to our game plan. If they get back defensively, we've got to rotate it, make them work on defense. We come out in the third quarter and a switch came on with Dave Dixon. His energy was just phenomenal," Alan Mullins recalls of Dave Dixon's on switch.

"At halftime, in the locker room, I went over to Greg Ponzer, and I said, 'The third quarter is ours'," Dave Dixon recalls saying. Greg Ponzer decided to start directing the ball to Dixon and see can happened. "A couple of minutes into the third quarter we were down 16. Miller called a timeout. Troy was worn out. Billy was worn out. Dave hadn't had a good tournament. We're all tired. But Miller calls a timeout. They made the announcement that we had just set a world record attendance for a high school basketball game. Dave Dixon heard that, and just got wound up. He started screaming. We couldn't hear Miller. Schadler couldn't shut him up. Nobody could shut him up. He just got locked in and intense. And we were down 16," Sean Dougherty recalls of the deficit.

"I told the guy that was guarding me, David Orme, 'You're going to have to get some help.' I said, 'You can't guard me.' When I told him that he said, 'I know'," David Dixon remembers of his smack talk. "They were holding their shorts bending over. Our legs were tired too. Orme asked me if my legs were tired and I lied and said no. But you could tell that his legs were tired," Dave Dixon recalls.

As fortune sometimes shines, the player who disappeared for three and a half games, rose to the occasion to save the day for his teammates who were nearly spent.

"I always met the players out on the floor because I didn't want the parents to hear what I was saying to them. Dixon is jumping up and down like a kangaroo. Ponzer looks at me like what's going on, and I said, 'I don't know either, Greg, but get him the damn ball. Let's keep getting it to him.' Dixon had fourteen that quarter," recalls Larry Miller of the Dixon explosion.

Simon Kenton outscored the Royals 12-2 to begin the third quarter and won the quarter 22-11. They led 47 to 46 at the end of the third period.

The Pioneers continued the pace into the fourth quarter. With 6:49 left, the Pioneers led 53-48. Billy Meier picked up his fourth foul. Kelly Middleton made seventeen straight free throws in the tournament, but he missed the front end of the one and one. Billy Meier began a spurt by scoring baskets and rebounding and the Pioneers stretched their lead 57-48 at 5:00. At this time, John Salyers of WHKK commented, "This is two ball clubs taken to the limit." Hardy Tribble remarked that maybe "Mason is a little bit more tired." John Salyers replied, "Down nine makes you more tired." The Royals couldn't score. As the Simon Kenton crowd roared, the Pioneers seized their largest lead 59-48 at 4:08 on a layup by Greg Ponzer. For the first time in the tournament, McKinley began missing shots. "He's a very tired young man," John Salyers commented. As the Pioneers maintained their lead 61-50 at 3:20, Dale McMillen commented Independence 61 - Mason County 50 and stated with excitement "Meier has gone to war."

As the double digit lead held 64-54 after a Ponzer free throw, Dale McMillen complimented the "people from Independence" for support of their team. Joe Stark, the Pioneer athletic director, led the cheers pacing back in forth and sweating near his seat.

As the score held 65-54 at the 1:43 mark, Dale McMillen commented: "Hopefully, sixty-four frustrating years hopefully to be erased." The Royals closed the gap to 65-60 with :56 seconds left, but then Greg Ponzer hit two free throws. Ron Coleman recalls hearing Greg Ponzer exhorting his teammates. He saw Greg pat Troy McKinley on the rear and told him "Come on big boy." Middleton answered with a basket, 67-62, with :45 seconds left. Mason fouled Ponzer again after Ponzer jumped for a rebound so high Dale McMillen claimed, "If Ponzer went any higher, he would have to get a license." As Alan Mullins made a free throw with twelve seconds left, Dale McMillen spoke of the school's explosion, the girls basketball team wreck, the coaches who had lost in the finals from the 9th Region. With :07 seconds left, Billy Meier fouled out, replaced by Dave Medley. Despite fouling a lot during the game, this was the first game Meier fouled out during the year. A free throw finished the score 70-63. The Pioneers won by seven. In celebratory excitement, Dale McMillen announced: "Simon Kenton has won the Kentucky State Tournament. The first time in history the 9th Region has won it. Before 21,287, the largest crowd to ever see a high school basketball game."

Hardy Tribble spoke into his microphone: "The most emotional one we've covered. They are a gutsy ball club." John Salyers recalled on the radio reading stories in the library about Carr Creek: "I hope sometime this is in a

Junior Kelly Dougherty #14 shoots vs. Bell-view

Tip-off, Sandy Ross #30 and Donna Voges #31

Coach Butch Hayes at the girls district tournament

The 1981 KHSAA
Boys State Tournament

The Pioneer Express

Ballboy, Doug Pelphrey at the state tournament. Doug later became the placekicker for the NFL's Cincinnati Bengals. (Courtesy of Ron Coleman)

Alan Mullins in their first round game vs. Knott Central

258

Greg Ponzer drives to the basket

Troy McKinley is about to seal the victory over Virgie by hitting this winning free. (Courtesy of Ron Coleman)

Linda Whittenberg, front row right and Bill Boyle, SKHS teacher, to her left, enjoying a spectacular Sweet Sixteen tournament.

Each time the Pioneers posted a victory, the scramble ensued to get another ticket for the next game and get closer to the crown.

Leading cheers in the enormous Rupp Arena provided new challenges for the Pioneer cheerleaders as well, but like their hardwood counterparts, they were up to it.

Going to state always provides for great times for friends in addition to getting out of school legally. Krista Isler, Tammy Elliot, and Jill Brueckner clown around in their motel room waiting for the next Pioneer game. (Courtesy of Mary Zimmerer)

Coach Larry Miller examines his teams play from the bench. (Courtesy of Ron Coleman)

Simon Kenton High senior Sharon Nie dressed in pioneer attire at the KHSAA tournament. (Courtesy of Ron Coleman)

Billy Meier boxes out for the rebound against a highly favored Louisville Moore team in the third round final four game. (Courtesy of Ron Coleman

Billy Meier becomes a big factor as he controls the rebound vs. Louisville Moore

MOORE HIGH SCHOOL — SEMI-FINALIST
1981 STATE BASKETBALL TOURNAMENT

(Left to Right) Mgr. David Gaskin, Mgr. Don Chism, Stepfon Moran, Ernie Dickerson, Michael Anderson, Steve Duvall, Ray White, Mgr. Roby Huebner, Mgr. Daryal Thomas. Second Row: Head Coach Tom Finnegan, Jim Hubbs, Chad Moore, David Rein, Brent Curd, Manuel Forrest, Dennis Phelps, Ernie Strasser, Kenney Brown, Aubrey Pitts, Swopes Thompson.

MAYFIELD HIGH SCHOOL — SEMI-FINALIST
1981 STATE BASKETBALL TOURNAMENT

(Left to Right) Front Row: Gerome Owens, Jamie Parrott, Jon Redd, Chris Graham, Jeff Flood, Ronnie Gray, Mike Jackson, Chuck Whitnell. Second Row: Mgr. James Redd, Jesse Moss, Cary Sherrill, Charles Parrott, Steve Moffitt, Joe Prince, Blaine Wastell, Frankie Sanderson, Mark Wiman, Mgr. Vince Dawson.

The McKinley's arrive early for the game.

As Pioneer spirit became irresistibly contagious, Rupp Arena fills up with fans before the championship game setting the world record for the largest attendance to ever watch a high school basketball game. (Courtesy of Ron Coleman)

SKHS Coaches Pelphrey, Schadler and Miller studiously watch others play, waiting off court for their next contest. (Courtesy of Ron Coleman)

MASON COUNTY HIGH SCHOOL — RUNNER-UP
1981 STATE BASKETBALL TOURNAMENT

Left to Right) Front Row: Brian Littleton, Mark Hester, Mark Crawford, Terry Jackson, Gary Beiland. Second Row: Dale Liles, Kelly Middleton, Allen Feldhaus, David Orme, Tony Pollitt, Willie Feldhaus, Charlie Jackson.

Coach Miller gives a pre-game radio interview at the tournament. (Courtesy of Ron Coleman)

Coach Miller directs his team all the way to the championship. (Courtesy of Ron Coleman)

Billy Meier battles for a jump ball vs. the Virgie Eagles (Courtesy of Ron Coleman)

Troy McKinley takes aim from way outside. (Courtesy of Ron Coleman)

Dave Dixon stretches for a rebound in the Finals against Mason County. (Courtesy of Ron Coleman)

Greg Ponzer lays it up on a fast break in the state championship game. (Courtesy of Ron Coleman)

Dave Dixon shoots a lay up vs. Mason Co.

Troy McKinley shoots in the paint for the state championship. (Courtesy of Ron Coleman)

Coach Larry Miller loads the trophy to take it back home to Independence.

A triumphant Billy Meier, Troy McKinley, and Dave Medley carry the spoils of their great victory.

Troy McKinley wears the newly cut net as he receives the All-Tournament and MVP awards following the state Championship game. It was his 18th birthday.

The battle has been won and the celebration begins.

The 1981 Kentucky State Champions and Cheerleaders

Coach Miller is hoisted onto the shoulders of Alan Mullins and Billy Meier and carried into the SKHS gym in celebration of their state championship. (Courtesy of The Kentucky Enquirer*)*

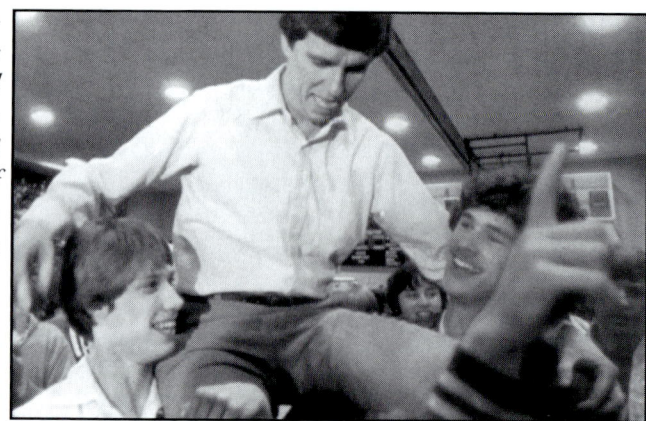

Below: *Gene Kavanough, an art student in the room during the explosion, celebrates in the car caravan from Lexington to the school following the championship. (Courtesy of* The Kentucky Enquirer*)*

Troy McKinley interviewed for the news

Greg Ponzer, in his football jersey, and Billy Meier are carried into the gym for the celebration

This 1981 yearbook's theme reflects the pioneer determination marked by their extraordinary basketball echievements. It's cover was designed by cheerleader Mary Zimmerer.

'81 PIONEER
Simon Kenton High School
Volume 44

'81
mz
NO STOPPING US NOW

David Dixon

John David Medley

Billy Meier

Sean Dougherty

270

Alan Mullins

Greg Ponzer

Troy McKinley

Troy McKinley went on to play for the University of Kentucky

book so my little girl can read it. They said Ponzer, Dougherty and Mullins couldn't hack it. They said Miller couldn't coach. They said he shouldn't play man to man. Maybe you just want to be a state champion." "I thought I was not going to live to see it," added Dale McMillen to John Salyers remark. John Salyers recalls the radio broadcast of the 1981 state tournament as 'the sport highlight of my life.'

"Thank you, God. Thank you. I love you," David Medley shouted to the ceiling as the final buzzer sounded.

"I've been hearing all year that there's no way we could win it. But I know coming in we could play with any of these schools. Our advantage tonight came on the inside game," stated Coach Miller stated regarding the win. "We were talking today about the so-called jinx in the Ninth Region. But we told ourselves there can't be any jinx on us and that we were just going to go out and do it," Troy McKinley told a throng of press now allowed to talk to him. "It took us a while to get some momentum. Once we got the ball to our big boys, we really started to roll," Greg Ponzer cheered.

Dave Dixon is proud of his performance in the finals. "Their coach was quoted in the paper: 'Well, we did a good job on McKinley, but Dixon hurt us.'"

"A tournament official told me if they voted after the championship game, there would have been three guys from Simon Kenton on the all-tournament team. I've still got one of the nets. I would have loved to have been on that all-tournament team," Dave Dixon reflects on his final game.

Unfortunately, there is no videotape of the finals game. Coach Miller asked to tape it and the KHSAA officials said they would take care of it. They never did. Allegedly, no one put the film in the cameras.

Larry Miller remembers after the game no one grabbed the basketball. He did. It remains on top of his television set in a glass case in his living room. The reporter, Gene McLean, who Larry recalled becoming upset regarding player interviews wrote the next day to begin his column:

"All week, young brash Simon Kenton coach Larry Miller did a perfect imitation of Joe Namath. Just like the former New Your Jets quarterback, who promised a Super Bowl Championship, Miller kept boasting of his unheralded, unranked team and kept promising a state championship. But just as it was with Namath, nobody really believed him. Until last night".

After the victory, Coach Miller shouted, "Amazing, amazing, amazing, we've done it. Amazing!" For anyone considering the win a fluke. "This was no fluke. You don't win four games in forty-eight hours on a fluke," pointed out Larry Miller. Every once in a while, a team can upset another. It's why a few Cinderellas make it a round or two in the NCAA tournament. But, these teams do not win four or six games and win the tournament. Simon Kenton defeated Knott County Central who beat Breathitt County, a team which lost only one game. The Pioneers defeated the #2 and #3 teams in the state, Virgie and Louisville Moore. Simon Kenton then bested Mason County who defeated the #1 team, Lexington Bryan Station. No, the Simon Kenton win resulted from a Coach and his players preparation and focus, not luck.

"I'm really proud to be part of the team that finally won it for this region. I saw a lot of people from other schools in our area down here rooting for us and I know that helped us," remarked Greg Ponzer at the time.

Troy McKinley's performance in Rupp Arena would earn him the Most Valuable Player Award for the tournament. A photograph shows Troy walking off the floor of Rupp Arena with the net around his neck, his MVP trophy in one hand and his all tournament team trophy in the other. Troy also earned a lasting place in the record books. In the ninety-year history of the tournament, Troy's one hundred and seventeen points over four games is ninth on the all time list. His sixteen field goals against Virgie is twentieth on the all time list for single games. His forty-seven field goals in the tournament places him sixth on the all time list.

Billy Meier would also make the All-Tournament Team. Dave Dixon was selected Honorable Mention All-State for the year.

Statistics for turnovers are not listed in the KHSAA record program, but it is difficult to believe if a point guard ever played every second of the four game state tournament and only had seven turnovers as Alan Mullins achieved during the tournament. This amounts to less than one turnover a half against the best teams pressing full court.

In the sixty-four year history of the tournament up to 1981, no team won the four games and the championship by a smaller total margin of victory of eleven than the 1981 Simon Kenton Pioneers. It was in fact the closest state championship in tournament history. Only the seven points over Mason County involved more than a one or two point victory.

Also, in the sixty-four year history of the tournament up to 1981, no high school game in world history was ever played before a larger crowd of 21,287 than the finals between Simon Kenton and Mason County. The same night as Simon Kenton's win, in Market Square Arena in Indianapolis, before a crowd of 17,490, Vincennes defeated Anderson at the Indiana State Championship, 54-52. The Kentucky crowd exceeded the Indiana crowd by 4,000.

Mason County would win a state championship in 2003 led by Chris Lofton who plays at the University of Tennessee. In 2006, as KHSAA honored the 25th anniversary of the Simon Kenton victory at the conclusion of third quarter of a state quarterfinal game, the Pioneer players and coaches walked to the center court as the public address announcer called their names. Half the crowd applauded, the other half sat in bothered silence. Of all teams to be playing at the time, and even trailing by a frustrating ten, was Mason County. Their fans still held a grudge. Mason County would lose the game to Owensboro Apollo.

"I'm really proud to be part of the team that finally won it for this region. I saw a lot of people from other schools in our area down here rooting for us and I know that helped us," remarked Greg Ponzer at the time.

Despite the accomplishment, Greg Ponzer offered an extremely mature comment at the time to the state press: "It was fun seeing so many people come to see good basketball. But the blast reminds me that this isn't all to life. I'm proud. But I'm a senior. I'm getting older. Life gets tougher after this."

Since the Pioneers' 1981 state tournament victory, no other team from the 9th Region or Northern Kentucky has managed to win the tournament.

CHAPTER 44
Cheerleaders at State

*"We've known each other since we were nine or ten,
Together we climbed hills and trees, Learned of love
and ABC's, skinned our hearts and skinned our
knees."*
 ~ From Terry Jack's song "Seasons In The
Sun"

The Simon Kenton cheerleaders accomplished an amazing physical, mental and emotional feat on their trip to state to cheer on the boys basketball team. The girls competed in the state cheerleading competition as a result of their winning the Ninth Region Cheerleading competition. They also competed in the Sweet Sixteen competition for the cheerleading squads for the basketball teams playing in the tournament. They also cheered their team on through four games in forty-eight hours. While the state held one of the competitions at the Memorial Coliseum, the other competition took place at the Fayette Mall. Cheering in two competitions and for four games in forty-eight hours left the girls exhausted and voiceless. They rushed from place to place. The girls competed, then rushed back to Rupp to cheer in the games. Despite the distractions and burdens upon their time, the cheerleaders earned third place in the Sweet Sixteen competition.

"We ran to and from the competitions back and forth across town. Don Schadler drove the bus for us. We used the team bus for the weekend. He hurried us over and dropped us off at Memorial Coliseum. He'd drive back to pick up the team," recalls Linda Whittenburg of the hectic schedule. "Then we rushed back to Rupp Arena. We moved constantly the whole weekend, back and forth. Due to time constraints, we ate on the bus in between our obligations."

"Ladies helped wash our uniforms because we only wore one uniform despite all the games and competitions. Shawna Cartwright and Connie Beech washed uniforms for us in between games and competitions. Joyce Miller helped, too. We were a poor bunch," Linda Whittenburg laughs.

"The girls' routine for competition mixed "Jailhouse Rock", "Old Time Rock-N-Roll", "Funky Town" and "Celebrate'. I became so sick of those songs. If I hear any of them on the radio to this day, I switch the channel. We also played Queen, 'We Are The Champions,' Linda Whittenburg recollects of them. Despite Linda's thoughts regarding the songs, the cheerleaders never tired of the songs. Greenup County, a Kentucky cheerleading powerhouse, cheered with a huge squad more common for today's cheerleading teams. The Simon Kenton team cheered with eight girls. "We all lost our voices," Tami Elliott recalls.

Bert Bennett, the Kenton County School Superintendent, mailed a letter to Ms. Whittenburg expressing more than appreciation for the awards:

"We are most happy that you finished on top for the year, but our pride is not limited by that fact alone. We have received many compliments regarding the deportment of your squad, both on and off the basketball court. They were gracious and ladylike at all times and this fact should be a continuing source of pride to you, their parents, their school, their community, and, certainly, it will be to us."

The years of rules, dedication, practice, spirit and talent paid off for the cheerleaders. "Despite having differences between them and me from time to time, we accomplished so much, all the while having so much fun. I loved them," Linda Whittenburg recalls of her squad.

The junior varsity cheerleaders for the 1980-1981 season included Joy McKinley, Laura Lauterwasser, Debbie Huesman, Sherry Mateoli, Sandy Jackson, Michele Michaels, Missy Chadwick, and Tami Kelley.

CHAPTER 45
Celebration

"Some are born great. Others earn greatness."
~ Shakespeare

As the horn sounded on the championship game, the Pioneers pulled off the impossible. They won the Kentucky State Championship. No one, except maybe Larry Miller, thought it possible. Who knows if Larry Miller really believed they would win. Only he knows. The cheerleaders, coaches, staff and fans stormed the hallowed Rupp Arena floor. Dave Medley ran to half court, kneeled down and kissed the floor. He then jumped up in the stands to embrace his mother and father in a victory bear hug.

In a sign of respect, deference and gratitude, each player crashed the stands and found his parents. "We had a good group of kids. Obviously, we also had a good group of parents," Alan Mullins explains.

"I remember my mom and dad sitting up in the corner of Rupp. A 12-foot concrete wall separated the seating sections. I remember running and hitting the wall four foot up with a foot, grabbing the rail, and jumping over the wall to reach my mom and dad. They lost their voices. They cried. It was just pandemonium," recalls Sean Dougherty of his Spiderman imitation.

"I knew how much it meant to my dad and mom, especially Dad. For all those years of bringing us down there to the tournament," Dave Medley said. "The fact we actually won the state tournament after all the years watching it as little boys seemed surreal."

Coach Miller missed out on the team's shared joy immediately after the game. "It's one of my only disappointments of the tournament. After the buzzer sounded, the television crews and press converged on me and I didn't get to enjoy it with the kids. I remember watching the kids walk around the court with the trophy. I remember Billy holding up the trophy and walking around the arena with the fans applauding. I hugged a few of them, but when they presented the trophies, I found myself talking to reporters conducting radio interviews," expresses Larry Miller with a small fragment of regret. The players, coaches, managers and ball boys, each took their turn cutting down the nets.

As the Regional victory fell on Coach Miller's birthday, the Pioneer state tournament victory coincided with Troy McKinley's birthday. The entire crowd at Rupp Arena sang happy birthday to Troy in celebration after the game. It's a birthday Troy will never forget. "The players all wanted to return back to the hotel. We stayed at the Holiday Inn North, which enjoyed an indoor pool. I avoided the party. A friend of mine, Robie Harper, a guy I coached under at Drakesboro, came up to my room to congratulate me. He sat on the Board of Control of the KHSAA at the time. He said, 'Larry, you don't want to go down to that party.' I said, 'What do you mean?' He said, 'They're doing things down there you wouldn't approve of'," Larry Miller laughs.

The fans threw most of the players into the pool, including Greg Ponzer. "I stuck the bottle of Jack Daniels in the front of my pants, and held a six pack of beer in my arms. I walked down to the party and the first person I run into is my dad, Vic Ponzer. He looked away. As far as I'm concerned, it was the biggest party in the history of man," Greg Ponzer recalls of the party. "They tossed Principal Bob Abell in the pool. Even the Coke machines found their way to the pool," laughs Greg Ponzer. Bob Abel explains he wasn't the least bit intoxicated at the party as rumored, but was so happy with the victory he couldn't stop smiling. Allegedly, the Holiday Inn asked the Pioneers to never come back.

Despite not drinking, someone handed Dave Medley a bottle of wine to hold as he walked around shirtless with only his sports coat and shorts on. Don Turney and Tom Blank from Covington Catholic gave him the bottle. The Pioneers old 'enemies' drove to Lexington to cheer the Pioneers on and party with their foes. Dave Medley avoided being thrown into the pool and "probably went to bed a little earlier than anyone else," Dave recalls.

Alan Mullins also avoided the pool, but received an odd request of a fan. "Jim Moore, my best friend through most of high school, had an older sister. I walked in the Holidome and saw a sea of people. Bodies everywhere. Jimmy's sister grabbed me, stuck a marker in my hand and said, 'come on, you've got to sign this.' 'Sign what?' I replied. She then raised her shirt up. I thought well, I guess this is what you have to do when you win a State Championship," Alan laughs.

Larry Miller excused the drinking as part of the times and place. "People are different. Northern Kentucky folks never thought anything about drinking. It wasn't a big deal then. I'm sure Billy Meier drank beer. Ponzer's dad ran a bar. McKinley was Baptist and I'm sure he never drank. I never saw Dave Medley take a drink, but he probably would. We'd have our coaches meetings in bars. They'd have open bar. The Carrollton bus crash later changed everyone's mind set. But at that time, people didn't think twice about drinking and driving back then. It was wrong, but it happened. Plus the parents brought the beer into the party. They claim Greg Ponzer sat at a table by the pool and people gave him beer which he stacked up," Larry Miller rationalizes. Years later in 1988, a drunk driver crossed the median on Interstate I-71 near Carroll County, Kentucky and hit head on a school bus of children returning from a Sunday trip to an amusement park. The crash killed twenty-seven and injured thirty-four severely, some with permanent disfigurement from burn injuries. Only sixteen escaped injury. The attitude in Kentucky toward drinking and driving changed forever.

Someone offered Billy Meier a bath tub of beer at the party. "After we won the tournament, we came back to the hotel. They're throwing players in the pool. They threw me in the pool too. I'm walking up soaking wet to my room to change. Dave Coppage from Coppage Construction, real good buddies with my dad, always watched the state tournament. The Coppages stayed in a room at the Holidome. Dave saw me walking down the hall. He grabbed me and told me great game. And he says, 'you want a beer'. And I said, 'well, heck yeah, I'll take one.' I walk in his hotel room and his bathtub is nothing but ice and beer. I grabbed one and opened it up. He encouraged me, 'get a couple, get a couple.' I start shoving them in my shirt. I stuck them in my pockets. I planned on taking them to Greg and Sean. I put them in my front pockets, in my back pockets and under my arms. I walk out with a 12-pack. After I leave, I'm trying to reach my room so nobody can see me. I run into Dave Schadler. He pops out of the coaches' door. He says, 'come in here, Coach wants to talk to you'. I walk in and I'm standing there with beers in my hands, beers in my pockets, beers in my shirt, beers everywhere. Coach Miller is talking to me about statistics. He tells me I played great. He didn't say anything about the beers. I walked out and walked down to the room. Dave Schadler caught me a few minutes later and he says, 'you know Miller asked me, Dave, are the boys drinking?'" Billy Meier laughs.

Andy Burns appeared for the victory party at the Holiday Inn. "In essence, once they beat us, we became big fans of Simon Kenton. I attended the state tournament and watched every game. We actually cheered for Simon Kenton. We drove over to the Holiday Inn Dome after the game to celebrate with them. What a magical moment for Simon Kenton. A magic moment for the Ninth Region," Andy Burns explains.

"The cheerleaders and players used the same bus to travel to and from everywhere on the weekend. Imagine, representing the entire region, and they send only one bus. I don't think anyone sat long the entire trip back. I also never got so sick of hearing the song 'Celebration'," Linda Whittenburg recalls of the bus ride home on Sunday. The weather for Sunday, March 22, 1981 for Northern Kentucky called for rain and a temperature as low as 35.

The bus traveled through Walton on the way back to Simon Kenton. Billy Meier recalls "beer bottles and rocks" being thrown at the bus. "There was stuff hitting the bus all the way through there," Billy Meier recalls of the gauntlet.

"The adrenaline still flowed. We played the same song "Celebration" over and over again. The caravan of 100 to 150 cars followed the bus. I also remember the weather wasn't that great," Sean Dougherty remembers of the caravan.

"The police picked us up at the Grant County line on I-75. They led the way to the Walton exit. We drove through Nicholson and up to the school. People stood on the side of the road holding signs. It was unbelievable. We reached the gym and you couldn't have packed another soul in the gym. The superintendent gave a nice speech. Others talked. I spoke a little bit," Coach Miller recalls.

Coach Miller walked to the microphone to chants of 'Mil-ler, Mil-ler, Mil-ler.' He told the crowd, "We played the best basketball of the year, and I thought we had the best player in the state." The crowd chanted, "Big Mac" to thunderous applause. The Coach's remarks drew the loudest applause. Regarding Manuel Forrest, the Coach said "He is phenomenal, but I don't know if he could play for us." Fans hoisted each player up and carried them into the gym as Roman conquering heros. Randall Wagner picked up and carried in Alan Mullins. Gene Kavanaugh was one of the players who carried in Billy Meier. Alan Mullins and Billy Meier carried Larry Miller into the gym. Greg Ponzer wore his #5 football jersey as he was carried in. Gene Kavanaugh couldn't control his excitement: "The whole experience of the explosion knocked us all down. We all felt sorry for ourselves. We needed something to pick us up. The whole town got behind this team," Gene yelled. When Dave Dixon spoke to the crowd, he stumbled on his words, unable to express his adulation. He finally simply stated: "There are no words to express it. It's just a feeling inside of you and that feeling is so great." Alan Mullins told the crowd: "If you feel the way I do right now, this is probably the best moment of your life. This is great. I hope it lasts forever." Randall Wagner never received the microphone, but he told the local press: "We've had death and dislocation. We've laughed and we've cried. Now we're going to really celebrate. This community has been so down from what's happened that this is just the greatest thing in the world," reiterated Randall Wagner after the victory.

"I really thought coming into the tournament we had a legitimate chance of winning," said Larry Miller at the time. "Not very many people agreed with me. We didn't receive much publicity outside the Ninth Region, so basketball fans down state didn't know anything about us. They know now. We have a great basketball team and I truly believed in my heart we were going to win."

"It was a spirit of caring about others which really helped pull it off. During the course of the year, many made sure the kids knew how special they were. They rose to the occasion. For Simon Kenton to come back and celebrate a new building, and then to celebrate a state basketball championship is special," said Neil Stieglemeyer of the win.

Mike Tolliver believed after the Walton game fate chased Simon Kenton. "I remember saying many times, it was the worst of times and the best of times. Through the loss of life and many injuries to the rebuilding. I remember everyone trying to make Simon Kenton whole again as best it could be. I believe we always thought basketball helped move us in the direction of having our own identity again. We felt violated after the explosion. The state championship helped pull it back together again," Mike Tolliver reflects.

Both the City of Independence and Kenton County passed proclamations honoring the Pioneers.The City of Independence made eight signs for every major road entering Independence, blue with white letters:

"Welcome to the City of Independence.
  Home of the Simon Kenton Pioneers.
1981 Kentucky State Basketball Champs."

Enthusiastic fans have confiscated every one of the signs. They hang as trophies on walls in homes somewhere. Considering new signs would suffer the same fate, the City hasn't bothered to replace them.

Bob Abel recalls Jake Menefee spent the state tournament in the hospital. Bob recalls after Larry Miller spoke at a Rotary meeting after the championship, Bob, Larry and Bert Bennett stopped at the hospital to visit Jake. Bob remembers Jake apologizing to Larry for his threats and conduct.

On the Monday after the win, Simon Kenton High School answered their phones, "Simon Kenton, State Champs, may I help you?" The school held a student body celebration later during the school for those few who may have missed the Sunday after celebration.

Mark Weidner drew a color print commemorating the state victory. It's a photo of each of the seven players and Coach Miller. It hangs in the Simon Kenton trophy case behind the trophy. Their jersey's hang close by and retired: McKinley - 40, Mullins - 12, Dougherty - 11, Meier - 41, Ponzer - 5, Dixon - 32 and Medley - 35. The coaches and players are deservingly forever immortalized in the Simon Kenton community.

CHAPTER 46
Complete Athletes

"If you aim at nothing, you'll hit it every time."
~ Unknown

The varsity basketball players at Simon Kenton High School excelled beyond the hardwood court. A review of their other athletic pursuits aids an understanding of why they became state champions in basketball.

Billy Meier starred in baseball and football. The Simon Kenton baseball coach, Coach Finn, slotted the big right hander as his number one starter. Billy threw over 90 mph. Billy played college baseball at Thomas More College. He also played the outfield. In football, Billy started at tight end on offense and defensive end on defense. He also won the job as placekicker. Imagine breaking the stereotype of a kicker at six foot six. Billy won Honorable Mention by *The Enquirer* for All Region for placekicker. *The Enquirer* selected him Second Team Tight End. *The Kentucky Post* named him First TeamTight End. *The Courier Journal* chose him Honorable Mention State for Tight End. Billy still preferred baseball to basketball. He attended Thomas More College on a basketball scholarship so he could also play baseball for them.

Sean Dougherty recalls playing baseball all summer as a youngster, not basketball. He played on baseball teams in the local area called boosters. All seven varsity basketball players played Taylor Mill Booster baseball in the summer. Sean not only played second base on the Simon Kenton baseball team, he started cornerback on the football team and ran track. His senior year, he won the 100% Runner Award. He also won the School Principal's Award for student/athlete. His senior year, he started at second base, started at cornerback and won with Alan Mullins, Dave Dixon and Jimmy Moore the 9th Region 1600 meter relay. They also set the school record. In football, Sean won the Coaches Award.

Greg Ponzer started at shortstop for the baseball team. As all baseball fans know, the shortstop is always one of the best athletes on the team. Greg started at safety in football where he led the team his senior year in interceptions, including a 100-yard interception return for a touchdown. He received the team's Most Valuable Defensive Back Award. He received the Captain's Award and was named Second Team All Region by *The Enquirer*. *The Kentucky Post* chose him First Team. He was selected Honorable Mention All-State by the *The Courier Journal*. He won the senior superlative Most Athletic as voted by his classmates.

Troy McKinley focused on basketball and tennis. Besides being the undisputed star on the basketball team, Troy played as the number one seed on the Pioneer tennis team. He lettered three years in tennis. His height proved valuable in launching a serve or playing the net. His senior year, rules forced Troy to choose not to play tennis because he played in basketball all-star games.

Dave Dixon played baseball growing up. In high school, he didn't play baseball or football, but starred in track. He won the Ninth Region 1600 meter relay with Sean Dougherty, Alan Mullins and Jimmy Moore. He also won the Ninth Region title as the best triple jumper and long jumper. He placed fourth in the Region with the quarter mile. He placed third in the state with the long jump. The track coach chose him as MVP. He also ran cross-country.

"When we competed in the Covington Catholic Invitational. I didn't know it, but I'm running against the best quarter-miler in the region, and we're shoulder to shoulder coming around the last curve. I'm a determined guy and I'm like leaning forward, cranking my legs as hard as they'd go. I thought, he's going to pass me. So I start leaning forward a little bit more. He's right on my shoulder. I lean forward a little bit more. I ended up down face first, just flat on the track," Dave Dixon laughs.

Alan Mullins played baseball, football and ran track. He won the "Most Improved Runner" Award from the track coach. In the Region, Alan won the 100 meters and placed second in 200 meters. Bottom line - he was the fastest runner in Northern Kentucky. The basketball team had a point guard who was the fastest player in the Region. Not bad. As a junior, Alan started at tailback for the football team where he led the team in rushing. His junior year, Alan received the school's Most Valuable Offensive Back Award, scored 19 touchdowns, finished fifth in the Ninth Region in rushing at 1,192 yards. *The Enquirer* newspaper named him Honorable Mention All Region. *The Kentucky Post* selected him Second Team. Alan also won the School's "I Dare You Award" for determination.

When Alan Mullins played basketball at Simon Kenton the next year, he recalls the anticlimactic nature of the year. He knew it would be a different season with no chance for a repeat. Alan earned a football scholarship to Western Kentucky University so he didn't concern himself with a future basketball career. He would play. Have fun. Move on. He would start as a sophomore as a receiver and be the most valuable offensive player at Western Kentucky. When he graduated, he would be second leading receiver in school history. At an open try-out in Atlanta, Alan received a contract with Winnipeg of the Canadian Football League. He survived to the last cut.

Dave Medley played baseball and football. However, he passed up football his senior year to play of all things for a "jock," the tuba in the marching band. It probably explains though why Dave Medley won the senior superlative "Most Talented" as voted by his classmates.

Billy Meier received a baseball scholarship to Thomas More College. (The college didn't offer basketball scholarships at the time.) Dave Dixon received a scholarship for basketball at Eastern Kentucky University. Troy McKinley received a basketball scholarship to the University of Kentucky. Greg Ponzer received a football scholarship to Hanover College in Indiana. Alan Mullins received a football scholarship to Western Kentucky University. Dave Medley received an academic scholarship to Western Kentucky University. Although he did not receive a scholarship, Sean Dougherty attended Northern Kentucky University.

Despite these extensive athletic accomplishments, the team will still always be remembered for their basketball accomplishments.

Billy Meier lettered in basketball for three years. He made the All State Tournament team in 1981. He made the 1981 Ninth Region All Tournament team in 1981. The *Courier-Journal* chose him Honorable Mention All-State in 1981. Like Billy Meier, Dave Dixon was a three year letterman and a Honorable Mention All State Team by the *Courier-Journal* in1981. Also in 1981, he was selected to the NKAC First Team, All Region All Tournament Team, Connor Invitational Team and Newport Catholic Invitational Team. Dave Dixon still holds the single season school record with Troy McKinley of 62.3% field goal percentage. His 45 points is also still a single game record for the school.

Troy McKinley is the most decorated basketball player in Simon Kenton's long history. He made all the teams Dave Dixon made and then a few more. In 1981, he made All-State First Team. He made All-Region, 1980 and 1981. He made All-District in 1979, 1980 and 1981. In 1981, the *Kentucky Post* and *Kentucky Enquirer* chose him Outstanding Player in Northern

Kentucky. He won the Most Valuable Player for the State Tournament. In an unprecendented feat, Troy led the region in field goal percentage, points average a game and free throw percentage in 1981.

CHAPTER 47
Quitting

"Be the hammer, never the nail."
~ Unknown

Coach Miller remained at Simon Kenton one more year after the championship season, but never coached the Pioneers again.

"We'd been dealing with the Board of Education and the superintendent for two or three years over coaching salaries. I'd completed research with other coaches, Afterkirk over at Dixie and Jim Mitchell at Scott. We all received the same salary, fourteen hundred dollars a year for head coach. The Boone County's freshman coach made more. Everybody received more than us, so we asked for a raise. The response was no. If you don't like it, go somewhere else. They didn't care," explains Larry Miller of the salary issue.

"We had a contract then like a union contract. Our education group met with them and negotiated. I couldn't convince them to push for any more money either."

"The end of June, the fiscal year, it came out, Afterkirk, Mitchell and I received a $70 raise."

"So I walked in with my resignation to Mr. Bennett, the superintendent. I explained to him what it was and he said, 'What if I go to the board and ask for more money for you?' I said, 'Would you actually do that?' 'Well, I'll have to think about it.' Then I said, 'Well, would the board actually give me more?' 'Well, I don't know.' I said, 'Well, that's what I thought.' I said, 'You can just keep my resignation.'

"Bert even tried to keep me from landing other jobs later. He told stories I demanded a raise. I didn't demand anything. When I didn't receive what I thought was just, I just said, I don't want to work here anymore, which I thought was fair. I didn't demand anything to stay."

Simon Kenton High School today (Courtesy of the author)

Simon Kenton High School Gym today. (Courtesy of the author)

289

The author, Eric Deters, and his wife, the former Mary Zimmerer to whom this book is dedicated.

The four cheerleaders from 1981 at their 25th class reunion in 2006. Left to right: Mary Zimmerer, Krista Isler, Tami Elliot and Jill Brueckner.

Robert W. Williams gravesite (Courtesy of the author)

The firehouse in Independence today and just as it appeared in 1980. (Courtesy of the author)

"Downtown" Independence today. The only addition since 1980-81 visible is the traffic light. (Courtesy of the author)

Ponzer's Tavern today. Note the "For Sale" sign in front. (Courtesy of the author)

Boone County's Gym today. Site of the famous Walton Verona game. (Courtesy of the author)

Current photo of 1980-81 SKHS cheerleaders today: **Front***: Linda Whittenburg.* **First Row***(left to right): Pam Meenoch, Krista Isler, Jill Brueckner, and Mary Zimmerer, (varsity cheerleaders).* **Second Row***: Lori Lautterwasser, Tami Kelley, Missy Chadwick, Deneen Rimer (varsity) Debbie Huesman, (junior varsity cheerleaders).*

The SKHS Coaches and players March, 2006 at the 25th anniversary of their championship victory in Rupp Arena. **Front Row** *(left to right): Tony Brosky, Sean Dougherty, Alan Mullins, Greg Ponzer and Coach Pelfry.* **Second Row**: *Coach Schadler, Larry Callahan, Dave Dixon, Tim Downs, Troy McKinley, Dave Medley, Billy Meier, and Coach Larry Miller. (Courtesy of the Kentucky High School Athletic Association)*

Dave Dixon and Jill Bruckner (The last page of the 1981 yearbook)

"I stayed on as a teacher at Simon Kenton. I taught over at Northern Kentucky University. I taught math at night in the Math Department. I still taught in the day at Simon Kenton. I only made $1,400 coaching basketball. At Northern teaching two classes, three hours, two nights a week – I made $2,000. It wasn't a lot of money, but it was only two nights a week, so I made more money. Joyce's dad was ill and she wanted to return closer to here. We received other opportunities, but Meade County was a nice job. I became head coach and math teacher at Meade the next year, the 1982-1983 school year."

The coach of Mason County received a new car for finishing second in the State Tournament. Larry Miller received a $70 raise and a hand towel with his name embroidered on it. Bill Pelfrey "hated to see it happen." Pelfrey would turn down Coach Miller's job to go into administration. Pelfrey became the assistant principal at Simon Kenton High School in 1983.

"If Larry stays at Simon Kenton, Scott Draud goes to Simon Kenton. (Scott Draud was a great player in the 1980's who played college basketball at Vanderbilt.) Simon Kenton had Darren Moore, who ended up being a decent high school player and could have been a great one. If Larry had stayed at Simon Kenton, they'd have been a dominating team," Dave Schadler believes.

"Kenton County had no vision. They didn't know what was important. Those guys all took something from Larry. Maybe from me, too, but I think especially from Larry. Larry Miller's not a politician. Larry Miller could never be a superintendent, regardless how smart he is and regardless of his leadership skills, because he's the kind of guy that will say, 'This is wrong, I'm not going to do it.' I was the same way," Dave Schadler recalls of the Miller resignation.

"Larry can be hardheaded, just as hardheaded as you can be, even about stupid stuff. The raise, he wasn't being stupid about. Joyce could tell him and I could tell him at times, 'This is ridiculous, back off,' and he would do it. But I never told him to back off on the raise because he was right," Dave Schadler explains of the raise issue.

Despite Larry Miller's recommendation, Dave Schadler was passed over for the head coaching job at Simon Kenton. The Board gave the position to Donnie McFarland. Dave Schadler tried to stay on as an assistant before quitting.

On July 24, 1982, the friends who loved them so much, his fellow teachers, threw a going away party for Joyce and Larry Miller at Mike and Faye Collins home. A winner left Independence only returning for the anniversaries of his team.

CHAPTER 48

The Career of Troy McKinley

"One crowded hour with a glorious life is worth an age without a name."
~ Colonel William Travis at the Alamo

Troy McKinley remarkably led the Ninth Region in 1980-1981 in scoring average, field goal percentage and free throw percentage. He also finished fifth in rebounds. "People talked about how Troy could score, but Troy was truly a remarkable passer," Dave Schadler recalls. During the Walton-Verona District and Louisville Moore games, McKinley proved his worth as a passer.

Troy remembers his first basketball team coached by Bob Wells. The team played games at Taylor Mill Elementary School as part of the Taylor Mill Booster youth sports program. "I thought we were pretty good. The scores were like 18 to 2 and 18 to 10. I just wanted to play. The score didn't matter at that age," Troy remembers. Troy would play on the same basketball and baseball team coached by Bob Wells with Sean Dougherty and Bob's son, Jeff, who later focused on wrestling at Simon Kenton.

"They played their first game at Taylor Mill School. They were only seven years old. They played with a full-sized basketball and ten-foot rims. We walked in and I'll never forget it. The score was four to two on the game before us. I looked up and they had four lights lit on the clock. I told Mary somebody forgot to clear the lights. We're three quarters early. The buzzer went off. I thought it was the end of the first quarter, but the game was over. Final score four to two," Bones laughs.

"At any rate, we put our team out there. Bob Wells coached them. He possessed the good sense to teach them basic fundamentals. They wouldn't double dribble. Kids were allowed to put the ball under their arm. The score was eight to two and Troy had all eight points. After the game, we walked to the car."

"Mary's crying and carrying on, and I asked, 'What's wrong?' She said, 'Did you hear what these women were saying about Troy? Big overgrown blond-haired kid. Said he's got to be in the fifth grade.' He was taller than everybody."

"I told Mary I don't know what lies ahead, but if he has any talent at all, you're going to hear those remarks. You have to let it roll off you. The next game, we won sixteen to four, and Troy scored fourteen points. His basketball career began there," Bones explains.

"Troy is an awesome player. He was champion material from the time we played in the Taylor Mill Boosters. My team played against Troy's team and they beat us every daggone year," Dave Dixon remembers of playing against Troy McKinley.

As far as Troy McKinley remembers, he loved playing basketball, but he never displayed flash. "Friends asked me, 'How many points did you average your senior year?' I said, 'twenty-five'. 'How many times did you shoot a game?' I said, 'Not very many.' 'What do you mean not very many?' I said, 'I just didn't shoot very many. We had a good team. I didn't have to shoot much'," Troy recalls of his shooting.

"I would have to check my most attempts in a game. It would be interesting to know. I wanted to shoot, but I didn't want to be labeled a ball hog. I didn't want that reputation. I would much rather win than to be called a ball hog. I believe my field goal percentage was 62 percent," Troy reflects of his accuracy. A review of all the games played in the 1980-1981 season and post-season reflect Troy never had a <u>single</u> off night. This is a rarity for a scorer in basketball.

"Reflecting on the scores from high school, I never forget we didn't have the three-pointer. Our junior year, we scored 101 points against a team without three-pointers. Many of those games were in the 70s. In today's game, even with the three-pointer, these high school games have high scores in the 50s," Troy points out. Bones McKinley remembers half of Troy's shots falling beyond the now three-point arc. "We were fast and the guards made steals, but it's just amazing to me the amount of points we scored," Troy recalls of the scores.

Troy McKinley's college recruitment followed an interesting route. "ESPN just began. We rarely saw a college basketball game on television. We only had four channels. A lot of these schools I didn't know where they were or anything about them," Troy recalls of college recruitment.

"I remember receiving a poster from Vanderbilt University and thought 'nice gym.' But I didn't want to go there. I've never even heard of Vanderbilt."

"After my senior year, Vanderbilt fired their coach. C. M. Newton was the athletic director. Coach Richard Schmidt hopped a plane one afternoon to visit me here in Independence."

Coach Miller remembers sending a tape of Troy McKinley to the University of Kentucky and not hearing anything back from the University. The day after the state championship, Troy McKinley became a University of Kentucky recruit.

"My buddies and I were out in my yard shooting basketball. Dad called me to the phone. He yelled, 'Coach Hall's on the phone.' I said, 'Yeah, whatever.' 'No, seriously, he's on the phone.' I'm like, 'No, he's not'," Troy remembers of the call.

Bones remembers the shock from Coach Hall to know Troy was already shooting basketball the day after the championship.

"They finally convinced me to come in the house and sure enough, Coach Hall from University of Kentucky was on the phone. He told me he watched me have a good state tournament. He told me how great a player he thought I was and all the recruit talk."

"The conversation lasted a few minutes. He asked me to visit. I also remember Coach Miller becoming angry at me because I wouldn't fly to Kansas for a visit," Troy recalls. Also, Joey Meyer from DePaul called Coach Miller, but Troy said, 'No thanks,' Larry Miller remembers. "Coach Miller told us before our senior year to write down a hundred colleges we'd like to attend. I said, 'What a hundred colleges?' I didn't even know ten," Troy laughs of the suggestion. "So I asked why?," Coach said, 'Because I will take videotape of you and send to every college you chose.' So he was very helpful. My list probably came to 12 or 15," Troy recalls of his Coach's offer.

Dave Schadler thought Troy should attend Western Kentucky and play for Clem Haskins. So why University of Kentucky? "Just too irresistible. I really liked Western. Because Louisville won the national championship, I attended Louisville's national championship banquet at Coach Crum's request. It was my recruiting visit there. I then visited Western and loved it. Came home. I announced to my parents I'm going to Western. Then I visited Kentucky. I guess it was just too irresistible, being Kentucky," Troy explains of his college choice.

On August 20, 1981, Troy McKinley signed his letter of intent to play at the University of Kentucky. Coach Joe B. Hall and Assistant Coach Joe

Dean both attended the signing. "Troy is an unusual player in that he is such an outstanding shooter," Coach Hall said at the time. "Not since Tom Parker have I seen such a fine shooter in high school. His great shooting ability is much needed on our team."

'He is an outstanding young man with fine character. He is an A student and a member of the National Honor Society. We're very pleased to have the state tournament's most valuable player coming to Kentucky. At 6-5½ , he is small for the forward position, but he has excellent work habits, and we believe he will work hard to elevate all phases of his game,' explained Coach Hall of his new recruit.

"I'm very excited and happy. I'll be playing the next four years at UK," McKinley said at the signing. "I want to thank the other colleges for showing interest in me - my parents, my teammates and my coaches for making it all possible. "I dreamed about playing for UK all my life. They've got good players, a beautiful campus and I really like Coach Hall."

"Unfortunately, I was definitely a tweener. The year I graduated from college, '85-'86, they instituted the three-pointer. Coach Hall focused on the inside game. I understood that from high school. In college, that game hurt me. Growing up, all those years, I never handled the ball. In college, I'm not tall enough to play forward. All the other forwards are six-nine and I'm six-five. I was not fast enough to play guard. No ball handling skills to play shooting guard and not tall enough to play forward," Troy explained about his college status.

"Kentucky shot 13 percent in the Final Four in Seattle against Georgetown. Paul Andrews and I, another good shooter who won the State Tournament the year after Simon Kenton, were sitting on the end of the bench and thought why doesn't Coach put us in. We could make one," Troy laughs.

"Georgetown not only had Patrick Ewing, they had this bald-headed player who was the best defensive player I've ever seen in my life. I think we were intimidated. They also had Patrick Ewing. He was massive and great. I always tell people, hey, I played against Michael Jordan at North Carolina. I didn't play, but I was there. I watched him dunk over everybody," Troy laughs.

From Troy's first game as a Taylor Mill Booster to his first away game at University of Kentucky, his mother and father never missed a single game. From 1938 to 1981, Troy and Dave Dixon were only the fifth and sixth basketball players to ever graduate from Simon Kenton and attend college on a basketball scholarship and remain four years. Shirley Elliott, Dave's uncle, was another at Tennessee Chattanooga.

Dave Dixon sums up Troy's shooting ability better than anyone with a simple story. "You can imagine, growing up with Troy and playing with him all those years, how many games of horse we played. We lived close by. We played a lot of summer basketball together, but I never remember winning a single game of horse against him. He is an awesome pure shooter. I had the quickness and athletic skills, but he was the shooter, a pure shooter. He's fantastic," Dixon states with admiration.

Another legend of Troy McKinley relating to horse is that Rick Pitino, during the time he coached Providence, allegedly bragged at a clinic, no one could beat him in horse, and Troy McKinley accepted the challenge and won.

CHAPTER 49
Where are They Now

"History will be good to me because I am going to write it."
~ Churchill

Larry Miller remains proudly and happily married to Joyce Thomas. Young Bart, three at the time of the 1981 state championship, became a first team all state player in Kentucky in high school and earned a full basketball scholarship to Marquette University in Wisconsin. Bart obtained a graduate degree at MIT and is an engineer in Atlanta, Georgia. He's six foot five, an inch taller than his father. The Miller's daughter Amanda stands five ten and plays at the University of Missouri - St. Louis. She's the third all-time scorer for Central Hardin High School near the Miller's home and is the school's all-time leading rebounder.

Since 1996, Larry worked as the assistant principal at Central Hardin High School. In 2000, a drunk driver hit his car T-boned at an intersection and nearly killed him. The accident leaves him with severe arthritis. His toleration of alcohol has changed with the times and his near untimely death.

Larry comes across Greg Ponzer at the state tournament games. Both attend every year. Bart was the same age as Troy's younger brother Jeff, and Larry caught up with Troy McKinley at Jeff's wedding. Larry also attends reunions of the team at Simon Kenton.

Troy McKinley has returned to school to obtain a teacher's certification. He plans to teach physical education. He's married to Donna Voges whom he dated during the state championship season. She was a junior in 1981 at Simon Kenton and also played basketball. The McKinleys have three children. A former ICU and trauma nurse at University of Kentucky, Donna is now a clinical educator for GlaxoSmithKlein. Troy became a Lexington,

303

Kentucky police officer after he graduated from the University of Kentucky. He retired after injuring his back in a pursuit chase on foot. Troy even tried his luck with a Chinese Restaurant - "Wok On In" in Highland Heights, Kentucky. In 2004, Troy coached the Boone County High School freshman boys. He placed Walton-Verona down as his first choice for student teaching since he lives in the area. "They told me they wouldn't let me come over there," Troy laughs. When asked about a future coaching basketball, he claims: "No, I'm just not into it." He would prefer to coach tennis and golf.

Sean Dougherty married his high school girlfriend from the 1981 basketball season, Sandy Whaley. They married after graduation. Sean won the principal award for outstanding student athlete, but his marriage would not be a joyful one. Shortly after the state tournament, Sean learned Sandy carried his child. But for the pregnancy, neither planned to marry. Sean believed marriage was the "right thing to do." "My mom was fine, but my dad didn't talk to me for three weeks," Sean recalls of his decision to marry.

Sean's marriage to Sandy would end in divorce. However, their daughter Jessica would be a basketball and softball star at Simon Kenton. Jessica played college softball at Northern Kentucky University. Now married, Jessica has given Sean a grandchild. As it happens many times in life, it all works out.

Sean married again. Despite a second divorce, his son Ryan from the marriage is an academic star. The third time has been a charm for Sean. He and his wife, Amy, have a son, Kyle. They live in Petersburg, Kentucky in Boone County. She works for Delta Airlines. Sean works at United Parcel Service where he holds a significant sales position.

Greg Ponzer and his wife, Debbie have four children. They live together in Independence, Kentucky less than two miles from Simon Kenton High School on the same street the Medleys lived. After starring at Hanover College in Indiana on a football scholarship where he also received a business administration degree, Greg accepted a job for Ashland Oil Company, Kentucky's largest corporation. Greg still works for Ashland as a sales representative. Greg would be the first person in the Ponzer family to attend college. Greg's son, Payton, ironically now plays basketball at Walton-Verona High School.

Billy Meier is married to Shelley Mullins. Each of them has a child from a prior marriage, Billy and Cody, and together they have a daughter, Madison. Billy works for Martin Homes Construction. He lives in Independence, a mile from Simon Kenton High School. At the end of Billy Meier's sophomore season at Thomas More College where he attended on a basketball scholarship and played basketball, he suffered a back injury after the driver of the team bus fell asleep, resulting in a crash. His injuries would end a storied athletic career.

Dave Dixon and his wife, Angela and they have two children, Mary and Adam. Dave works in marketing at Siemens Energy Automation. He graduated from Eastern Kentucky University where he played basketball on a scholarship. He obtained a degree in computer science with minors in business and math. He earned his MBA from Thomas More in 1998.

Dave Medley is divorced with two children, Ryan Elizabeth and Olivia Claire. He is the promotion and marketing manager for WKYT, a CBS affiliate in Lexington, Kentucky. He started out pre-dental on an academic scholarship at Western Kentucky University before finishing in broadcasting. He and Alan Mullins both attended Western Kentucky during the same years.

Alan Mullins is divorced with one son, Tate. Alan was a school psychologist at Boone County High School before landing the head basketball coach position for boy's varsity at Pyle High School. He graduated from Western Kentucky University on a football scholarship. He missed the final cut to make a professional Canadian Football League team. Alan worked as a school psychologist at Heath High School in McCracken County in Western Kentucky when Michael Carneal shot and killed three students in 1997. Alan returned to Northern Kentucky in 1998.

Linda Whittenburg would teach at Simon Kenton until 1990. After her years at Simon Kenton, Linda taught three years at the School for Creative and Performing Arts in downtown Cincinnati. The founder of the school, Bill Dickinson, hired her. She left when he departed. She now owns her own business, Cabin Arts, in Burlington, Kentucky in Boone County. Cabin Arts is a full-service quilt shop with quilt supplies, notions, patterns and fabric. Cabin Arts also teaches quilting courses. Cabin Arts is a restored 1850's log cabin. Her husband, Dan, owns a business next door, Superior Imports.

Tami Elliott tried out for the University of Kentucky cheerleading squad. She made it to the final cut, but came up short to make the team. She faults her last minute decision to try out. Tami received her nursing in psychology degree at the University of Kentucky and currently works as a school nurse in central Kentucky. Divorced, she lives in Paris, Kentucky with her 13-year-old daughter, Bria.

Mary Zimmerer attended Ringling School of Art in Sarasota, Florida, one of the finest art schools in the country. She finished seventh in her graduating class at Simon Kenton. She pursued a career as a graphic designer in

Florida and Cincinnati, Ohio. She is married to me, the author, Eric Deters. Together, we have six children. She has three sons, Cory, 18, Cole and Cameron, 15-year-old twins. Cory attends Northern Kentucky University. Cole and Cameron attend Scott High School. I have three children, Erica, 17, Charlie Ann, 16, and Parker 14. Erica and Charlie Ann attend Simon Kenton. Charlie Ann is a cheerleader. Erica is an honor student. Parker attends Summit Middle School where he plays football and basketball. Mary not only cares for the six children; she quilts and pursues other artistic endeavors. I brag I'm married to a beautiful and sweet 'Martha Stewart'.

Jill Brueckner is married to Keb Bright and has twin boys, Chase and Logan. She lives in the same house on Pelly Road in Independence where she grew up next to Mary Zimmerer. Jill obtained her nursing degree and works as a nurse at a Cincinnati hospital.

Krista Isler lived in Nashville, Tennessee with her daughter before moving back this year to Northern Kentucky. She works in sales with Drees Homes.

Pam Meenach is married to Gary Schneider. They live in Independence a couple of miles from Simon Kenton. They have four children, Grant, Jake, Ben and Jessica. Pam is Vice President of Atkins Company. She recalls her senior year, after the 1981 season, as being completely anti-climatic and boring.

Tonda Hignite lives in Florida. She runs her own dance studio. For her own reasons, Tonda refused repeated requests for an interview.

Deneen Reimer is married to Todd Wolsing. They have two children, McKaila and Alex. They live in Taylor Mill, Kentucky, a town adjacent to Simon Kenton. Deneen is a teacher at Ft. Wright Elementary School in Kenton County.

For her own reasons, Charlotte Woods refused repeated requests for an interview.

After Larry Miller resigned his position as head coach, Coach Schadler applied for the job. He didn't get it. The Athletic Director, Joe Stark, coached Dave in high school and Dave thought Joe could have gotten Dave the job if Joe wanted. It disappointed Dave not to receive the opportunity. He left Simon Kenton, but later returned as the assistant principal. Dave later received his Doctorate in Educational Administration at the University of Kentucky.

"I was assistant principal for five years. Mike Tolliver allowed me to be involved in the basketball program. I hired Dan Trame. Trame got things going again. I felt like I was a part of that. We got the tradition going again. I was offered the principal's job at Williamstown, which is a little independent school in Grant County. I knew Mike wasn't going anywhere so I took that job. I was the principal there for eight years," Dave Schadler said of his career path.

Manuel Forrest attended the University of Louisville and played for Denny Crum. He wrecked his knee and never made it to the NBA. He played pro basketball in Argentina where he still lives.

Andy Burns and his wife, Kennon, have two children, Cameron 14 and Drew 10. His wife received eleven high school letters and is in her high school Hall of Fame. She swam competitively at Miami University in Oxford, Ohio. Andy attended Northern Kentucky University on a basketball scholarship. He would play against Dave Dixon again who played at Eastern Kentucky University.

Andy Burns did his student teaching at Simon Kenton High School with Tim Moore in 1986. Andy's a project manager for a heavy hauler rigging company moving transformers for utility companies.

Sandy Williams, Robert's mother, and Tracy, his sister, moved to Chicago where they live.

The 1981 graduating class held commencement exercises in the new gymnasium. It was the first time graduation had been in the school in eleven years. The class overcame obstacles never before faced by their school or almost any school. Russ Hilmandolar, the valedictorian, addressed his class. He used the word "phenomenal" in his speech as a tribute to Coach Miller who Russ claims used the word "phenomenal" all year to describe the basketball team. Diane Schadler spoke to the class as the Class President. She focused on how her class accomplished so many firsts. The Class of 1981 proudly walked out of their graduation to "Celebration."

In 1995, Ron Dennis's son, Billy made it to the state tournament with Simon Kenton and Troy McKinley's brother, Jeff. Jeff McKinley would later play at Louisville for Denny Crum. Tony Brosky was a reserve on the 1981 team. His little brother, Nick was on the 1995 team too. Nick would later die in a car accident. The Pioneers lost to Marshall County, a team they beat earlier in the year. They blew a huge lead. Their star player, Jeff Krohman, missed two free throws. He never missed. He holds many records at Simon Kenton, including breaking Troy McKinley's scoring record for a career at the school. He's the only Pioneer to score over 2,000 points. Jeff Krohman would later play at Kentucky Wesleyan. He now coaches the Simon Kenton boys freshman team.

No other Ninth Region team has won the state tournament. Holmes made it to the finals in 1990 and lost to Louisville Fairdale 77 to 73. In

1997 Highlands made it to the finals and lost 71 to 59 to Louisville Eastern. In 2006, Covington Catholic lost in the first round. Most Ninth Region teams never move past a round or two. The Pioneers of 1981 accomplished what no team in over 90 years was able to achieve: a boys varsity basketball championship.

CHAPTER 50
Lucky Seven?

"Luck is the residue of design."
~ Branch Rickey

Ron Coleman suggested the title of this book to be "Lucky Seven." The reason for Ron's suggestion is based upon a long discussed connection to the 1980 - 1981 year events surrounding Simon Kenton connected to the number 7. Someone who studies numerology may be intrigued by the relationship to events in this story to the number 7. A current popular television series is called *Numbers*.

Seven holds significance in the Christian Bible. I personally always believed the number three and seven must be lucky, special or divine based upon the connection to the stories from the Bible. The references are countless. With respect to the number seven, it all begins in Genesis with creation taking 7 days and the Sabbath, a day of rest, falling on the seventh day. The number 7 appears throughout the Old and New Testament. I grew up the third son of 7 sons at 333 Green Road which I always believed was a blessing. Friends recently changed their phone number because it contained three sixes (666) in a row and they were having terrible luck.

For those who enjoy number games, please consider the following connections this story has to the number 7:

1. As reflected first on clocks blown from the wall, the explosion on October 9, 1980 occurred at 7 minutes to noon.
2. Seven players played the central role in the team's success.
3. The team's worst loss involved a 7 point loss.
4. There was 7 seconds on the clock when Andy Burns missed the free throw leading to the Greg Ponzer layups to tie the game.

5. Simon Kenton forced 7 turnovers on Walton in the last 3 minutes of the game when they trailed by eight.
6. There was 7 seconds on the clock when Troy McKinley made a free throw to seal the Virgie game.
7. There was 7 seconds on the clock when Coach Miller called the play resulting in Troy McKinley's pass to Billy Meier to win the Moore game.
8. The Pioneers won the Moore game 71 - 70.
9. The Pioneers won the Mason game 70 - 63, a 7 point margin and Billy Meier fouled out with 7 seconds remaining.
10. Simon Kenton is 7 miles from the Walton city limits.
11. Simon Kenton is 7 miles from Scott High School where Simon Kenton attended night school.
12. The District championship game fell on March 7.
13. The Region championship game fell on March 14, 14 being 7 x 2.
14. The Pioneers scored 77 points in the Region championship game.
15. The State Championship game fell on March 21, 21 being 7 x 3.
16. Prior to Simon Kenton's state victory, 7 teams from the 9th Region lost in the finals.
17. Alan Mullins only had 7 turnovers in the state tournament.
18. In 1981, Knott County suffered a mine explosion on Pearl Harbor Day, December 7.
19. Greg Kroth, the team manager, calculated he spent 7 years in hospitals.
20. At night school, Simon Kenton's day ended at 7:10.
21. Mary Zimmerer finished ranked 7th in her 1981 class.

(I left this list at 21 so it would be a multiple of 7!)

One can always play with numbers, but it's hard to ignore the oddity and 'twilight zone' presence of the #7 in the story. Providence or coincidence? Only God knows.

There is also a surreal Simon Kenton and Walton - Verona connection. Maybe it's coincidence based upon the two schools being in close proximity to each other.

1. Bob Medley played basketball at Walton. His son Dave played at Simon Kenton.
2. Dwight Searcy played basketball at Walton. He taught at Simon Kenton.
3. Joyce Miller taught at Walton before coming to Simon Kenton.
4. During 1981, Bill Boyle taught at Simon Kenton. He is now the

superintendent at Walton.

5. Andy Burns, the Walton Bill Buckner, student taught at Simon Kenton and would have played at Simon Kenton, but for his father's death. He also traced his roots to Simon Kenton.

6. Troy McKinley wanted to student teach at Walton - Verona, but was not accepted.

7. Ron Coleman, 1981 Simon Kenton Booster President, finds his daughter, Shawna, teaching at Walton - Verona.

8. The current principal at Simon Kenton, Dan Sullivan, is married to Walton player John Anderson's sister, Julie. Dan's dad, Dan, refereed the Walton/Simon Kenton game.

9. Simon Kenton practiced at Walton after the explosion.

10. Robert Williams took art lessons in Walton.

11. Andy Burns' girlfriend attended Simon Kenton and Dave Dixon's girlfriend attended Walton. They were the two centers in the 1981 game.

Providence or coincidence? Only God knows.

CHAPTER 51
Final Chapter

"As the light fades from the screen, From the famous final scene."
~ From Bob Seger's "Famous Final Scene"

After Greg Ponzer's college career at Hanover, he attended Northern Kentucky University for one class. Greg needed one credit to receive his degree from Hanover.

One day, Greg found himself alone shooting basketball inside the Northern Kentucky University Student Convocation Center. His high school and college playing days were over. In a surreal moment, Andy Burns from the Walton Bearcat team of 1980-1981 strolled into the gym. There they were. Two warriors from a fabled basketball game in the faded memory of local basketball fans. As often happens in any situation among competitors, Greg asked Andy if he wanted to play a game of H-O-R-S-E. Andy good naturedly accepted the challenge as Greg shot first. As the players made baskets and missed shots, the score remained close. Soon they found themselves deadlocked on the final letter. Greg held the basketball and the next shot. As if he had never left behind his 'stick it in the eye' bravado from the time he came out of the pile of Covington Catholic players at the Regional Finals with Tom Blank's blood on his elbow, Greg coolly and calmly dribbled the ball to the free throw line. He stood behind it. He dribbled the ball a few times as he crouched slightly forward. As he bounced the ball its final preliminary bounce, he looked up and turned to Andy.

"Hey, Andy," Greg sarcastically asked. "Let's see if you can make one this time."

As Greg lifted the ball to shoot, he lost sight of Andy Burns. As the shot fell through the net, Greg turned smiling back toward Andy Burns. Andy wasn't there. Andy was walking to the exit door. Tears were flowing out of Andy's eyes and down his cheeks as he quietly walked out of the gym, never to shoot the free throw.

THE KENTUCKY
High School Athlete

SIMON KENTON HIGH SCHOOL
K.H.S.A.A. BASKETBALL CHAMPION — 1981

(Left to Right) Front Row: Cheerleaders — Michele Michaels, Tami Kelley, Debbie Huesman, Joy McKinley, Sandi Jackson, Sherry Matteoli, Lori Lauteruasser, Missy Chadwick. Second Row: Cheerleaders — Deneen Reimer, Mary Zimmerer, Tami Elliott, Krista Isler, Linda Wittenburg, Jill Brueckner, Pam Meenach, Charlotte Woods, Tonda Hignite. Third Row: Mgr. Niki Repka, Jeff Hester, Tony Brosky, Joey Brueckner, Tim Downs, John Meier, Rob Jennings, Robbie Heeager, Doug Norton, Dave Gray, Mgr. Dave Magee, Ass't. Coach Bill Pelfrey. Fourth Row: Head Coach Larry Miller, Stat. Joey Friemuth, Sean Dougherty, Greg Ponzer, Dave Medley, Billy Meier, Dave Dixon, Troy McKinley, Larry Callahan, Jeff Williams, Alan Mullins, Greg Kroth, Ass't. Coach Dave Schadler.

Member Of National Federation of State High School Associations

Official Organ of the
KENTUCKY HIGH SCHOOL ATHLETIC ASSOCIATION

APRIL, 1981

1981 Boys' State Tournament Box Score Information

Game 1 — Session 1

Todd Central — Fred Harper

no	player	min	fg	fga	ft	fta	reb	a	pf	tp
50	Woodard	29	5	12	3	3	9	1	4	13
42	Glass	30½	6	14	2	2	5	4	4	14
44	Smith	31	6	13	8	8	9	0	3	24
40	Burks	31	5	11	1	2	5	0	3	11
12	Rager	15	0	6	0	1	1	0	3	0
22	Harper	17	0	1	3	4	0	2	3	3
14	Leavell	1	0	0	0	0	0	0	0	0
20	Cope	1	0	0	0	0	1	0	0	0
30	Harris	½	0	0	0	0	0	0	0	0
34	Naylor	1	0	0	0	0	1	0	0	0
52	Woodard	2	0	0	0	1	0	0	0	0
54	Shanklin	1	0	0	0	0	0	0	0	0
	Team						0			
	Total	160	24	57	17	21	31	7	20	65

Boyd County — Eugene Clark

no	player	min	fg	fga	ft	fta	reb	a	pf	tp
25	Sisler	30	7	24	0	0	4	2	2	14
41	Vanhoose	8	2	3	2	2	7	0	3	6
45	Eiswick	14	4	6	4	6	5	0	4	12
31	Fannin	23½	4	11	0	0	9	1	3	8
21	Sisler	18	2	3	0	1	4	4	3	4
43	Salyer	1	0	1	0	0	0	0	0	0
11	Stai	24½	1	4	2	2	1	0	0	4
55	Wells	24	8	13	9	13	14	0	0	25
53	Walter	14	1	4	0	0	1	2	1	2
35	Litteral	1	0	0	0	0	0	0	0	0
51	Griffith	1	0	0	0	0	0	0	0	0
33	Sisler	1	0	0	0	0	0	0	0	0
	Team						2			
	Total	160	29	69	17	24	46	9	16	75

Game 2 — Session 1

Mayfield — Roger Fields

no	player	min	fg	fga	ft	fta	reb	a	pf	tp
52	Parrott, C.	25½	11	20	4	4	12	1	5	26
50	Sanderson	26½	3	5	4	7	12	1	4	10
32	Prince	21	4	9	4	7	6	0	5	12
24	Flood	31½	3	11	7	8	6	7	2	13
20	Graham	28	2	5	2	2	4	1	5	6
40	Wastell	6½	1	2	0	1	4	1	0	2
30	Jackson	½	0	0	0	0	1	0	0	0
22	Owens	7	1	2	0	4	2	2	2	2
12	Gray	12	0	2	0	0	1	1	1	0
14	Moffitt	½	0	0	0	0	0	0	0	0
4	Parrott, J.	½	0	0	0	0	0	0	1	0
44	Sherrill	½	0	0	0	0	0	0	0	0
	Team						2			
	Total	160	25	56	21	33	50	14	25	71

Laurel County — Chuck Broughton

no	player	min	fg	fga	ft	fta	reb	a	pf	tp
32	Karr	21½	0	10	4	8	10	2	5	4
33	Andrews	31½	5	7	4	7	9	0	4	14
44	Stidham	23	4	7	2	2	1	0	4	10
14	Maxie	28½	1	12	5	7	4	4	2	7
25	Bowling	22½	2	14	8	8	8	0	1	12
10	Sawyer	12	2	3	0	0	0	2	4	4
21	Bruner	7	1	3	0	1	0	0	2	2
34	Rose	2½	1	2	0	0	0	0	3	2
35	Smith	½	0	0	0	0	0	0	0	0
41	Reed	2	1	2	0	0	3	0	0	2
51	Bowling	7½	1	1	1	2	2	0	0	3
55	Prince	½	0	0	0	1	0	0	0	0
	Team						3			
	Total	160	18	61	24	36	40	8	25	60

Game 3 — Session 2

Bryan Station — Bob Barlow

no	player	min	fg	fga	ft	fta	reb	a	pf	tp
20	Conner	29	5	9	2	2	9	0	3	12
31	Berry	22	6	11	6	6	8	1	3	18
12	Clay	26	7	13	0	0	4	1	1	14
00	Byrd	28	8	12	1	2	2	5	4	17
13	Southworth	17	2	4	0	0	2	0	1	4
10	Williams	8	0	2	0	0	0	0	1	0
11	Routt	2	1	1	0	0	0	1	0	2
14	Stevens	1	1	1	0	0	0	1	1	2
15	Sykes	9	1	2	0	0	0	1	2	2
30	Taylor	2	1	1	0	0	0	0	1	2
32	Weathers	2	0	0	0	0	1	0	1	0
25	Barber	14	1	1	0	1	0	0	1	2
	Team						3			
	Total	160	33	57	9	13	28	8	18	75

Allen County — Gary Shelton

no	player	min	fg	fga	ft	fta	reb	a	pf	tp
35	Harper	31	11	21	3	9	11	0	3	25
45	Brown	27	0	2	2	3	3	1	3	2
31	Spencer	26	1	3	1	2	7	0	0	3
40	Hall	25	0	6	1	2	3	0	5	1
30	Rippy	30	3	11	1	2	2	0	2	7
22	Pardue	5	0	0	2	2	1	0	1	2
11	Graves	4	0	1	0	0	1	0	0	0
54	Pardue	1	0	0	0	0	0	0	0	0
53	Harper	2	1	1	0	0	0	0	0	2
32	Keen	7	0	0	2	3	3	0	1	2
44	Meador	1	0	0	0	0	0	0	0	0
50	Harwood	1	0	0	0	0	0	0	0	0
	Team						0			
	Total	160	16	45	12	23	31	1	15	44

Game 4 — Session 2

Shelby County — Tom Creamer

no	player	min	fg	fga	ft	fta	reb	a	pf	tp
14	Sullivan	32	7	15	1	3	6	2	3	15
40	George	24	3	5	2	2	5	0	4	8
54	Stoner	32	4	10	2	4	9	0	1	10
32	May	32	4	12	1	6	8	0	3	9
50	Chambers	15	1	4	0	0	3	2	3	2
10	Vandertoll	0	0	0	0	0	0	0	0	0
34	Mason	0	0	0	0	0	0	0	0	0
12	Moore	0	0	0	0	0	0	0	0	0
22	Marshall	0	0	0	0	0	0	0	0	0
20	Jones	25	4	6	0	2	5	0	3	8
24	Sullivan	0	0	0	0	0	0	0	0	0
30	Wiley	0	0	0	0	0	0	0	0	0
	Team						0			
	Total	160	23	48	6	17	36	4	17	52

Mason County — Allen Feldhaus

no	player	min	fg	fga	ft	fta	reb	a	pf	tp
33	Middleton	28	5	11	3	7	6	2	4	13
5	Jackson	32	6	11	0	0	3	0	2	12
40	Orme	32	6	11	0	0	4	0	2	12
44	Feldhaus	31	5	12	2	4	8	3	2	12
4	Jackson	32	1	5	2	2	3	2	2	4
52	Pollitt	0	0	0	0	0	0	0	0	0
13	Crawford	1	0	0	0	0	0	0	0	0
12	Feldhaus	4	0	0	0	0	0	0	0	0
15	Littleton	0	0	0	0	0	0	0	0	0
21	Hester	0	0	0	0	0	0	0	0	0
10	Bekand	0	0	0	0	0	0	0	0	0
51	Liles	0	0	0	0	0	0	0	0	0
	Team						1			
	Total	160	23	50	7	13	25	7	12	53

Game 5 — Session 3

Moore — Tom Finnegan

no	player	min	fg	fga	ft	fta	reb	a	pf	tp
43	Brown	31	12	23	0	0	9	1	3	24
51	Thompson	23	4	7	0	1	8	0	2	8
53	Forrest	32	12	26	4	8	10	2	4	28
25	Anderson	25	1	7	6	6	1	0	1	8
11	Hubbs	27	0	0	0	1	4	4	1	0
35	Davis	0	0	0	0	0	0	0	0	0
21	Pitts	0	0	0	0	0	0	0	0	0
41	Rein	0	0	0	0	0	0	0	0	0
15	Dickerson	5	2	2	0	0	0	0	0	4
55	Phelps	17	0	1	0	0	3	0	3	0
5	White	0	0	0	0	0	0	0	0	0
00	Strasser	0	0	0	0	0	0	0	0	0
	Team						1			
	Total	160	31	66	10	16	36	7	14	72

Butler — Mike Durham

no	player	min	fg	fga	ft	fta	reb	a	pf	tp
11	Lucas	32	2	4	0	3	4	0	4	4
20	Betts	29	2	3	0	1	3	3	3	4
25	Epperson	32	10	21	3	7	9	1	4	23
10	Robertson	26	9	15	4	5	2	0	5	22
21	Porterfield	31	4	0	0	0	5	5	1	8
13	Maier	0	0	0	0	0	0	0	0	0
14	Ward	0	0	0	0	0	0	0	0	0
22	Williams	0	0	0	0	0	0	0	0	0
24	Jacobs	10	1	1	0	0	3	0	1	2
30	Becker	0	0	0	0	0	0	0	0	0
31	Wolfe	0	0	0	0	0	0	0	0	0
32	Ebel	0	0	0	0	0	0	0	0	0
	Team						2			
	Total	160	28	53	7	16	39	9	18	63

315

Game 6 — Session 3
Owensboro — Randy Embry

no	player	min	fg	fga	ft	fta	reb	a	pf	tp
22	Hunter	32	11	18	6	7	6	0	4	28
44	Johnson	15	3	5	4	9	5	0	1	10
32	McCormick	24	1	3	1	5	6	0	3	5
14	James	32	3	10	2	2	2	1	2	8
12	Southerland	17	0	3	0	0	2	1	5	0
10	Loucks	21	3	8	3	4	6	0	2	9
21	Miller	0	0	0	0	0	0	0	0	0
24	Taylor	16	1	3	0	0	1	1	2	2
34	Webb	0	0	0	0	0	0	0	0	0
40	Wilson	0	0	0	0	0	0	0	0	0
42	McFarland	0	0	0	0	0	0	0	0	0
52	Pewitt	3	0	0	0	0	1	0	0	0
	Team						5			
	Total	160	22	50	16	27	36	3	20	60

North Hardin — Ron Bevars

no	player	min	fg	fga	ft	fta	reb	a	pf	tp
20	Valentine	31	8	16	5	7	12	2	5	21
52	Murray	30	6	11	0	1	5	0	3	12
50	Burrow	13	3	10	2	4	3	0	5	8
25	Jeter	32	6	17	2	4	8	0	1	14
14	Watts	32	0	1	4	4	3	1	2	4
51	Barker	15	-0	1	0	2	3	0	2	0
21	Spilman	6	0	0	0	0	2	0	2	0
15	Gates	0	0	0	0	0	0	0	0	0
23	Deaton	0	0	0	0	0	0	0	0	0
10	Sutton	0	0	0	0	0	0	0	0	0
12	Allen	1	0	0	0	0	0	0	0	0
24	Peterson	0	0	0	0	0	0	0	0	0
	Team						1			
	Total	160	23	56	13	22	37	3	20	59

Game 7 — Session 4
Virgie — Bob Osborne

no	player	min	fg	fga	ft	fta	reb	a	pf	tp
50	Osborne	22	3	5	0	0	2	0	5	6
22	Johnson	30	4	8	4	7	16	4	1	14
42	May	31	13	18	12	14	22	0	4	38
20	Rowe	30	7	18	5	6	4	10	2	19
44	Napier	31	3	7	0	0	3	2	3	6
32	Jarrell	9	0	1	1	2	0	0	1	1
12	Newsome	2	0	0	2	3	0	0	1	2
40	Casebolt	1	0	1	0	2	1	0	1	0
34	Osborne	1	0	1	3	4	3	0	0	3
24	Tackett	1	0	0	0	0	1	0	0	0
14	Belcher	1	0	0	0	0	0	0	0	0
30	Gould	1	0	0	0	0	0	0	1	0
	Team						2			
	Total	160	30	58	29	38	54	16	19	89

Clay County — Bob Keith

no	player	min	fg	fga	ft	fta	reb	a	pf	tp
30	Brown	25	4	8	4	7	5	0	2	12
20	Hampton	27	2	7	2	6	5	0	2	6
42	Bowling	31	4	13	0	2	6	0	3	8
24	Corum	30	8	18	4	4	4	3	3	20
14	Roberts	29	8	15	4	6	2	1	5	20
34	Combs	2	0	0	0	0	0	0	1	0
32	Combs	13	2	4	0	1	5	0	4	4
52	Griffin	1	0	0	0	0	0	0	1	0
10	Combs	1	1	1	0	0	0	0	0	2
50	Cornett	0	0	0	0	0	0	0	0	0
54	Hall	0	0	0	0	0	0	0	0	0
12	McWhorter	1	0	1	0	0	0	0	2	0
	Team						0			
	Total	160	29	67	14	26	27	4	23	72

Game 8 — Session 4
Knott Central — Harold Combs

no	player	min	fg	fga	ft	fta	reb	a	pf	tp
44	Collins	32	10	19	8	8	11	1	4	28
24	Stamper	32	8	18	4	7	5	0	1	20
34	Conley	32	4	6	2	4	7	0	1	10
30	Combs	22	0	1	0	0	0	1	4	0
14	Adams	24	0	3	4	5	4	0	5	4
22	Moore	0	0	0	0	0	0	0	0	0
50	Collins	0	0	0	0	0	0	0	0	0
54	Steele	0	0	0	0	0	0	0	0	0
10	Christian	13	0	2	0	0	2	1	5	0
12	Slone, A.	0	0	0	0	0	0	0	0	0
52	Slone, J.	5	0	0	0	0	2	0	0	0
20	Slone, I.	0	0	0	0	0	0	0	0	0
	Team						0			
	Total	160	22	49	18	24	31	3	20	62

Simon Kenton — Larry Miller

no	player	min	fg	fga	ft	fta	reb	a	pf	tp
40	McKinley	32	14	25	0	1	7	2	3	28
41	Meier	21	5	8	2	4	10	2	3	12
32	Dixon	28	2	5	4	8	6	0	4	8
5	Ponzer	32	2	12	1	3	3	3	4	5
12	Mullins	32	2	5	1	3	1	1	3	5
11	Dougherty	15	2	4	2	4	0	3	3	6
35	Medley	0	0	0	0	0	0	0	0	0
33	Callahan	0	0	0	0	0	0	0	0	0
42	White	0	0	0	0	0	0	0	0	0
14	Jennings	0	0	0	0	0	0	0	0	0
3	Brosky	0	0	0	0	0	0	0	0	0
21	Downs	0	0	0	0	0	0	0	0	0
	Team						0			
	Total	160	27	59	10	23	27	11	20	64

Game 9 — Session 5
Boyd County — Eugene "Jeep" Clark

no	player	min	fg	fga	ft	fta	reb	a	pf	tp
24	Sisler, Kent	27	12	30	3	8	9	1	4	27
40	Vanhoose	22	1	4	1	3	8	0	2	3
44	Elswick	22	2	6	1	1	6	1	4	5
30	Fannin	25	5	12	0	4	0	2	10	10
20	Sisler, Kevin	14	2	7	0	0	0	1	3	4
42	Salyer	1	1	1	0	0	0	0	0	2
10	Stai	16	1	4	1	3	2	0	0	3
54	Wells	15	2	4	4	4	7	0	5	8
52	Walter	18	1	3	0	0	1	2	1	2
34	Litteral	0	0	0	0	0	0	0	0	0
50	Griffith	0	0	0	0	0	0	0	0	0
32	Sisler	0	0	0	0	0	0	0	0	0
	Team						3			
	Total	160	27	71	10	19	40	5	21	64

Mayfield — Roger Fields

no	player	min	fg	fga	ft	fta	reb	a	pf	tp
52	Parrot	28	11	17	1	3	14	0	5	23
50	Sanderson	28	5	7	3	9	5	0	3	13
32	Prince	32	8	16	0	1	12	0	2	16
24	Flood	32	1	11	7	8	3	3	3	9
20	Graham	32	4	7	0	1	5	2	4	8
40	Wastel	8	0	0	2	3	3	0	0	2
30	Jackson	0	0	0	0	0	0	0	0	0
22	Owens	0	0	0	0	0	0	0	0	0
12	Gray	0	0	0	0	0	0	0	0	0
14	Moffitt	0	0	0	0	0	0	0	0	0
4	Parrott	0	0	0	0	0	0	0	0	0
44	Sherrill	0	0	0	0	0	0	0	0	0
	Team						2			
	Total	160	29	58	13	25	44	5	17	71

Game 10 — Session 5
Bryan Station — Bob Barlow

no	player	min	fg	fga	ft	fta	reb	a	pf	tp
20	Connor	25	4	6	2	2	7	0	4	10
31	Berry	31	12	f16	6	6	10	1	5	30
12	Clay	32	10	22	0	0	2	1	2	20
00	Byrd	27	1	10	2	4	1	1	5	4
13	Southworth	11	0	1	0	0	4	0	3	0
10	Williams	12	0	2	0	0	1	0	2	0
11	Routt	0	0	0	0	0	0	0	0	0
14	Stevens	0	0	0	0	0	0	0	0	0
15	Sykes	20	0	3	0	1	2	0	1	0
30	Taylor	0	0	0	0	0	0	0	0	0
32	Weathers	0	0	0	0	0	0	0	0	0
25	Barber	2	0	0	0	0	1	0	2	0
	Team						2			
	Total	160	27	60	10	13	30	3	24	64

Mason County — Allen Feldhaus

no	player	min	fg	fga	ft	fta	reb	a	pf	tp
33	Middleton	32	7	10	10	14	7	2	2	24
5	Jackson	32	5	9	0	0	3	1	1	10
40	Oreme	29	3	9	3	4	8	0	4	9
44	Feldhaus	32	7	13	6	9	8	2	3	20
4	Jackson	32	2	4	2	2	4	0	2	6
52	Pollitt	0	0	0	0	0	0	0	0	0
13	Crawford	2	0	0	0	0	0	0	0	0
12	Feldhaus	1	0	0	0	1	0	0	0	0
15	Littleton	0	0	0	0	0	0	0	0	0
21	Hester	0	0	0	0	0	0	0	0	0
10	Beiland	0	0	0	0	0	0	0	0	0
51	Liles	0	0	0	0	0	0	0	0	0
	Team						6			
	Total	160	24	45	21	30	36	5	12	69

Game 11 — Session 6
Moore — Tom Finnegan

no	player	min	fg	fga	ft	fta	reb	a	pf	tp
43	Brown	26	5	12	0	0	8	0	0	10
51	Thompson	23	3	8	2	4	7	2	3	8
31	Forrest	28	8	22	10	12	16	4	2	26
25	Anderson	21	7	9	1	3	4	0	3	15
11	Hubbs	19	1	1	3	5	3	0	1	5
35	Davis	3	0	1	0	0	0	0	0	0
21	Pitts	2	0	0	0	0	0	0	0	0
41	Rein	3	0	0	0	0	2	0	0	0
15	Dickerson	14	1	2	1	2	0	0	4	3
55	Phelps	17	2	3	1	3	8	0	3	5
5	White	2	0	1	0	1	1	0	0	0
53	Strasser	2	0	1	0	0	1	0	0	0
	Team						2			
	Total	160	27	60	18	30	52	6	16	72

Owensboro — Randy Embry

no	player	min	fg	fga	ft	fta	reb	a	pf	tp
22	Hunter	18	5	9	3	8	3	1	5	13
44	Johnson	22	5	10	0	0	8	0	3	10
32	McCormick	25	1	3	2	5	3	0	4	4
14	James	25	1	7	2	5	2	0	4	4
12	Southerland	27	4	6	0	3	2	1	2	8
10	Loucks	18	1	3	2	2	1	0	3	4
21	Miller	5	0	2	0	0	0	0	2	0
24	Taylor	8	2	8	1	2	1	0	0	5
34	Webb	3	2	5	0	0	2	0	0	4
40	Wilson	2	1	1	0	0	1	0	1	2
42	McFarland	5	1	3	0	0	2	0	1	2
52	Pewitt	2	0	0	0	0	0	0	0	0
	Team									
	Total	160	23	57	10	25	30	1	25	56

Game 12 — Session 6
Virgie — Bob Osborne

no	player	min	fg	fga	ft	fta	reb	a	pf	tp
50	Osborne	29	1	2	4	5	3	3	3	6
22	Johnson	26	3	6	1	1	7	0	5	7
42	May	32	12	20	7	12	13	0	1	31
20	Rowe	32	13	25	4	5	0	1	4	30
44	Napier	24	2	4	0	0	2	0	3	4
32	Jarrell	1	0	0	0	0	0	0	0	0
12	Newsome	16	0	0	5	0	0	1	4	5
40	Casebolt	0	0	0	0	0	0	0	0	0
34	Osborne	0	0	0	0	0	0	0	0	0
24	Tackett	0	0	0	0	0	0	0	0	0
14	Belcher	0	0	0	0	0	0	0	0	0
30	Gould	0	0	0	0	0	0	0	0	0
	Team									
	Total	160	31	57	21	29	25	5	20	83

Simon Kenton — Larry Miller

no	player	min	fg	fga	ft	fta	reb	a	pf	tp
40	McKinley	32	16	27	7	8	13	0	2	39
41	Meier	32	8	18	2	3	9	0	4	18
32	Dixon	14	5	8	0	0	4	0	5	10
5	Ponzer	15	1	4	5	8	0	1	4	7
12	Mullins	32	1	4	0	0	4	3	2	2
13	Dougherty	23	3	4	1	2	2	1	4	7
35	Medley	12	0	1	1	4	4	0	0	2
33	Callahan	0	0	0	0	0	0	0	0	0
42	White	0	0	0	0	0	0	0	0	0
14	Jennings	0	0	0	0	0	0	0	0	0
3	Brosky	0	0	0	0	0	0	0	0	0
21	Downs	0	0	0	0	0	0	0	0	0
	Team						1			
	Total	160	34	66	16	25	37	5	23	84

Game 13 — Session 7
Mayfield — Roger Fields

no	player	min	fg	fga	ft	fta	reb	a	pf	tp
52	Parrott	24	5	10	1	2	3	0	5	11
50	Sanderson	23	3	10	0	0	4	0	2	6
32	Prince	21	2	3	0	5	5	0	5	4
24	Flood	31	6	15	0	0	3	4	2	12
20	Graham	31	3	7	5	6	0	3	0	11
40	Wastell	13	4	6	1	3	2	0	4	9
30	Jackson	1	0	2	0	0	1	0	1	0
22	Owens	12	0	1	0	0	1	1	1	0
12	Gray	1	0	1	0	1	0	0	0	0
14	Moffitt	1	0	1	1	2	2	0	0	1
4	Parrott	1	0	0	0	0	1	0	0	0
44	Sherrill	1	0	0	0	0	0	0	2	0
	Team						1			
	Total	160	23	56	8	19	23	8	22	54

Mason County — Allen Feldhaus

no	player	min	fg	fga	ft	fta	reb	a	pf	tp
33	Middleton	31	5	10	13	13	7	0	1	23
5	Jackson, C.	24	5	7	0	0	4	1	5	10
40	Oreme	29	7	11	1	2	9	0	4	15
44	Feldhaus	31	4	10	8	8	8	1	1	16
4	Jackson, T.	28	1	2	2	2	3	1	5	4
52	Pollitt	2	0	0	0	0	2	0	0	0
13	Crawford	5	0	0	0	0	0	1	0	0
12	Feldhaus	6	1	2	3	4	0	1	1	5
15	Littleton	1	0	0	0	0	0	1	0	0
21	Hester	1	0	0	0	0	0	0	0	0
10	Beiland	1	1	1	4	4	0	2	1	6
51	Liles	1	0	0	0	0	0	0	0	0
	Team						3			
	Total	160	24	43	31	33	37	7	18	79

Game 14 — Session 7
Moore — Tom Finnegan

no	player	min	fg	fga	ft	fta	reb	a	pf	tp
43	Brown	12	2	10	0	2	0	1	4	4
51	Thompson	22	2	5	0	0	1	0	2	4
31	Forrest	32	18	41	11	14	11	0	3	47
25	Anderson	31	4	6	1	3	1	0	4	9
11	Hubbs	30	0	0	2	2	1	1	3	2
35	Davis	0	0	0	0	0	0	0	0	0
21	Pitts	0	0	0	0	0	0	0	0	0
41	Rein	10	0	0	2	2	2	0	1	2
15	Dickerson	1	0	0	0	0	0	0	0	0
55	Phelps	22	1	1	0	0	5	0	3	2
5	White	0	0	0	0	0	0	0	0	0
53	Strasser	0	0	0	0	0	0	0	0	0
	Team						1			
	Total	160	27	63	16	21	24	1	17	70

Simon Kenton — Larry Miller

no	player	min	fg	fga	ft	fta	reb	a	pf	tp
40	McKinley	32	10	14	13	14	8	1	3	33
41	Meier	32	7	10	1	5	12	0	4	15
5	Dixon	25	6	11	1	2	5	0	5	13
32	Ponzer	25	3	8	0	1	10	4	2	6
12	Mullins	0	0	0	2	2	1	1	2	2
11	Dougherty	14	1	3	0	0	0	0	2	2
35	Medley	0	0	0	0	0	0	0	0	0
33	Callahan	0	0	0	0	0	0	0	0	0
42	White	0	0	0	0	0	0	0	0	0
14	Jennings	0	0	0	0	0	0	0	0	0
3	Brosky	0	0	0	0	0	0	0	0	0
21	Downs	0	0	0	0	0	0	0	0	0
	Team						2			
	Total	160	27	46	17	24	38	7	18	71

Game 15 — Session 8
Mason County — Allen Feldhaus

no	player	min	fg	fga	ft	fta	reb	a	pf	tp
33	Middleton	27	7	15	6	7	4	0	4	20
5	Jackson	32	6	20	1	2	1	0	4	13
40	Orme	31	6	10	0	1	8	0	3	12
44	Feldhaus	31	5	17	1	2	13	3	3	11
4	Jackson	31	2	6	2	2	2	0	5	6
52	Pollit	2	0	1	0	0	0	0	0	0
13	Crawford	1	0	0	1	2	0	0	0	1
12	Feldhaus	5	0	1	0	0	0	1	0	0
15	Littleton	0	0	0	0	0	0	0	0	0
21	Hester	0	0	0	0	0	0	0	0	0
10	Beiland	0	0	0	0	0	0	0	0	0
51	Liles	0	0	0	0	0	0	0	0	0
	Team						5			
	Total	160	26	70	11	16	33	3	20	63

Simon Kenton — Larry Miller

no	player	min	fg	fga	ft	fta	reb	a	pf	tp
40	McKinley	32	7	17	3	3	11	1	2	17
41	Meier	29	5	8	6	9	9	0	5	16
32	Dixon	28	8	10	2	3	6	0	4	18
5	Ponzer	32	4	9	5	10	9	5	4	13
12	Mullins	32	2	4	2	5	4	4	0	6
11	Dougherty	6	0	1	0	1	0	1	1	0
35	Medley	0	0	0	0	0	0	0	0	0
33	Callahan	0	0	0	0	0	0	0	0	0
42	White	0	0	0	0	0	0	0	0	0
14	Jennings	0	0	0	0	0	0	0	0	0
3	Brosky	0	0	0	0	0	0	0	0	0
21	Downs	0	0	0	0	0	0	0	0	0
	Team						1			
	Total	160	26	49	18	31	40	11	16	70

About the Author

Eric Deters is a 43-year-old attorney who practices law in Kentucky, Ohio and Florida. He is married to the former Mary Zimmerer, a cheerleader for the 1981 Simon Kenton Pioneers. He has three children, Erica, Charlie Ann and Parker, and three stepchildren, Cory, Cameron and Cole. In 2006, the Kentucky Trial Court Review named Eric one of the most prolific trial attorneys in Kentucky. This is his second book. He is the co-author of Saving Grace, another nonfiction work. He has also founded his own agency, Deters Media Agency.

DEDICATION

In addition to the dedication to Mary Ann Zimmerer and my three children, I want to dedicate the book to every teacher, staff member and student attending the 1981 Simon Kenton school year. Obviously, I could have interviewed a thousand more people. Everyone of these individuals who possess their own stories from 1980 - 1981 are named here. They lived this story.

Bob Abell, Principal
Mike Tolliver, Assistant Principal

Faculty and Staff
Mary Abell
Laura Hasenstab
Dave Schadler
Robert Abell
Tom Hatley
Don Schadler
Jean Ammon
Tim Hiatt
Beverly Searcy
Heidi Atkinson
Carolyn Hilliard
Dwight Searcy
Regina Baldwin
Vaughn Hilliard
Jean Shotwell
Carol Barker
Eugene Keith
Todd Shupe
Pam Barns
Martha Lockhart
Pat Slusher
Connie Beach
Niki Locklear
Carolyn Smith
Alice Bowen
Phyllis Lonneman
Steve Smith

Ken Bowen
J.B. Losey
Joe Stark
Bill Boyle
Cal Lyon
Rommie Starks
Jackie Cain
Portia Malott
Janice Sulkes
Shawna Cartwright
Steve Massey
Marylon Taylor
Nancy Clagett
Joyce Miller
Doug Watson
Mike Collins
Larry Miller
Sharon Webb
Dan Daniels
Tim Moore
Jane Webster
Carolette Depew
George Mullins
Ron Wells
Robin Farris
Wynell Northcutt
Linda Whittenburg
John Finn

Nancy Platt
Kathleen Whiley
Carl Fitzer
Ray Powers
Carol Williams
Gary Goldsberry
Jean Reed
Marilyn Young
Tom Hamilton
John Rich
Lynn Hanen
Gerry Scaringi

Custodians
Peggy Bradley
Willie Kidwell

Cafeteria Ladies
Annie Caldwell
Liz Nunnery
Lucille Cambell
Marie Payne
Bert Elstrum
Carol Pierce
Fern Elswick
Joan Rutherford
Pearl Haines

Betty Sargent
Sherri Hammonds
Veronica Schmitt
Bert Kirt

SENIORS
Oma Acree
Sharon Ahlers
Kaye Ainsworth
Patsy Angel
Vernon Arnold
Dan Ashcraft
Tammy Ashcraft
Judith Atkinson
Mary Bach
Shelia Bachmann
Sue Bachmann
Paula Baldwin
Jay Ball
Karen Bates
Angela Baugh
Lisa Baynum
Thomas Beemon
Kevin Beighle
Diane Berry
Linda Borne
David Bowen
Kelly Bowlin

Steve Bowling
Anita Boyer
Pearl Branstutter
Donna Breeden
Glen Bridges
Gregory Brown
Michael Brown
Jill Brueckner
Tony Burden
Arvil Bush
Brent Butler
Sandy Cain
Kim Caldwell
Claude Casson
Gina Caudell
Kim Chadwell
Margie Chan
Jennifer Chapman
Marc Chapman
Michael Cheeks
Adam Childers
Ronnie Clark
Gina Cocco
Shawna Coleman
Richard Collins
Vickie Cooper
Bob Creekmore
Rodney Curtis
Jody Cuzick
Sherry Damon
Terri Darrell
Jerome Daugherty
Scott Davis
Tim Day
Patti Keatherage
Diana Dedden
Darren Dehner
Lisa Dirr
David Dixon
Barbar Dorgan
Sean Dougherty
Todd Downs
Karl Durden
Michelle Dyer
Bonnie Ecklar
Christina Eddins
Denis Egger
Shirley Elbert
Tami Elliott
Kimberly Engle
Lori Ernest

Barbara Evans
Kathy Evans
Jeff Eversole
Rusty Eversole
Cathleen Feagan
Patty Ferguson
Francie Ficke
Doug Fisk
Laura Florence
Sheri Fowler
Greg Frank
Jo Ellen Freeman
Kevin Friedman
Lisa Fuehner
Bill Funke
Mike Gabbard
Tammy Garrison
Terri Gauck
Jennel Gibbs
Anita Gillum
G. Lane Godby
Jeffrey Goecke
Sandy Graham
Randy Haggard
Tammy Hamilton
Lynne Hammons
Mike Harden
Rod Harmon
Joseph Havey
Steven Heeger
Laura Hegener
Carl Hellmann
Russ Hilmandolar
David Honaker
David Hopkins
Beverly Hubbs
Keith Huelsman
John Huffaker
Eric Hummeldorf
Joey Humphery
Debbie Hurst
Krista Isler
Don Jackson
Sherri Jackson
Tracie Jacquillard
Michelle Jarman
James Johnson
David Jones
Connie Jump
Mark Kannady
Gene Kavanaugh

James Keith
Sheila Kemper
Todd Kew
Robert Kiely
Deborah King
Sarah King
Kenny Kleisinger
Angela Kloeker
Donna Klotz
Daniel Koch
D. Kordenbrock
Lisa Kordenbrock
Greg Kroth
Donna Larison
Donna Lawson
Jack Lemming
Juli Leugers
Monica Liming
Angela Loesing
Robert Lunsford
Kim Maddox
Jim Mann
David Mardis
Leroy Mason
Melissa McKinley
Troy McKinley
David Medley
Billy Meier
David Moore
Darice Mullins
Freda Mullins
Kevin Mullins
Martina Mullins
Paula Mullins
Kimberly Muth
Jaye Nantz
Roger Neumeister
Lisa Newman
Sharon Nie
David Noem
Missy Noland
Michelle O'Banion
Lisa Oliver
Don Osbourn
Angela Parker
James Payne
David Pennington
Paul Perkins
Harvey Pickett
Eric Pierson
Greg Ponzer

Sherry Porter
Brenda Raleigh
Glenda Raleigh
Pamela Raleigh
Rebecca Reed
Robert Reel
Anne Richardson
Eric Richardson
Deborah Richter
Joan Richter
Donna Ridner
Patricia Roberts
Bobby Roland
Linda Rose
Jamie Ross
Debbie Rump
Gary Rump
Marty Rump
Randy Rump
Joe Schmiade
Denise Schroeder
Karen Schuchart
Doug Schulte
Robin Schulz
David Scott
Denise Sebastian
Doug Setters
John Sharon
Kimberly Sharp
Steve Simpson
Melanie Slaughter
Martha Smiley
Darren Smith
Ervin Snodgrass
Michele Sorrell
Elliott Speaks
Brian Stephens
Michelle Strain
Mike Stutler
Bruce Taylor
Jeff Taylor
Kimberly Thomas
David Thompson
Sandy Thompson
Loretta Tiryung
David Trinkler
A. Wayne Turner
Williams Turner
Steve Vinson
Scott Wallin
Tammy Ward

Crystal Watson
Petra Webster
Kati Weiland
Jeff Wells
Laura Whaley
Saundra Whaley
Gregory Whiteker
Jeffery Whittaker
Vernon Wiley
Lore Williams
Debra Wittrock
David Wodraska
Becky Wolfe
D. Wolfinbarger
Keith Wood
Sandy Workman
Susan Wright
Brian Wyatt
Terry Yancey
Sandra Yeager
David Yelton
Mary Zimmerer

JUNIORS
Jessee Allen
Tina Alsip
Tony Ashcraft
Robert Ayers
Scott Bagby
Jill Baird
Jeff Baldwin
Danny Ball
Sonnie Bates
Mary Beach
Kim Beighle
Kem Belcher
Rod Bell
John Bishop
Melissa Blanken-
ship
Paul Bledsoe
Angie Booth
Rick Bowen
Tony Bowling
Angie Bradley
Greg Braunwart
Brenda Brown
Sandy Brown
Cathy Bullard
Larry Callahan
Tony Callen

Alan Campbell
Karen Carpenter
Tammie Casson
Karen Chambers
Rivers Chapman
Annette Cheek
Margeret Cheesman
Sandy Cheesman
Danielle Childress
Doug Clark
Jamie Clark
Susan Clark
Duffy Coker
Bill Coldiron
Barry Cole
Lisa Coleman
Daryl Collins
Jamie Combs
Bob Conklin
John Cook
Gordon Cooper
Randy Cooper
Shelly Copeland
Robbie Coppage
Jeff Craven
Steve Crawford
Verna Crisp
Dave Cully
Sandy Curtis
Keith Daly
Christy Daugherty
M. Deatherage
Kelly Dougherty
Angel Durnell
Gina Edmondson
Rick Elliott
Connie Fahey
Marc Figgins
Tony Finnel
Randy Flexner
Holly France
Donna Freeman
Joey Freimuth
Jerry Freking
Danny Fuehner
Dan Funke
Bob Gadker
Cindy Garera
Todd Garvin
Alicia Gee
Sharon George

Adam Gibson
Jennifer Gilley
Karen Glacken
Pam Glass
Cathy Goecke
Julie Goodridge
Sherry Grant
Rick Grimes
Pam Grizzell
Karina Gulley
Tammy Haggard
Denise Hall
Linda Hambrick
Kelly Hamilton
Robbie Hamilton
Tera Hamilton
Bryan Hamlin
Kim Harmaning
Connie Hart
Matt Heeger
Nancy Heeger
Lori Helmick
Tonda Hignite
Alan Hodge
Lisa Holbrook
Debbie Holt
Sherry Howard
Tracey Howell
Jackie Hopper
Russell Hubbard
Kim Huff
Tom Jacquillard
Brian Jameson
Kelly Johnson
Jennifer Jones
Steve Kannady
Bob Keith
Chester Kemper
Robbie Kilgore
Eddie King
Cathy Kitts
Mary Kloentrup
Kevin Knight
Scott Kresser
Jennie Krolage
Sean Lafferty
Joe Lowe
Daryl Lynn
Chriss Lytle
Phyllis Magee
Mike Maher

Mike Martin
Dave McIntosh
Melissa McKenney
Tom McNay
Pam Meenach
Barry Miller
Butch Miller
Randy Miller
Tim Miller
Mike Mintken-
baugh
Robert Mobley
Jimmy Moore
Lisa Morgan
Melissa Morgan
Alan Mullins
Tina Mullins
Art Muth
Tina Muth
Danny Nagle
Tammy Napier
Darlene Nevels
Jim Noel
Les Overbay
Vicki Perkins
Sharon Phillips
Betty Piercefield
Gina Piercefield
Rodney Polly
Dick Pompillio
Deneen Reimer
Vicki Rice
Lori Richardson
Diane Richter
Tyrone Roberts
Brent Robinson
Connie Rogers
Kim Rogers
Cheryl Roland
Teresa Roland
Carol Roth
Remona Rowe
Greg Rump
Sue Russell
Lisa Salyers
Jeff Sargent
Wanda Saylor
Tina Schadler
Mike Schalck
Jeff Scherder
Brad Schlueter

PIONEER SPIRIT

Mike Schoborg
Anita Schoonover
Tom Schulte
Lanny Setters
Ronnie Shafer
Tom Shaw
Todd Shumate
Tim Sipple
Albert Sizemore
Devell Sizemore
Lorna Smiley
Tammy Smith
Tim Smith
Renee Sorrell
Eric Speaks
Barry Stamper
Laura Stein
Donna Steins
Curtis Stephens
Paula Stephens
Cindy Stephenson
Steve Strain
Robert Strayer
Tina Taphorn
Glenn Thoemer
Teri Thomas
Crystal Trapp
Jackie Truett
Randy Underwood
Debbie Vicars
Donna Voges
Khaun Vu
Greg Wainscott
Carrie Walton
Terri Walton
Laura Warrington
Sally Washum
Missy Wayman
Mike Webster
Teresa Webster
Bernie Wesselman
Lynne West
Robert White
Beverly Willenborg
Jeff Williams
Robert Williams
Missy Wilson
Tony Wolfe
Todd Wolsing
Charlotte Woods
Angie Yeagel

Stephanie Yeager
Mischelle Young

SOPHOMORES

Gary Adair
Jeff Ainsworth
Sonny Ainsworth
Niel Alsip
Greg Armstrong
George Arnett
Marie Ashcraft
Mary Ashcraft
Christa Atkins
Terry Audass
Marcy Bachman
Torrie Barhorst
Diana Beach
Angie Beck
Darren Belew
Zinda Bell
Karen Bennett
Jimmy Bergman
Mike Berry
Jeff Borne
Steve Borne
Brenda Bostrom
Cheryl Bradford
Robin Branham
Tracy Brewer
Robby Brinkley
Julie Brooks
Tony Brosky
Joana Brown
Joey Brueckner
Robin Brunker
Denise Burns
Rhoda Burns
Joey Butsch
Becky Caldwell
Pat Campbell
Bryan Carpenter
Holly Carson
Bradley Carter
Tense Casey
Jeff Casson
Sonya Casson
Missy Chadwick
Chuck Childers
Terri Clark
James Coker
Alicia Collinsworth

Janet Combs
Kathy Combs
Lisa Cooper
Terry Cooper
Carmen Cornelius
Sheila Daly
Wanda Darrell
Deborah Daugherty
Nila Dekelaita
John Dehart
Donnie Dotson
Tim Downs
Michelle Drennon
Dean Dressman
Jerry Dye
Bennie Dyer
Angie Durr
Lisa Eastridge
Marc Eaton
Rita Eggleston
Jerri Ehlman
Debbie Ellis
Teresa England
Mitch Engle
Jackie Ernest
James Evans
Lisa Ewing
Tim Fair
Raymond Ferrell
Karen Figgins
Jeff Fightmaster
Brenda Filer
Donald Finnell
Gloria Focke
James Fogle
Sherry Freking
Robert French
Wally Fultz
Rita Funke
Jenny Gadker
Donald Gauck
Darrin Gilvin
Lorie Ginn
Scott Glass
Doug Goodridge
Donna Gosney
Richie Gouge
David Gray
Clint Green
Gary Green
Mary Gripshover

Jimmy Grizzell
Sam Grizzell
Terry Hall
Stephanie Hamilton
James Harmeling
Robbie Heeger
David Hegge
Doug Henderson
Rod Herper
Jeff Hester
Karen Hiles
Teresa Hobb
Jeff Hodge
Crystal Holbrook
Chris Hooten
Cassie Hopper
Toni Hopper
Larry Hubbard
Debbie Huesman
Jim Huff
Kurt Hummeldorf
Kem Humphrey
Phil Hurley
Pamela Hurst
Rhonda Hutchins
Chrisy Iha
Terry Iha
Traci Ishmael
Sandy Jackson
Tim Jackson
Monica Jarman
Rob Jennings
Janet Johnson
Chris Jones
Paula Jones
Julie Jump
Reeford Justice
Cliff Kaninenberg
Tami Kelley
Bill Kelley
Shelley Kenney
Patty Kiely
Sheri Klaserher
Jude Kloeker
Melody Lambert
Lori Lauterwasser
Robbie Lawson
Joey Lee
April Leffler
Lekkey Liggett
Scott Liming

322

Ronda Lipscomb
Carol Littlefield
Jeff Lorenzen
Cuncray Louden
Mia Lowe
James Lynn
Kim Magee
Donald Martin
Sherry Matteoli
Andrea Maxwell
Bill McCall
Evelyn McCauley
Debra McClure
Charlotte McCubbin
Debra McCubbin
Salena McDaniels
Joy McKinley
Lori McNay
Debbie Meece
John Meier
Dawn Meyer
Michele Michael
Karen Miller
Dovon Mitchell
Dale Mullins
Roge Mullins
Rhonda Napier
Chris Neal
Pamela Nebel
Donna Nolan
Jimmy Noland
John North
Doug Norton
Dave Nowack
Penny O'Neal
Lisa Parker
Pamela Patrick
Eric Patton
Tanya Pemberton
Anita Perkins
Jennifer Perkins
Sherry Peters
Susan Pierce
Tim Platter
Beth Plunkett
Angie Polley
Jeff Pope
Greg Powell
Mark Rawls
Lisa Reel
Michelle Reneau

Jimmy Reusch
Glenn Riggs
Kenny Rippe
Darren Roland
John Rose
Amy Rump
Karen Rusk
Jenny Sabie
Todd Sanders
Kevin Saddrock
Sherri Sandusky
Tony Sargent
Eric Satchwell
Bill Saylor
Harold Saylor
Terry Saylor
John Schaffer
Glenn Scott
Peggy Seng
Todd Setters
Karen Shaw
Brian Shipman
Becky Simmons
Alice Smiley
Linda Smith
Karen Smith
Karen Somers
Sara Speaks
Lisa Spencer
Melissa Stallsworth
Meil Stambaugh
Donna Stein
Lori Stephens
Linda Stith
Lisa Storms
Laurie Strain
Brian Strange
Deanna Stull
Charley Tashiro
Kenneth Thoemer
Linda Thomas
Steve Thomas
MikeThompson
Stephen Traylor
Julie Trenkamp
Scott Trenkamp
Carol Turner
Dennis Ward
Keith Warren
Wade Webb
Pete Webster

David Webster
Diane West
Jennifer Wheeler
James White
Tia White
Theresa Whittaker
Tim Whittamore
Robin Whittrock
Roy Willenborg
Marty Wilson
Connie Winan
Donna Wodraska
M. Wolfinbarger
Robin Woodbury
Greg Workman

FRESHMEN
Kim Allen
Paul Angel
Donna Ante
Tony Antrobus
Ricky Arthur
Rocky Arthur
Michael Ashcraft
Kim Audas
Greg Bach
Michael Bach
Elizabeth Bachert
Brent Baldwin
Marty Banar
Danny Barns
Ray Barton
Tim Barton
Jackie Bates
Jeff Baugh
Rhonda Beagle
Jennifer Beeman
Diane Bell
Lisa Bishop
Annette Black
Julie Black
Jesse Blackaby
Wayne Blackburn
Davie Boling
Betty Bowen
Elaine Boyer
Doug Branch
Frank Branstutter
Kim Broaddus
Tina Brooks
Glenda Brown

Keith Brown
Steve Bryson
Suzie Bullard
Todd Burkett
Bradley Butler
Shelly Caldwell
Kim Carter
Chuck Childers
Lane Claypool
Doveye Coldiron
Darren Collins
Steve Collins
Raejea Collinsworth
Lisa Compton
Danny Cook
Delene Cook
Tonya Cooper
Tammy Cox
Teresa Creekmore
Diana Curry
Saprina Dalton
Geoia Damico
Jimmy Daut
Sheila Davis
Connie Dedden
Cheryl Dannis
Sharon Dingus
Donna Douba
Lorie Doud
Belinda Duncan
Lanna Duncan
Donna Dunn
Laura Dunn
Ginia Durr
David Dutill
Caraleah Dyer
Michelle Eckerle
Jeff Egger
John Eibeck
Faith Elam
Shonnie Elberts
Marcilla Embry
Michelle Endres
Debbie Etherington
William Faulkner
Scott Fetters
Lisa Finnell
Myrtle Fletcher
Margie Fogle
Eric French
Darren Fuehner

PIONEER SPIRIT

Linda Fuller
Joe Funke
Steve Galloway
Karen Gatman
Robert Gauck
Brian Gee
Randy Gibbons
Frank Glaza
Paul Glenn
Debbie Goetz
Jim Gosney
Jim Graber
Denna Grant
Regina Grant
Chris Greene
Beth Gregory
Sandy Grimes
Terry Gripshover
Kay Grizzell
Ray Guffey
Paula Haley
Kim Hall
Tracy Gallon
Leeroy Hancock
Richard Hanser
Willard Harnweling
Bobby Jo Hartke
James Havey
Sharon Helmer
Regina Henderson
Mike Hensley
Lisa Hinkle
Christine Hoffman
Robert Hoffman
Don Holleran
Kay Holt
Christina Hondker
Betty Howard
Kathy Hubbard
Michael Hughes
Wendy Hurt
Keith Iles
Tabatha Isaacs

Martina Isler
Cheri Johnson
Kimberly Johnson
Tony Johnson
Rebecca Julick
Rodney Kannady
Jennifer Keeton
Teresa Keith
Alice Kelly
Kelly Kelly
Kirk Kelsey
Chris Kiely
Jane Kincaid
Dennis Kindoll
James King
Teri King
Toni King
Tonya King
Jeff Kite
John Kloeker
Mark Koors
Tara Koors
Kevin Krebs
Mary Kresser
Johnny Landrum
Lisa Larison
Teresa Lay
Nancy Loesing
Chalee Lorenzen
Kelly Lytle
Darin Magee
David Magee
Tracy Magee
John Malott
Sharon Mardis
Jeff Martin
Lori Matteoli
Trudi Maxwell
Billy McBee
Rodney McClure
Sharon McDaniel
Jeff McDannold
Leslie McKenzie

Teresa McNeese
Shawn Meade
Larry Meiman
Amy Miller
Laura Miller
Scott Miller
Teresa Miller
John Milner
James Mitchell
Lisa Moore
Todd Moore
Tonya Moore
Amy Morgan
Bill Morgan
William Mueller
Elizabeth Myeller
Melody Myers
Jack Neal
Carol North
Jerry Olivier
Mary Beth Orr
Michele Pemberton
Dwight Penick
Eugene Petty
Carolyn Perry
Stefanie Perry
Amy Pierce
Jeff Piper
Ralph Pope
Joe Price
Michael Price
Betty Raleigh
Stephen Raleigh
Jeff Rankin
Lori Reel
Sandra Remley
Jim Rennekamp
Nicki Repka
Dwight Rice
Glenn Riggs
Lisa Rogers
Jamie Ross
John Ross

Kelly Roth
Barbara Rowe
Mike Rowe
Ann Rump
Cindy Rutherford
Samantha Sally
George Scherder
John Schmiade
Chris Schoborg
Diane Schulte
Lori Setters
Angela Sexton
Ricky Sexton
Lance Sharp
Shari Shelley
John Shoemaker
Candy Shouse
Gina Smith
Edwin Stahl
Scott Stephens
Elaine Stetter
Pamela Storms
Christine Strain
Sheri Straus
Russell Strayer
Bobby Sturdiuant
Keith Sturdiuant
Jill Stutler
Kyle Tackett
Jeannie Taylor
Sandra Tipton
Brian Tomlin
Christi Trego
Lillian Trinkler
Karen Truett
Richard Turner
Bill Waymer
Angie Webster
Mary Wells
Patty Yelton
Joe Zimmerer

Index